# 'When the Banks Closed, We Opened Our Hearts'

Hundreds of personal
memories and photos of
the Great Depression,
from readers who recall the days
when families drew closer and
refused to let tough times defeat them.

FAMILIES PULLED TOGETHER and helped one another when tough times struck. Extra places were often set at the family table for aunts, uncles, cousins and more distant relatives who were temporarily out of work and needed a place to stay until they got back on their feet.

Corbis/Horace Bristol

**'When the Banks Closed, We Opened Our Hearts'**
**Copy Chief** Deb Warlaumont Mulvey
**Photo Coordinator** Trudi Bellin
**Layout Designer** Monica Bergwall
**Proofreader** Vicki Jensen
**Assistant Photo Coordinator** Mary Ann Koebernik

**Reminisce**
**Editor** Bettina Miller
**Art Director** Cheryl A. Michalek
**Associate Editor** John Burlingham
**Editorial Assistants** Blanche Comiskey, Melody Trick

**Home & Garden**
**VP, Editor-in-Chief** Karol K. Nickell
**Executive Editor** Heather Lamb
**Creative Director** Sharon K. Nelson
**Product Development Editor** Rachael Liska

**The Reader's Digest Association, Inc.**
**President and Chief Executive Officer** Mary G. Berner
**President, North American Affinities** Suzanne M. Grimes
© 1999 Reiman Publications, LLC
5400 S. 60th St., Greendale WI 53129

**Reminisce Books**
International Standard Book Number:
0-89821-257-X

Library of Congress Catalog Number:
98-68486

**On the Cover:** WPA workers in Seattle, Washington gladly accepted some hot soup cooked and served by a sympathetic woman during the Depression years. (Photo: Corbis/*Seattle Post-Intelligencer* Collection; Museum of History & Industry)

For additional copies of this book or information on other books, write Reminisce Customer Service, P.O. Box 5294, Harlan IA 51593-0794; call 800-344-6913; e-mail *rpsubscustomercare@custhelp.com*. Visit our website at *Reminisce.com*

# Contents

*Curbis/Underwood & Underwood*

**POOR TO THE CORE.** The stock market crash and ensuing Depression came as a jolt to folks who were once financially secure. Many had to "learn to live poor" in a hurry, resorting to such entrepreneurial pursuits as selling apples on the street.

# Prologue

*By Clancy Strock, Contributing Editor, Reminisce Magazine*

BACK IN 1990, Reiman Publications decided to launch a new kind of nostalgia magazine, one written by its readers. We had a hunch people might enjoy fellow readers' personal recollections, but we had no idea just how well such a publication would be received. Happily, *Reminisce* became North America's most popular nostalgia magazine.

Soon, mailbag after mailbag of memories poured in, and *Reminisce* editors discovered something surprising. Many of the best stories were about the Great Depression. But they weren't the tales of sorrow and pain you might reasonably expect.

Instead, what people remembered most vividly was the way families looked after each other…and how even total strangers were ready to help someone in trouble. The folks who shared these stories obviously felt some well-deserved pride at having survived a terrible decade with honor and dignity.

### We Put the Best in a Book

In 1992, we gathered the best of those memories into a hardcover book titled *"We Had Everything But Money"*. It was the first in a series of *Reminisce* books, a priceless collection of oral history as told by the people who lived it.

*"We Had Everything But Money"* turned out to be the most popular book of stories ever compiled by Reiman Publications. More than 250,000 people purchased copies, and 7 years later, orders are still coming in every day.

That steady pulse beat of interest, plus the fact that our first volume didn't seem to dent our well of reader memories from the Depression years, led us to consider printing another book about the Depresssion. The result is in your hands.

*"When the Banks Closed, We Opened Our Hearts"* is our second heartfelt book about the

**OUR 1992 REMINISCE BOOK of reader-written memories, "We Had Everything But Money", remains a runaway best-seller. Our readers' continuing interest in the 1930s led us to produce this second book of Depression-era memories, "When the Banks Closed, We Opened Our Hearts". It is the essential companion to the first book, and we hope you enjoy it.**

**DEPRESSION-ERA MEMORIES remain vivid for Clancy Strock, who grew up during the 1930s. He routinely reads and edits such recollections in his role as Contributing Editor for Reminisce, North America's most popular nostalgia magazine.**

Depression, and we've tried to include aspects about those trying years that we didn't cover in *"We Had Everything But Money"*.

These stories need to be told if our children and grandchildren are to know how much courage and just plain goodness is found in the human spirit when it's put to the test.

### Happy Memories from *Orphans*?

For example, many people told us about the years they spent in orphanages. Their parents simply had no way to feed and clothe the children. Can you imagine the heartbreak when weeping children and sobbing parents were torn apart and strangers hauled the kids off to an orphanage?

But Chapter Six, We Called the Orphanage "Home", isn't sad, it's triumphant. It may even start you to thinking about one way some of today's juvenile problems could be handled.

In Chapter Four, you'll recall the reason trash disposal wasn't much of a problem 60 years ago. Recycling was a way of life.

And while John Steinbeck gave us an eloquent novel about the "Okies", who headed west in search of a better life, just wait until you come to the *first-person* memories in Chapter Eight. These folks actually lived *The Grapes of Wrath*.

Although I grew up during the Great Depression, there are stories in this new volume that surprise even me. For one thing, as those days have faded into the mists of my memory, I developed a vague sense that Franklin D. Roosevelt and his New Deal programs "cured" things in fairly short order.

Far from it. The Depression stayed with us for a full 10 years.

Don't get me wrong, Roosevelt's visionary "Alphabet Soup" programs ended hunger, put people back to work, restored faith in our financial institutions, corrected a bunch of social evils and quite possibly saved our nation from an all-out revolution. No small feat.

But what made the facto-

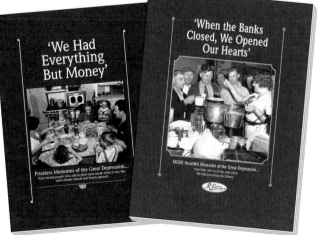

'We Had Everything But Money'

Priceless Memories of the Great Depression...

'When the Banks Closed, We Opened Our Hearts'

MORE Heartfelt Memories of the Great Depression...

ries hum again, created world markets for our farm products and made unemployment just a bad memory was World War II. As you'll read in this book, the Great Depression still hung over America like a dreary fog as late as 1940.

The assortment of topics touched upon in this new volume make it an essential companion to the first. Like all *Reminisce* books, it's filled with first-person memories and family-album photos...stories from people like you.

In all *Reminisce* books, I've written the prologues and chapter introductions. My wife calls me "the tour guide", and that's not a bad description of where I fit in. As you reach each new chapter, there I stand, describing what you're about to find behind the next door.

### How Could Kids Understand?

But when I finished reading the memories destined to fill this new book, I was struck by a realization: My children—and *especially* my grandchildren—would find these stories virtually incomprehensible.

*"So the banks closed? Why didn't you just use your credit card?"*

*"No television, computer games or CDs? What did you do for fun?"*

*"Six years old and picking beans to earn money for the family groceries? Couldn't you just call for a pizza?"*

*"Three families crowded together in a three-bedroom house? You mean kids had to share their room?"*

See my problem? That decade of the Great Depression is beyond the ken of anyone who didn't experience it. Yet I want my grandchildren to know about it, both because of the important lessons that can be learned and also because of what it reveals about the deep-down strength of the human spirit.

I want them to understand the real meaning of this book's title: *"When the Banks Closed, We Opened Our Hearts."* I'm not sure the history books they study in school do a good enough job of explaining the unique qualities that define the strengths in people. History teaches things that have happened. It doesn't necessarily explain much about the people who made it happen.

As I pondered this, the face I saw in my mind's eye was that of my 12-year-old granddaughter, Katie. She's inquisitive and bright...a perfect audience for the stories in this book.

Not that my other grandchildren—Tim, Dana, Andrew, Beky, Brian, Jenna, Erin and Megan—aren't also "above average", as Garrison Keillor so tactfully puts it. But writing is easier for me when I'm talking with just one person.

So, I elected Katie, and hope that I've not eternally alienated all the others and their parents.

As we journey through the chapters in this book, I hope to give Katie some personal family memories of those tough years. Like the contributors to this book, I'm part of the last genera-

**LEARNING'S A KICK!** Katie Strock, 12, of Minneapolis, Minnesota knows lots about soccer and her schoolwork. Thanks to her Grandpa Clancy's "letters", she'll likely come to learn a lot about life during the Depression. You can read Clancy's letters to Katie at the beginning of each chapter in this book.

tion that experienced the sharp teeth of the Great Depression.

By 1932, as I recall, things had gotten pretty bad on our little farm in northern Illinois. We depended for our living on selling the eggs, corn and milk we produced. But growing a crop suddenly cost more than what we got when we sold it. We were flat broke.

Then in 1933, the banks closed. Even kids who'd put their pennies and nickels into school-sponsored thrift programs found that their savings were gone. Our parents couldn't believe they were cleaned out, except for whatever cash was around the house.

Eventually, most everyone got their money back, but not their faith in banks. For many years after that, lots of people kept their money hidden under the mattress or buried in a jar out back or just carried it around in their pockets. *Anywhere but in a bank.*

I'm sure my grandchildren can't imagine a time when *everyone* is penniless. To them, a financial crisis is when they don't get their overly generous allowances on Monday morning.

Everyone we knew was just as poor as we were, and many were worse off.

### No Jobs, No Income

One family in every three didn't have any source of income. And the ones who did find work were making near-starvation wages.

During most of those Depression years, nearly everyone had kinfolk living with them. These relatives had lost their jobs, couldn't pay the rent, had no money for food and had nowhere left to turn. So relatives took them in, sometimes just for a few months...sometimes a lot longer.

In today's affluent times, we read about homeless people and are embarrassed when we encounter them holding up signs on street corners. But they are strangers.

What made the Depression homeless different was that they were *us!*, for pity's sake. They were Uncle Bernie, the carpenter...and Cousin Walter, the accountant...and Uncle Earl, the once well-to-do salesman.

I hope neither Katie nor any of my grandchildren have to live through a time like the Great Depression. I hope they never know what it's like to futilely search the house for a nickel for food. I'm sure they'll never be put in orphanages because their parents can't afford to take care of them.

But I hope that by learning how bad things once were, they'll better appreciate how good life is for them today. And I especially want them to know that people have unsuspected reserves of courage and generosity and kindness.

And finally, Katie, I hope you'll always open your heart to those less fortunate. You'll see why when you read the stories in this book. ⬚

# CHAPTER ONE

# Bank Closures Shook Our Trust

***NO SECURITY ANYWHERE.*** **During the first 3 years of the '30s, bank failures wiped out the savings of millions of Americans and led to a massive loss of confidence in the country's financial institutions. (Photo: Brown Brothers)**

# From the desk of Clancy Strock

Dear Katie,

When I was your age, a bank was a big, solid-looking building with bars on the windows and a uniformed guard standing inside. In the back was an awesome place called "the vault" where, I was pretty sure, they kept everyone's money (including my $8.45). With its enormous steel door, that vault was awfully impressive.

But today the "bank" where we get our money is often a little place in the local shopping mall. The cash is inside a contraption about the size of a big television set. Feed it a plastic card, punch in some magic numbers and it spits out money.

Well, whether we're talking about an impressive building or an electronic marvel ready to serve you 24 hours a day, consider this: **What if tomorrow morning not a single bank anywhere opened its doors, and none of those cash machines had any money?**

Ah, you say, just use your VISA card. Good idea, but during the Great Depression, credit cards hadn't been invented.

Well, you say, why not write a check? That's what Mom and Dad do when they pay their bills. Another fine idea, Katie. But when the banks close their doors, no one will take their checks.

Just imagine a world where one morning no one has any money, except the few dollars in their pocketbooks. How do you buy groceries and gas? How do you pay for your school lunch? How do you get into a movie or buy clothes or even get an ice cream cone?

Without money, how could your dad pay the people who work for him? And if they didn't get paid, would they keep coming to work?

It's hard to imagine, isn't it? But it actually happened during the Great Depression. Eventually most of the banks reopened. Some never did, though, and people who had savings accounts with them lost everything they'd worked so hard for all their life.

As a result, lots of older citizens never trusted banks again. Some actually buried their money in cans or jars out in the back-yard. Others hid it under the floor or in their mattress. That's why even now we sometimes read of money being found in the strangest places.

One of the first things President Roosevelt did in 1932 was to have Congress pass laws to protect people from bank failures. The results can be seen in the bank ads in your local newspaper. Some-where near the bottom you'll see a little "FDIC" emblem and the words "FDIC insured". That means the government will pay off bank customers should the bank ever go out of business.

People can't lose their life savings. That's one good idea to come out of the chaos that occurred "the day the banks closed".

*Your Grandpa Clancy*

# Dad's Strong Leadership Kept Small Bank Open

*By Frederick Olson, Wauwatosa, Wisconsin*

FROM 1925 until his death in 1938, my father was president of Wauwatosa State Bank, outside Milwaukee, Wisconsin. Banks had closed during previous panics and depressions, but the Great Depression was particularly harsh on financial institutions.

Few Americans had participated in the orgy of stock-market speculation that preceded the crash, but many had deposited their savings in banks for a rainy day. For many people, it was now pouring.

By '31, banks were hard-pressed to pay off depositors on demand, and many were forced to close. Depositors were increasingly nervous and angry. "It's our money," they'd say. "Why can't we get it out?"

Unfortunately, the prosperity of the 1920s made some bankers less prudent than they should have been with other people's money. There was no federal insurance for deposits, as there is today.

**RIDING OUT THE STORM. Scenes like the one below were common at banks as panicked depositors withdrew their life savings. The prudent practices of Frederick Olson's father (shown at right with 16-year-old Frederick and his mother) helped his bank survive the squeeze.**

As the Depression deepened, so did my father's concern. As a bank officer and director, he had a substantial investment in bank stock. If the bank closed, he would not only have to forfeit the value of his stock, but match its value in cash to pay off depositors.

But worries about his own liability were incidental. My father's primary concern was for the depositors. During one tense period, my father almost dreaded going to work, lest he find a long line of depositors demanding their money. I suspect those worries shortened his life.

"Runs" on banks could occur whenever another local bank closed. No matter how strong a bank was, it couldn't withstand the demands of a large number of depositors for their cash—it had too much money tied up in loans and investments.

A bank's best safeguard was a reputation for solvency and conservative practices, and my father's bank had that. But it wasn't easy to maintain a tiny bank when big banks were in trouble and the bank down the street was going through the wringer.

## The Lender of Last Resort

In 1931, President Herbert Hoover persuaded Congress to create the Reconstruction Finance Corporation, a federal lender of last resort for financial institutions and businesses. Banks threatened with liquidation were encouraged to use their assets to obtain RFC loans.

Every bank in Milwaukee County that survived the Depression borrowed from the RFC sooner or later—except my father's. He filled a valise with about a quarter-million dollars in bank securities and took them by train to Chicago to gain prior RFC loan approval in case of an emergency. But his bank never had to ask the RFC for the money, and he was justifiably proud of that.

When FDR took office, he ordered all banks temporarily closed on his inauguration day to forestall further runs until each bank could be reviewed and approved for reopening. On that historic Saturday morning, my father sweated out the closing order. He had little cash in his pocket, but because of his position, he felt he couldn't withdraw even a few dollars from his own account to tide us over the weekend.

Wauwatosa State Bank reopened after a government agency reviewed its balance sheet and assets. Later that year, my father asked the state banking commissioner for permission to pay a dividend—an almost unprecedented request. The bank was making money in spite of the Great Depression. ▨

**ON THE FRONT LINES.** Shown here with his 1929 Pontiac, George Biringer returned thousands of dollars to scared depositors during the bank run of '32 (see story below).

## FDR's Order Ended Banker's Nightmare

REMEMBER THE RUN on the banks in 1932? I was 22, working in a teller's cage at First National Bank in downtown Chicago. Deposit insurance was unknown at the time, and banks in the outlying areas were closing overnight.

All of the banks in downtown Chicago were ordered to stay open at all costs. Thousands of depositors were lined up around the bank where I worked, awaiting their turn to withdraw their money. Policemen were brought in to maintain order.

Then Federal Reserve trucks brought in millions of dollars to expedite the payouts. All of us worked many extra hours to clear up all the additional paperwork.

After 3 days of this tumult, President Roosevelt declared a moratorium and closed all banks until people could come to their senses. When the banks opened again, all was quiet, and business went on as usual.

—*George Biringer*
*Bella Vista, Arkansas*

## Scrip Kept Businesses Operating in Idaho Town

IN MARCH 1933, a couple of days after President Roosevelt ordered the banks to close, I found myself printing "money".

As soon as the banks closed, the Chamber of Commerce in Preston, Idaho held a special meeting. Some method of exchange was needed to keep the stores operating, so they decided to print scrip.

I ran it off on a hand-fed platen press at the newspaper and print shop co-owned by my dad. The scrip was printed on check stock so changes couldn't be made without marring the scrip, which was signed by Chamber representatives.

If a store owner balked at accepting scrip, a couple of Chamber representatives would visit him and guarantee payment as soon the banks reopened.

My payment for running the press was, of course, in scrip.

—*Dale Roe*
*Centerville, Utah*

**THE MAN WITH A PLAN.** President Franklin Roosevelt was willing to try just about anything to get the country's economic health back in order. Some of his ideas worked—and some didn't—but his confidence never wavered.

**DAD'S "SAFE" DEPOSIT.** Dorothy Weinberger's father (above, with Dorothy's mother) always knew where his money was.

## Former Depositor Found Bibs Safer Than Banks

MY GRANDMOTHER opened a savings account for me in the amount of $10, quite a sum for a small child in 1924. When the bank closed, my money was gone. On March 19, 1936, I received a check for 31¢.

My parents lost every penny in their savings and checking accounts. They had written a check for $700 a few days before the bank closed, but it hadn't cleared.

From then on, my dad always carried our family savings in the upper pocket of his bib overalls. He fastened the pocket shut with a big safety pin.

His friends kidded him about his "bank", but many of them kept their savings in the same way. For many years afterward, no one felt safe depositing what little money they had in a bank. —*Dorothy Weinberger*
*Artesian, South Dakota*

## Teller Saved Newsboy From Financial Jam

MY YOUNGER BROTHER had a paper route and paid the newspaper by check every week. When the bank closed unexpectedly, he wondered how he was going to make his payment. He'd just made a deposit the day before.

A couple of days later, the teller who'd taken his deposit called and asked my brother to come to his house. When my brother arrived, the teller gave him an envelope—with the money he'd deposited inside.

—*Kathleen Maney, Ottumwa, Iowa*

**WHAT FRIENDS ARE FOR.** Curly Moore (at right below) was a good friend of the engineer he's standing beside. The two men, with a little help from an "angel", found a way to protect their life savings.

## Cryptic Advice Saved Railroad Worker's Savings

MY FATHER, "Curly" Moore, was a very careful man as far as money was concerned and kept all his savings in a bank. He believed in banks, though many of his friends didn't. Some of them buried their money in coffee cans in their backyards, while others just hid their cash under mattresses.

Dad was a fireman on a switch engine, and the engineer was a good friend. They kept their money in the same bank. One day Dad told the engineer he'd saved enough to buy the lots for sale next to his home.

At the time, there were no hints that any banks were going to close. But some banks knew it was coming—including the one where Dad and the engineer had their savings. The engineer's sister worked there. She'd warned him what was going to happen but made him promise not to tell anyone.

The engineer simply told Dad to take his money out of the bank. He couldn't elaborate without breaking his promise to his sister. "You must trust me," the engineer said.

My father respected this man, so he followed his advice. He withdrew his money, bought the lots as planned and made money by selling potatoes, tomatoes and strawberries. —*Tressa Hamilton, Chandler, Arizona*

## Businessman Left in Lurch

MY FAVORITE UNCLE repaired automobiles for a living, and when the banks closed, he was left with only the cash in his wallet.

He was a very busy businessman, with parts and supplies being billed to him, and now he couldn't get to any of his funds. He had very little money to even buy food, let alone pay other expenses.

Something else I'll never forget is my grandmother storming about the president of a failed local bank. Her cousin was a teller there, and Grandma couldn't understand why the president hadn't warned her to take some of her money out rather than continue to put more in. —*Marcella Lewis
Lady Lake, Florida*

**TIME OF TURMOIL.** Marcella Lewis (at right with her mother, Pearl) was old enough to witness the bad times firsthand.

## Children Raced to See Hole Where Bank Had Been

IN 1932, our fourth-grade teacher told us school was being dismissed for the rest of the day because the local bank had gone under.

All the kids in Avella, Pennsylvania were familiar with coal mine cave-ins, so we assumed the bank had been swallowed up by a cave underneath. We thought that would really be something to see!

So four or five of us boys walked downtown to see where the bank "went under". We expected a big hole in the ground, but the bank was standing as usual.

I found out what "going under" actually meant when I was informed I'd lost my life savings—$2.50. It had taken me 2 years to save that amount in the school savings program. Later, I learned most families in our town had lost everything. —*Thomas McCready Salem, Connecticut*

**BUNDLE OF JOY.** Marian Guthrie's son Franklin, born in 1930, was a godsend to his parents—and to the doctor who delivered him (see story below).

**AN ECONOMICS LESSON.** Much like the eager schoolchildren shown below, Thomas McCready (at left) and his classmates were initially excited when they'd heard that the local bank had "gone under".

J.C. Allen and Son

## Delivery Fee Was Doctor's Christmas Gift

OUR FIRST CHILD was born at our home in Miami, Florida on Dec. 17, 1930. The doctor came by to check on me every day. On Christmas Eve, I prepared a Christmas card for him, with his $50 fee tucked inside.

When the doctor arrived that day, he told us the Biscayne Bank in Miami had closed. He'd lost all his money. All he had was some change his wife had put on top of the icebox. He later told me they wouldn't have had Christmas dinner if I hadn't paid him.

—*Marian Guthrie, Sarasota, Florida*

## Crosley "Transaction" Helped Family Make It Through

OUR FAMILY'S spell of bad luck began before the Depression. My father, a railroad engineer, died in 1927. Mother and we three kids foundered for a few years.

Mother remarried 4 years after my father's death, but her new husband lost his job. We moved out to a small farm, which was wonderful for all of us. Mother kept our old home in the city and still had some money in the savings and loan—but that was closed.

That savings and loan partially reopened from time to time, and we'd make the 90-mile drive back to see if Mother could withdraw some or all of her money. She never could.

One of those refusals really hurt, because we had our hearts set on buying a radio. Mother wasn't very assertive, but that dear woman somehow got the savings and loan to transfer her money directly to a radio dealer down the street. We went home with a gorgeous new Crosley!

On cozy winter nights, we would sit around listening to *One Man's Family* and *The Little Theater Off Times Square*. The savings and loan remained closed and the Depression went on, but we managed to live through it listening to our Crosley. —*Jean Greene Seattle, Washington*

**MOM MANAGED SOMEHOW.** Jean Greene's mother "withdrew" a Crosley radio from her local bank (see story at left).

# A Banker's Trust Set the Course for His Life

*By Art Uecker, Chula Vista, California*

MY ORIGINS are in South Dakota, but like so many of my generation during the Depression, I rode the rails, followed the crops and survived the Dust Bowl days as best I could.

I can still recall the night I awoke in a small tent in a logging camp in Chester, California to torrents of rain assaulting my tent. Small rivulets flowed around my bedding as I wondered whether this was all that life would ever hold for me.

Two years later, in 1937, I was in National City, California trying to convince a man named Hodkins to rent me a spot under a shade tree for the small trailer I had. But Mr. Hodkins was adamant—he would not rent. Sell yes, rent no. The purchase price was $108, to be paid off a few dollars per month, so when I handed him my $8 down payment, I was giving up my entire life savings.

When we shook on the deal, I became the owner of 1 acre of land in National City. For me, the land was a dream come true—and also the beginning of a new life.

My next purchase was a mixer to blend concrete and make blocks. In time, my block business was successful enough that I had the courage to approach a bank for a loan to build a small house.

I'll never forget the banker's words, "You have an honest face." I left his office in a daze. I had nothing, yet this man had faith in me and had given me money, something I'd had very little of up to that point in my life.

The cost of constructing my little house (I did all the labor) was $550. The outside measurements were 20 by 24 feet, but it had two bedrooms, a bath, kitchen and living room.

In 1939, I built two more houses on that acre, selling each for $2,500. At last, I felt that the sun was shining on me. The sale of those houses enabled me to repay the bank, make a profit and set a course for my life.

I was a building contractor until 1956—and I'm proud to say that those first three houses I built are still being used as family residences today. ▨

"MY COUSINS played 'Bonnie and Clyde' in the car behind my Aunt Rose in this picture," recalls Tressa Hamilton of Chandler, Arizona. In an era when banks folded often, there was lots of sympathy for those two infamous outlaws.

## College Education Cut Short

I CERTAINLY remember when the banks closed. I was a junior (below) at the University of Wisconsin and heard the news on the radio in my room.

I immediately sent a telegram to my mother in Nebraska. I remember exactly what it said: "Is my money and yours safe?" Well, it wasn't.

Between my sophomore and junior years, I'd taken a year off to work in my dad's jewelry store and had put my salary of $7 a week in the bank. I never got to attend college for my senior year. There was no money anywhere.

Although I did not graduate, I went on to take evening and summer college classes most of my life. I now have a certificate of achievement from Drake University in Des Moines for accumulating enough credits for a master's degree. It looks like a diploma, and I'm very proud of it.

*—Elsie Block, Des Moines, Iowa*

A DREAM COME TRUE. During the depths of the Depression, Art Uecker's bad luck finally changed for good when he invested in a piece of land and built this house.

# Graduation Dress Dilemma Had An Unlikely Solution

*By Elizabeth Alexander Redwood, Tulsa, Oklahoma*

IN 1931, I was a high school senior in the small town of Sandia, Texas. I was proud that I'd be graduating in the spring because so many kids my age had to drop out of school to help support their families.

When my adult half brother came home for a visit in February, he told me to let him know when it came time for me to graduate because he'd like to buy my graduation dress.

During the Depression, caps and gowns weren't used because people didn't have the money for rental fees. But the truth was that my family had no money for anything but food—and sometimes not even enough for that.

A month before our graduation, I wrote to my brother, then anxiously watched the mail for a reply that never came. Later, we found out that he'd gotten married during that time.

My mother would have made my graduation dress, but we had no material to even do that. There were only three graduating seniors in all of Sandia—all girls—and the other two had already had their dresses made.

Finally, with only a few days left until graduation, I was walking downtown and went past the bank. I remembered hearing that people were sometimes able to borrow money from banks, so, in desperation, I pulled open the heavy door and walked in.

I was so distressed that my throat constricted, causing me to speak in an unnatural falsetto, but I did manage to squeak, "Mr. Slabaugh, will you loan me some money to buy my graduation clothes?"

At first he looked surprised, and I thought he seemed nervous as he turned around and busied himself at the counter. (I noticed his shoulders were shaking, but I couldn't see his face.)

I quickly explained that as soon as cucumber season started, I'd be able to work and pay my loan. When he asked me how much money I needed, I told him $25, thinking I'd start high and settle for whatever he'd loan me.

To my utter surprise, Mr. Slabaugh handed me $25. That heavy bank door seemed much lighter as I hurried back out into the sunlight with my money.

With it, I bought a pink taffeta dress for the graduation and a green crepe dress for the baccalaureate service. I even had enough left over to buy matching shoes for each outfit.

On graduation night, I beamed at Mr. Slabaugh as he gave each one of us girls a bouquet of roses from his garden. That summer, I did go to work in the cucumber harvest and I did pay my creditor back.

But it was only when I didn't receive a receipt for my final payment that I realized I hadn't borrowed $25 from the bank at all—I'd borrowed it from kindly Mr. Slabaugh. ⊠

**PENNIES NOT ENOUGH.** Elizabeth Redwood needed a dress for her high school graduation, but where was she going to come up with the money?

---

## Student Savings Program Benefited the Whole Community

A BANK in my hometown of Auburn, Indiana came up with a wonderful idea during the Depression. The Auburn Automobile Company was about the only industry in town, so we'd been hit hard.

Each student in the city schools—about 900 of us—were to "bank" something at school every week, even if it was only a penny. We could save for college, or items like class rings, yearbooks and graduation clothes. We'd learn banking skills, and our money would keep the bank from closing its doors.

Classrooms competed with each other to get the most participants and biggest deposits. One student per row served as "teller", and a student from each class acted as courier, taking the room aggregate to the principal's office. The rooms that won honors were justifiably proud.

Printers were paid to make passbooks. The bank was able to meet its expenses and make a few loans. Money began to filter through the community again. But the real wonder was that this program gave everyone hope.

When I graduated from high school in 1932, I had over $400 in my school bank account. With a college scholarship, that was enough to pay my interurban fare to the university, buy a few clothes and pay some fees. The school banking venture was a wonderful learning experience.
—*Betty Hicks, Eufaula, Alabama*

# CHAPTER TWO
# Alphabet Soup

***ACRONYM HEAVEN.*** **After Roosevelt's New Deal was passed, there were a bewildering number of new government programs and most had their own acronyms. This photo shows an NRA parade in New York City in 1933. (Photo: Brown Brothers)**

# From the desk of Clancy Strock

Dear Katie,

By the time the Depression reached bottom, something had to be done and done *fast*. The biggest problem was the lack of jobs.

To add to the problem, the country didn't have much in the line of welfare programs. No unemployment insurance. No family assistance programs. No health insurance. No Social Security checks for the elderly.

President Roosevelt asked a group of bright people to come up with creative new ways to get the country moving. They quickly developed several programs with long-winded names such as the Civilian Conservation Corps, Public Works Administration and Works Progress Administration. Eventually these programs came to be known by their initials--CCC, PWA and WPA for example.

The scoffers lumped all these efforts together and called them "alphabet soup". To the surprise of many, the alphabet soup programs began to turn things around. One of the very best was the CCC. It took several million young men off the streets and put them to work improving our country.

The CCC workers got new clothes and shoes, hearty meals and health care and were paid $30 a month. However, they only got $5 of it. The rest went home to Mom and Dad. It doesn't sound like a lot of money, but for many families, it was a fortune.

The CCC men planted millions of trees, cleaned up rivers and streams, developed parks and campgrounds and cleared beaches, just to name a few improvements they made. Five years ago, Gramma and I spent 3 nights in a wonderful park in the Ozarks of northwestern Arkansas. We hiked beautiful trails, stayed in a fine cabin and were lulled to sleep at night by water running over a nearby stone dam.

Beside the dam was a monument with a brass plaque that carried the names of all the CCC men who built the park--a legacy we were enjoying 60 years later.

And last summer when you and your dad and brother Brian had that great canoe trip in the Boundary Waters of northern Minnesota, you can thank the CCC boys for getting things started in that area.

Meanwhile, the PWA poured money into building new hospitals and courthouses and schools and dams and bridges and harbors. Those projects made jobs for millions of workers and left America a better place for everyone.

Looking back today, it's hard to quarrel with the results. And those of us who lived through the worst of the Depression sometimes wonder whether a little "alphabet soup" might fix some of today's problems, too.

*Your Grandpa Clancy*

AN EXPERIMENT THAT WORKED. Some say that the CCC was the most successful government program ever instituted.

Brown Brothers

# CCC Workers Left Legendary Legacy

*By Joe Marinangeli, Arlington, Virginia*

THE Civilian Conservation Corps left this country a legacy that should long be remembered.

I know about the CCC because I was there. I started out as an enrollee in 1935 and ended up as commander of the last camp, located in Rock Creek Park in Washington, D.C.

From the CCC's inception in 1933 until it was disbanded in June 1942, nearly 4.5 million young men served in over 4,500 camps across the nation.

Some called them the "tree army"—they planted more than 3 billion trees in reforestation projects, and another 45 million trees and shrubs in landscaping and erosion-control projects.

*"On average, they gained 16 pounds in their first 6 months..."*

But CCC workers didn't just plant trees. They constructed 3,500 beaches and installed 5,000 miles of water-supply lines. They restored almost 4,000 historic structures, built 4,650 fish ponds and developed or built more than 800 state parks.

They constructed dams, picnic shelters and cabins. They erected more than 46,000 bridges and thousands of miles of roads. It would be impossible to list all the projects the CCC completed. Even Camp David, the Presidential retreat, was once a CCC camp.

Most enrollees were sent to camps many miles from home and worked 8 hours a day for room, board and $5 a month. Another $25 was sent to their families. The Army ran the camps and provided health care, education, recreation and discipline. Work projects were supervised by other government agencies, such as the Parks Service and Department of the Interior.

Enrollees worked hard and ate well on a daily ration allowance of 35¢. On average, they gained 16 pounds in their first 6 months of enlistment. While many enrollees were young men, the CCC also provided work for 225,000 World War I veterans and some 85,000 Native Americans.

The work could be dangerous, and a number of men perished. Nearly 300 CCC men lost their lives in a 1935 hurricane in the Florida Keys. Others died during the blizzards of 1936-37 or were killed in the New England hurricane of 1938.

Historians say the CCC may have been the most productive organization our country ever knew—an experiment that paid off for both the workers and the economy. It gave enrollees new hope, determination to succeed and a zest for living that served them well when they returned to civilian life.

Minnesota banker Tom Sweeney wrote about his CCC experience in a book called *Echo Trail*. This excerpt expresses beautifully what the CCC was all about:

"…The knowledge acquired in the CCC transformed us into what surely became the best generation in our nation's history…invincible in battle, humane in victory, resolute in our quest for a better world, conscientious toward our environment, strong in our belief in God and our country. We made contributions to our society of man that have never been equaled. The CCC set the stage for us and we, like Shakespeare, found it to be the whole world. No American youth left that stage without becoming a better man."

# Letter Vividly Describes CCC Life in National Park

IN SUMMER OF 1937, Washington Congressman Charles Leavy received a letter from William Nowlin, a landscape architect directing a CCC camp in Mt. Rainier National Park. On July 8, 1937, the Congressman read excerpts from that letter on the floor of the House of Representatives, saying it was "superior to any description I could give of the national parks and the CCC".

The text was submitted by CCC alumnus Bud Wilbur of San Diego, California, who says he found this "treasure" in the Hawaii State Archives.

Dear Judge Leavy:

All's quiet along the Chanapecosh except the raindrops pattering on my tent. It can rain so easily here. The clouds seem to hang on the treetops and release the moisture so gently, so cheerfully and so unceasingly. The sun is always on the point of breaking through but never quite succeeds. This is the seventh day of rain.

All week, these CCC Arkansas boys have worked out in the woods uncomplainingly, until yesterday. They put on those Army rainproof clothes—tin pants, they call 'em. They lean them up against a stump, climb up on top and jump into them.

They are about as stiff as a suit of armor, like the knights used to wear, except the armor had joints at the knees and elbows. They do not clank or ring, but when they walk, it makes a noise like filing a saw.

One of my "gang", a little fellow weighing about 100 pounds, came out to work the other day without his "tin pants" and I sent him back to get them. There was only one pair left—size 44.

## Had a Sense of Humor

Well, he got into them, bent the bottoms up so that he could walk, found a piece of half-inch rope to hold them up and gathered moss enough to fill them out around the waist. He also made himself a wig and some whiskers of moss and reported "ready for duty". These boys have a sense of humor.

There is such a variety and contrast to this work. One day we are planting delicate, lacy ferns on the bank of a stream and laying a carpet of green moss around them, and the next day we will be digging with a steam shovel or using a "cherry picker" to replace weathered boulders, weighing about a ton, to keep campers from driving where they are not supposed to.

Then we build stone fireplaces, plus huge log tables so heavy the people can't move them around…and we stencil, carve and burn signs on the face of cedar logs cut in half…build trails and footpaths…and haul gravel in dump trucks to surface roads.

Believe me, these boys are workers. They average over 20 years old, and most have more than a year's experience in national park work (which is a lucky thing for me). The hardest task is to have work enough to keep them busy. I assign them a job I think will last all day, and in a few hours the leader will come and ask what to do next.

## CCC Built Character

I hope they make the CCC permanent, even if they have to discontinue the Army and Navy. It's a great character-building institution. They get better training than in any school or college. I think it is the greatest thing the present administration has done.

We have no horizon here. Just trees everywhere. I like these tall hemlocks and firs. Your eyes follow them upward to a little patch of blue sky or gray sky and maybe a white cloud. "To contemplate the sky is good for the soul," somebody said.

I wish you could see this river. It is not a large river. It is small enough to be friendly. You can walk on one bank and enjoy the verdure on the other side. On a hot day, when the glacier silt comes down, it turns milky white; when

**HARD WORK AND FRESH AIR. Like many CCC crews, these young men building a road near Lancaster, California lived and worked outdoors—no matter what the weather.**

Brown Brothers

rain is falling, the water is green and white; and at times it appears blue and white. It is always in such a hurry and is always singing.

About a mile from here there is another stream called Laughing Water Creek. Follow along the trail for a little ways and suddenly you will feel a cool breeze and hear a sort of musical roar. A few steps more and the water seems to leap at you from the treetops.

Halfway down it separates into spray and mist; then it collects itself from the rocks and ferns into liquid form once more and goes giggling and gurgling down the mountainside.

There is a cedar swamp not far from here where there are many venerable cedars 12 to 16 feet in diameter at the base. There is one where these trees have grown together that measures 26

feet. Douglas firs 6 feet in diameter are common. The hemlocks and white pines are more slender, but very tall.

There is an undergrowth of vine, maple, three kinds of huckleberries and ferns everywhere. There are lots and

---

*"They get better training than in any school..."*

◈

---

lots of flowers, but they are so perfectly blended with ferns and moss that they are unnoticeable. You have to search for them. It's quite a shock to go out into civilization and see poppies, peonies and other highly colored flowers—they seem artificial, gaudy, like Christmas tree decorations.

There are plenty of brown and black

bears here, but they are wild in this corner of the park and we don't see them often.

There is a bird called a vireo that stays in the trees around my tent, and every morning about 2:30, he starts to blow a police whistle. I hope he swallows it someday. This is a fine place to sleep, however, and eat.

We have a baseball team, but we have to go 42 miles to find an open space big enough for a diamond, and a ball over the outfielder's head is lost forever in the jungles.

When these boys are dressed up, ready to go to a dance or somewhere, they might be so many boys from any college in the country. They are tall, husky and fine-looking lads and they dress nicely... Sincerely, your friend,
William S. Nowlin

# CWA Provided Temporary Relief to Starving Miners

*By Robert Cloyd, Lafayette, Indiana*

TO ORDINARY CITIZENS at the point of starvation in 1932, it seemed that Congress and President Herbert Hoover didn't have the foggiest idea how to ease the Great Depression—or even the inclination to try.

The only poor relief in our poverty-stricken mining town of Clinton, Indiana was free Red Cross flour and the "miners' commissary". Every other week, the miners' union distributed whatever foodstuffs it could put together. The union wasn't in much better financial condition than its unemployed members, and while the handouts were gratefully accepted, the quality was often questionable.

### Waited for Pork and Cork

Men would stand in line for hours to receiver their "miners' rations". This usually consisted of a 2-pound slab of fat bacon; a pound each of sugar, margarine, rice and navy beans; a pound of coffee, which was laced generously with ground cork; sometimes a pound of cornmeal; and maybe a couple of tins of canned milk.

All that put together wouldn't fill a 1990s grocery bag, and it certainly wouldn't feed a family for 2 weeks. But it was better than nothing.

Shortly after President Franklin Roosevelt's inauguration in 1933, Congress created the Federal Emergency Relief Administration and appropriated hundreds of millions of dollars to fund the Civil Works Administration.

The CWA, largely ignored in history books, never received the recognition accorded its successors like the WPA, CCC and PWA. It operated less than 12 months in 1933 and '34, but the temporary relief it provided was a true godsend to the hundreds of hungry people in our town.

A hastily arranged office was provided, and men requesting relief were required to sign up for work. A group was selected each day to perform menial tasks like sweeping sidewalks and streets, rak-

*SCRIP SURVIVAL.* Robert Cloyd recalls a true government godsend to his Indiana town.

ing leaves and cleaning ditches. At the end of the day, each man received scrip for $3 in groceries.

The men could work only once every 10 days to 2 weeks. They'd laugh at each other good-naturedly as they leaned on their brooms, rakes and shovels doing these make-work jobs. But they eagerly grabbed the $3 scrip at the end of the day.

That scrip meant each man's family would have something to eat, at least once a day, for a week or more. In 1933 and '34, it took two people to carry home the groceries that $3 would buy. ⊠

**FOND MEMORIES.** Lillian Carter recalls the National Youth Administration was good to her (story below).

## NYA Paid Teens to Learn Valuable Skills

AT 16, I became a charter member of the National Youth Administration in Bamberg, South Carolina. When I started in 1935, my pay was $11 a month. It later rose to $16.

I was allowed to keep my money, as long as I shared with my sisters. For instance, if I bought a new dress for myself, I had to buy dresses for my sisters the following month.

We girls were taught cooking, sewing, crafts and how to get along with other teenagers. The boys learned carpentry and shop skills.

In the beginning, I rode the school bus to the program headquarters in Bamberg. After about a year, the girls were required to take turns "living in" Monday through Friday. We lived in a house rented and furnished by the government, with a strict but fair housemother.

The program was a lot of fun and had a great impact on many young people. It certainly had a positive influence on my life.
—*Lillian Carter*
*Augusta, Georgia*

## Employee on Dam Project Forgot His WPA "Alias"

AT THE HEIGHT of the Depression and the dust storms in 1934, I tried to get hired on the WPA's huge Fort Peck Dam project on the Missouri River in Montana. I hitchhiked across the state line several times to apply, but only Montana workers were being hired.

One day I was visiting a chum in Montana. He'd just received notice that a job was waiting for him at the dam, but he couldn't take it. He had to stay home and help out on the farm.

I asked him for the notice and went straight to the employment office. I was the 10th man hired on the first phase of the dam project and promptly forgot that I'd gotten the job under someone else's name.

When the boss lined us up and started assigning duties, he looked at me and said, "Everett, you unload the truck."

I looked behind me. Who was he talking to?

The boss repeated the order. Still no response. So he walked over, punched me in the chest and said, "I mean you, Sleepy." Everyone else just howled with delight.

The name stuck with me throughout my 4 years on the job. Today, more than 60 years later, old friends still call me Sleepy.
—*Earl Keehn*
*Puyallup, Washington*

## Agriculture Program Left Some Farmers Brokenhearted

I REMEMBER THE AAA program President Roosevelt started to help farmers and regulate production.

In 1933, the Agriculture Adjustment Administration paid farmers in west-central Texas to plow up some of the cotton they had planted and then destroy it.

The government also bought surplus cattle, collected them in pens and shot them. I recall seeing a man using a rifle to destroy what must have been 100 head of cattle in a single pen.

The farmers who owned the cattle could keep the meat for home consumption or give it away, but they were not allowed to sell it.

A large number of people in our community benefited from this free meat. But my dad never forgot the experience of plowing up beautiful green cotton or killing his cattle.
—*Calvin Drake, Duncanville, Texas*

**TOUGH TIMES.** Calvin Drake, posing on his horse, recalls crops being plowed under.

### Family of Seven Lived on $3 a Week

PRAISE THE LORD for the WPA—it kept lots of people from starving. Daddy worked for the WPA 2 days a week in Dodson, Louisiana, earning $1.50 a day.

Sometimes he got a third day's work, but not often. Can you imagine raising a family of seven on $3 a week?

Daddy also made money by trapping wild animals and selling the hides. One woman would give him 25¢ for every opossum he brought her. Mother once made a quilt top and sold it for $2.

There was also a CCC camp about 10 miles away where a movie was shown every Saturday night. A neighbor sometimes rounded up all the kids who wanted to go and drove us there so we'd have some entertainment.
—*Dorothy Howard, Houston, Texas*

**BONANZA!** Dorothy Howard's department store job earning 20¢ an hour seemed like a fortune to a teenager.

**GO NORTH, YOUNG MAN.**
William Menth never made
it to California.

I WAS 15 when I left home to join the CCC. It was my first train ride. What a thrill it was to eat in the dining car! I'd been told I was going to California but ended up in Walker, Minnesota on a cold, snowy night. Off we went to camp, where we were issued blankets and sheets.

During inspection the next day, I was asked where my other sheet was. I told the man it was under my mattress. How did I know I was to sleep between two sheets? I never did at home.

Camp was 7 miles from town by the road, but only a mile away if you walked across a frozen lake. I never could get used to the sound of ice cracking under my feet,

but if you wanted to go to the show, you only had two choices.

While in Minnesota, we planted more pine trees than Carter had little pills. There must be quite a forest there now.

I served in a total of four camps. The last was in Springfield, Missouri, where we did soil conservation work and built the Roaring River Trout Farm, which remains an Ozarks tourist attraction to this day.

The CCC was great—three meals, clean quarters and plenty of discipline, which was good for some of us. After serving for 2 years, I went on to a bigger camp— the U.S. Navy. —*William Menth* *Kansas City, Missouri*

# Struggling Newlyweds Found Jobs with WPA

*By Elizabeth Mason, Lodi, California*

DURING my senior year in high school, in 1936, the school superintendent recommended my best friend and me for jobs with the National Youth Administration. We both came from large families, so it really helped with our school expenses.

We had to work a certain number of hours in exchange for pay of $6 a month. I spent most of my hours in the principal's office, typing and running errands.

After graduation, I found work as a waitress in a nearby town. There were very few jobs for single men, so my boyfriend joined the CCC. We decided to wait for things to improve before we got married.

When Elven finally got a steady job in our hometown grocery store, he borrowed his grandparents' Ford and drove to the town where I was working. We were married there in the Baptist parsonage, then returned to our hometown and rented a two-room house.

On our second Saturday in our new home, Elven came

*"What a great day it was
when we were approved..."*

home from work dragging his feet. The boss had let him go. The boss' brother, who had two small children, had lost his job and was hired to take Elven's place. I can't remember much about eating our dinner that night.

My parents still had four children living at home, so we had no choice but to move in with Elven's parents. What a great day it was when we were approved for WPA jobs! We were both so grateful to get work.

We rented a small homemade trailer house, and I started working for a doctor's wife. My pay was $1 a day, plus lunch. Elven worked at a quarry, and he enjoyed it, although it was hard and dangerous work. The rock was quarried by hand. Later, the rocks were used to build a stone wall surrounding our county courthouse.

There was no shame in WPA work, and the men soon took other jobs as the economy improved. There's always pride in doing a job well. ▨

**WELL DONE.** Elven and Elizabeth Mason (below) know firsthand about the crucial difference programs like the WPA could make. The wall Elven is proudly sitting on at left was made from stone he helped quarry while working for the WPA.

# Brothers' CCC Service Meant Health for The Whole Family

*By R.J. Greth, Reading, Pennsylvania*

A LOT OF PEOPLE were poor to the point of desperation during the Depression, and my folks were no exception. Dad not only lost his job, he developed a devastating illness that meant he *couldn't* work.

Though my brother John and I were the only children still at home, poverty brought two of my sisters back in those dark times. Neither John nor I could find employment. There wasn't even money to buy Dad's medicine.

When President Roosevelt established the Civilian Conservation Corps, John and I joined up as soon as possible.

I still remember the relief in my parents' eyes when they learned they'd be getting $50 a month from our efforts. It wasn't much, but it meant food and medicine.

Although my primary goal was helping my family, I can honestly say joining the CCC wasn't a sacrifice. For the first time in years, I had clothes that weren't rags. And food! Most of us boys ate everything in sight for the first few months. The food was better than good —it was delicious. And there was always plenty of it, no matter how hungry you were.

The work was hard for a skinny, undernourished 17-year-old. At first, I was put on a road-building crew, breaking rocks with a sledgehammer.

When I transferred to a surveying crew, I got along much better. We were assigned to measure and identify trees in the national forests of Virginia. That meant days in the woods, hiking up and down hills. I learned to pace myself and really liked being outdoors.

I joined the church in the town near our camp and got to know a lot of the local people. Those Appalachian mountain people were unlike any folks I'd known before. They pretty much lived off the land and what they could grow on their small farms in the hollows. To this day, I remember them fondly.

My best memory of all was hitchhiking back home to Pennsylvania for the first time and walking unannounced into the kitchen in my new CCC uniform. Mom got up to hug me so fast she spilled her coffee. Dad shook my hand until I thought it would drop off.

They sure looked good to me after months away, but my joy wasn't just in seeing them again. It was knowing that they were actually better off than they had been before. The CCC had given all of us a new lease on life. ⊠

**GROWING BOYS.** By the time Richard Greth's sister Melva visited him at his CCC camp (above) he'd already started to fill out from hard work and his "three squares" a day. In the photo at left, Richard is standing at far left with his CCC buddies.

---

**GYM DANDY.** This impressive structure looks great over 60 years later.

## Rock Gymnasium Remains a Source of Pride

WHEN MT. CROGHAN High School's rock gymnasium was completed by the WPA in 1936, it was said to be one of the finest in South Carolina.

The stones to build this structure were gathered from the fields and hauled in by interested citizens. The construction project required many workers and provided desperately needed income for struggling families.

After the Mt. Croghan schools closed in the 1960s, the gym stood vacant for several years. The property later was deeded to the town, and today the building is in excellent condition.

The "rock building" is not only a local landmark but a source of pride. It holds many memories for those who remember the positive impact its construction had on our community.

—*Gene Sellers, Mt. Croghan, South Carolina*

*HOME SWEET TENT.* Members of the CCC's "reforestation army", like Fred Haggerty in the story below, spent an awful lot of time living outdoors in tents like this. Despite the hardships, most recall those days with fondness.

## Camp in Forest Taught "Hard Joes" to Fit in

THE COAL MINES in our Pennsylvania town shut down in the early 1930s, leaving our family of nine with no regular income. Dad and three of us boys worked the old coal banks for leavings. We could gather half a ton in a morning's work.

Then came the CCC, and my brother and I joined. An Army truck picked up 30 men from our area and moved us to Fort Hoyle. After 30 days of boot camp, we were outfitted in World War I uniforms, including wrap leggings.

In August, our company of 100 men was sent to a cleared area of national forest. "Cleared" meant only that there were no big trees. We still had to clear out the bushes, snakes and porcupines to put up our tents. When we got things in shape, we were turned over to the forest rangers.

First we built a road at the foot of the tree-stripped, eroded slopes. Then we started planting trees in two-man teams. This continued until December, when we couldn't make so much as a dent in the frozen ground.

We were in the same tents until February. It was below zero many times, but there was very little sickness. We had a lot of "hard Joes" in our outfit at the be-

ginning, but there was not much discord in the months that followed.

My family received $25 a month and I got $5. Nowadays that wouldn't keep the wolf away for a week, but back then it made a huge difference.

We worked for our welfare and did something good for the forest. When I went back 20 years later to see what had grown, I couldn't even get in there with a car because of the trees.

The 18 months I spent in the CCC were probably the most healthful part of my life. That's what they should do with guys today who can't seem to fit in. My dad and the police were glad to see me go...and just as glad to see me come home.                          —*Fred Haggerty*
*Elm, Pennsylvania*

## Government Workers Took Pride in Their Labors

MY FATHER, grandfather and father-in-law all worked for the WPA. This program not only created jobs, it enabled many communities to undertake projects that otherwise would have cost millions of dollars.

Pittsburg, Kansas and several other towns in the area still have brick streets laid by WPA workers. The men also dug farm ponds, and they built dams with hand-carried rocks and bricks. The cement was stirred by hand with small crank-type mixers.

Everything was done by hand, so these projects took many months to complete. It was backbreaking work, but the men were proud to earn their wages, and they took great pains to do the job right.

The CCC built lakes and dams and created gorgeous state parks that are still in use today. Former open-pit coal mines were stocked with fish. Access roads were built and the surrounding area beautified with trees and picnic tables.

These programs kept many families from starving and allowed struggling men to accept help without damaging their pride. They weren't handed anything. They had to work hard for everything they got, and they took pride in that.     —*Lois Curnutt, Odessa, Texas*

## Things Went Swimmingly After WPA Came to Town

THE WPA BUILT many roads and bridges around our area. But what I enjoyed most was the swimming pool built in my hometown of Chappell, Nebraska.

The kids had nowhere to swim in dryland wheat country, so the pool was a welcome addition. It really improved life in our small community, and parents and kids alike still enjoy it.

Since Dad worked for the WPA, we received commodities like flour, dried fruit, cornmeal, cheese and cod-liver oil. We kids hated that cod-liver oil, but it must have helped us. We never got colds and were a pretty healthy bunch.

The WPA provided an income for our family and allowed Dad to keep his pride intact by working instead of just getting a handout.     —*Dlores DeWitt*
*Colorado Springs, Colorado*

*SUCCESS STORY.* Dlores DeWitt's family (she's the tall child at right) was kept healthy, both fiscally and physically, by WPA benefits.

# Kids Learned the Value of Working Hard

*By Raymond Larson, White Cloud, Michigan*

IN THE 1930s, President Franklin Roosevelt started a myriad of government programs to try to lift the country out of the Depression.

Many adults worked on WPA projects in my hometown of Ramsay, Michigan. They installed a badly needed sewage system and built a 5-foot dam to create a swimming pond.

### Snow Jobs

In the winter of 1935-36, the NYA put teenagers to work shoveling snow—a continuous job in an area that received an annual snowfall of 200 to 300 inches.

We were paid 50¢ a day and worked 2 or 3 days a week. That paid our way to the movies and skating rink, with a little left over for a bottle of soda pop and a candy bar.

In 1939, I joined the CCC, which *really* put me to work

**MUCH TO BE PROUD OF.** Residents of this CCC camp in northern Michigan improved the area.

building trails and a park at the mouth of the Black River on Lake Superior. Camp Norrie was located on the Wisconsin-Michigan border near Ironwood, Michigan.

### Six-Month Hitch

Most of the boys were between 18 and 25 and signed up for a 6-month hitch. We made about $30 a month. We could keep $8 of that and had to send the rest home to our parents.

Camp rules were strict. On weekdays, we got up at 6 a.m. By 7, we were loaded onto trucks for the 25-mile trip to Black River Harbor. We quit at 4 p.m. and rode back to camp.

By the time supper was over, it was usually dark. We dried our clothes over the wood stoves and had a couple of hours to spend at the small library and recreation room, which had one pool table and a radio.

Saturday was inspection day, and our barracks had to be clean and neat. If the

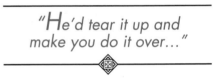

*"He'd tear it up and make you do it over..."*

inspector couldn't bounce a coin off the blanket on your bed, he'd tear it up and make you do it over.

On Sunday, we could walk a couple of miles to town and take in a movie if we had a dime to spare. Sometimes we just window-shopped and whistled at the girls. Those who lived close enough to camp could hitchhike home.

Working in a CCC camp taught us discipline and hard work, which prepared us for things to come.

---

### Solo at CCC Camp Put Audience in the Spirit

AS A TEENAGER, I played in a quartet called "The Novelty Four"—three accordion players and one guitarist.

We played at reunions, anniversary parties, church socials and other events. The sponsor would pass the hat, and we'd pick up a bit of change. A little went a long way in those days, so we always jumped at the chance to play.

In June of 1936, my group was asked to play at a CCC camp, where the Women's Christian Temperance Union was putting on a program.

The other group members could not play on that date, so I was asked to come to play a couple of solos.

As I stood backstage waiting to perform, I could see the boys were bored with the WCTU speaker's message. After working all day cleaning up the mess from a recent flood, they weren't too interested in hearing about the dangers of demon rum.

A lady standing backstage with

**LET THE FUN BEGIN.** Mary Toland (in the center of the back row) enjoyed playing her accordion.

me had noticed the boys' boredom, too, and began looking through my music. Suddenly her face lit up. With a twinkle in her eye, she handed me a piece of sheet music and dared me to play it.

When the speaker introduced me, I walked onstage and began playing *Roll Out the Barrel*. Believe me, the boys who had dozed off woke up in a hurry. It was great to see smiles on those tired faces.

The WCTU speaker wasn't too pleased at first, but eventually even she saw the humor in the situation.

—*Mary Toland*
*Citrus Heights, California*

# CCC Worker Kept Journal Of His Arizona Experiences

**COOK'S TOUR.** Charles Eiser spent much of his time in Arizona in the Hulalapai Mountains cooking. Pumps above were part of the camp's service station.

**COME 'N' GET IT!** After helping cook the food, Charles had to let the men know it was time to eat. At left he's about to ring the "dinner bell". The photo above shows a couple of Charles' friends posing with their truck, while the photo at far left shows Charles relaxing in the doorway of his barracks.

CHARLES EISER joined the CCC in January 1940 and was sent to Kingman, Arizona, which had a main camp and two "side camps". Charles was sent to Buck and Doe side camp in the Hulalapai Mountains, near the south rim of the Grand Canyon.

His wife, Dorothy, of Bensalem, Pennsylvania, sent these excerpts from Charles' journal between April and June:

**April 2:** It's a very nice day and the sun is out. The mountains are full of snow and very beautiful. I had mechanics class today.

**April 3:** I carried wire today and got scratched up a bit. Boy, have I got an appetite.

**April 8:** We finished our last job yesterday and then went to a different part of the state. It's a 1-1/2-hour ride, and there is a mining camp or town called Producers Mines. It's in very beautiful country.

**April 9:** A very hard day. We had to dig holes 2 feet deep into solid rock, and boy, was it hard. One hole a day. Very tired tonight.

**April 11:** Saw some pretty flowers I had never seen before. I never thought there were so many flowers in the desert.

**April 19:** Working in camp at present. I started a mechanics class, me being the teacher. Here's hoping they come. I saw Indians riding and roping in camp today.

**April 27:** What a day—everybody went to the main camp except six of us. We baked doughnuts until 1:45 a.m.

**April 29:** Everybody was happy until the Army inspector came unexpectedly and caught the kitchen in a mess about 11:30 a.m. Three of the KP's got sent down the main camp. I happened to be working pretty good, so I stayed.

**May 10:** The company went to a forest fire school today.

**May 29:** I am still in the side camp on KP. Today went arrow-hunting and found some good specimens.

**June 3:** Well, here I am, cooking at Buck and Doe, one day on and one day off. My first day was pretty good. In fact, I ate the food myself.

**June 14:** First cook was sick the last few days. I cooked supper for him today. We leave Buck and Doe tomorrow. Indians joined us for dinner. Heat 115°.

**June 19:** Main camp. Woke early. Went to work hauling rocks. Saw our little Indian boy friend for the last time. He cried when we left. We turned in our clothes tonight. ⊠

**JOB SUITED THEM. Carl Crumpton's four older brothers bought the clothes they're wearing from their CCC earnings.**

## In Family of 12, Half Worked for The Government

THOSE "alphabet soup" programs put soup on our family's table and clothes on our backs.

Of the 12 members in our family, half worked for the government. My dad worked on roads for the WPA. He wasn't paid much, but the job entitled us to government commodities—primarily food staples.

Mom worked for the WPA, too, as a cook in the lunch program at the elementary school in Ogden, Kansas.

But what helped us most was having my four oldest brothers in the CCC. Each brother served in a different state—Edward in Washington, Earl in Minnesota, Elmer in Kansas and Albert in Oregon.

The boys planted trees, fought forest fires and built windbreaks, shelterbelts and dams. In exchange for their work, they received food, shelter and clothes, and each was allowed to keep $5 of his monthly $30 pay. The rest was sent back home.

The money from those four boys in the CCC helped support the six kids and two parents back home. We had food, clothes, and the books, papers and pencils we needed on our desks at school. Being poor was normal to us during the '30s...we never knew anything else.

—*Carl Crumpton, Topeka, Kansas*

## Bag Lunch and Brute Force Only Prerequisites for This Workshop

AS A YOUNG FARM couple with small children, we needed many things we couldn't afford—like beds and bedding. When we heard the WPA was going to conduct workshops to supervise the making of mattresses, we decided to apply.

We were accepted and told to bring a bag lunch for the day. Everything else would be furnished. The cost of the materials for each mattress would be $4.

When we arrived, the blue and white ticking was already sewn together on three sides, ready to fill. It was up to us to prepare the filling, which came in the form of large rolls of hard-packed cotton.

We were given long wooden flails, which we beat the cotton furiously with until it fluffed up. Then layer after layer was inserted into the ticking until it was at least 8 inches thick. The fine dust from the cotton almost choked us, and we

were covered from top to toe with fine brown dust. We looked like Pillsbury doughboys.

When the mattresses were finally filled, we stitched the fourth side shut. The final job was to stabilize the filling by running long strands of strong thread all the way through the mattress with a 5-inch needle. It was strenuous work, but our need for mattresses drove us to do our best.

We made two mattresses that day, and they outlasted any other mattress we ever had.

—*Annette Oppegard St. Paul, Minnesota*

## CCC Camp Construction Provided Jobs, Too

I WASN'T a member of the CCC, but I did work on the construction of two CCC camps in Washington State—one south of Carnation, the other east of North Bend.

At Carnation, I helped lay pipeline to bring water to the camp—which is another way of saying I had a job as a ditch digger. We must have dug a mile-long trench for that 2-inch pipe. At North Bend, my job was keeping carpenters supplied with materials for studs and rafters.

Though I was fortunate to get these jobs, they were only temporary. From the time the footings were dug for the North Bend camp, it took only 14 days before it was ready for occupancy.

—*La Monte Harris, Shawnee Mission, Kansas*

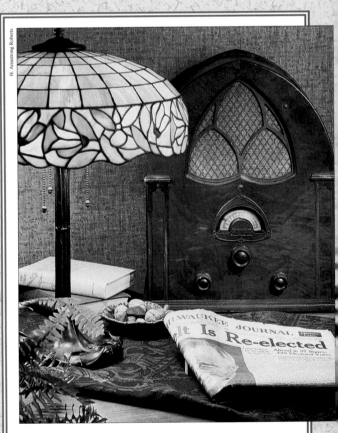

H. Armstrong Roberts

**THE "SOUP" MAKER. President Roosevelt's re-election in 1936 and again in 1940 ensured that the array of social programs instituted and administered by the government to combat the Depression would stay in effect for a bit longer.**

## WPA Taught Sewing, Secretarial Skills

THE FIRST WPA projects in Fall River, Massachusetts provided jobs for heads of families, with lots of heavy labor. As the program grew, so did the need for office workers to handle the paperwork. Training sites were opened to teach women and teenagers office skills and accounting.

The city also established sewing centers. Women learned to make shirts, pants and housedresses, which the welfare department gave to needy families. They weren't designer clothes, but with this assistance, my folks didn't need to buy me anything to wear to school except shoes.

The sewing centers didn't inspect clothes before sending them out, so some items were returned because of flaws. At first, these clothes weren't repaired or recycled—they were simply thrown out with sewing remnants.

This was a bonanza for me. After the centers closed at night, I'd go through the trash to salvage rags to sell for pocket change.

The WPA provided our city with many benefits. Before long, we had a skilled labor force and a thriving economy.

—*Stanley Batog, Ocala, Florida*

## CCC Saved the Day When School Roof Caught Fire

THE CCC came to our town in 1935 and established a camp near the city limits. The camp boosted our community's economy, and the whole county benefited from its work.

In 1938, I learned firsthand how efficient the workers could be in an emergency. I was teaching in a two-room country school when a man ran in one winter afternoon. "Lady, I hate to tell you," he said, "but your schoolhouse is on fire." Then he ran upstairs to alert the teacher and students there.

When we got outside the building, we saw the roof was ablaze. But a CCC truck was there with a crew, ladders, buckets, ropes and an ax.

Some men were on the roof, knocking off burning shingles, while others filled buckets from the school's well. The buckets were attached to ropes and drawn to the roof, and the fire was soon extinguished. If these men hadn't seen the fire and been equipped to help, the building would have been destroyed before help could have been summoned.

A few years ago, while my husband was in the local hospital, his roommate mentioned that he'd served in the CCC camp here in the 1930s. When I told him about the crew that saved our schoolhouse, he said, "I was one of those men."

—*Roberta Johnson, Russellville, Kentucky*

## WPA Road Crew Made Travel Possible Year-Round

THE WPA not only helped my brother and many of our neighbors by giving them jobs, it also transformed our roads, which were almost impassable in winter, to routes we could travel anytime.

*"BASIC" TRAINING.* Before heading to a northern-Minnesota CCC camp in the fall of 1933, Jim Donavan (left) and Avery Burgoon received indoctrination at Fort Snelling, Minnesota. Jim lives in El Cajon, California today.

Before the WPA, all roads in our area were mud, with axle-deep ruts in the rainy season. Sometimes the only way to travel was with horses and a wagon.

My brother, Leroy, started working on a WPA bridge crew in 1939. The workers built hundreds of small concrete bridges that made new gravel roads possible.

The gravel was poured into road forms about 8 feet wide and 6 inches deep, just like the forms used for pouring concrete. It took a year or two for the gravel to pack down, but it was still 10 times better than what we were used to. The WPA also cut down brush, cleaned the ditches and widened the roadbed.

—*Donald Catt, Flat Rock, Illinois*

*CATT PACK.* Donald Catt (the bareheaded kid on the left in the front row) does not recall those Depression days as being particularly unhappy for the kids in his family. While it was true they had little money, no one else did either, so folks got by the best they could.

# Chit-Based Welfare System Kept Families Fed

*By Stanley Batog, Ocala, Florida*

**AN EGG A WEEK.** Welfare in Stanley Batog's day meant that your family got food—but no money—based strictly on need.

WELFARE during the Great Depression was very different than the system we know today. I know, because I grew up a "welfare child" in Fall River, Massachusetts in the 1930s.

In those days, a welfare system was community based. Those working in the welfare office were your neighbors. They had intimate knowledge of any applicant and could readily see any change in circumstances.

This welfare system didn't involve cash. Once on the welfare rolls, a family would report to the neighborhood office every Monday to receive their chits or vouchers. The vouchers were based on the number of family members and their ages.

There was a milk voucher for children, and one for eggs and butter (each person was allotted one egg a week). These vouchers could be traded only on Tuesdays. The Wednesday vouchers were for meat, with the amount and weight based on family size.

Thursday's vouchers were for use at welfare distribution points, where families picked up a month's supply of various items. One Thursday it might be canned goods; another Thursday, staples like flour, sugar, oatmeal and rice; and on another, fruits and vegetables.

Those who volunteered at the distribution sites could take home extra items that were left at the end of the day.

Volunteers were also the first to find out which Thursday would be "clothing day", when clothes from the WPA's new sewing centers were distributed. I made a point of skipping school on those Thursdays so I could be among the first in line.

> *"I made a point of skipping school to be among the first in line..."*

The Friday chits were always for fish, and the fish market determined what you got. Most weeks it was bony mackerel. Our family didn't eat fish, so we gave our chits to French or Portuguese families in neighboring tenements.

As Fall River's economy began to pick up in the late '30s, more people were able to find work. The local welfare office always knew who was working and reduced their chit amounts gradually until the family was off the welfare rolls.

Though I was a welfare child, it never hampered my ambitions. In fact, that experience was the catalyst that drove me to a very rewarding life.

**SIGN 'EM UP!** Although this looks like a military recruiter's office, it's actually a group of young men hoping to become part of the Civilian Conservation Corps. You'll notice that many of them are smiling. That's because just about all of them could expect their situations to improve markedly once they became part of the CCC. A steady job—even if it only paid $30 a month—was a rare find indeed during the Depression.

## NYA Program Ended "Biscuit Lunch"

FOR A BOY growing up on a Texas cotton farm, the National Youth Administration was a big help.

The NYA was founded in 1935 to give job training to unemployed young people. It provided part-time jobs that allowed many students to stay in school instead of dropping out to help support their families. The director of our state program was a young man named Lyndon Baines Johnson.

For my job, I arrived at school by 7 a.m. to start fires in six coal stoves and a small kerosene heater. During the last class period in the afternoon, I brought in buckets of coal and kindling for the next day. I was paid $6 a month, half of which was turned over to my parents to buy food for our family of six.

In high school, I began helping the custodian one class period each day to pay for my lunch. The new school lunch program was supported by rations from the county relief office, and vegetables and meat donated by local farmers.

Before this program began, my lunch was usually a biscuit with jelly.

*—James Bentley Sr., Nampa, Idaho*

## FDR "Tuned in" to the Common Man's Plight

OUR FAMILY of four lived in Branson, Missouri in 1937, and we were about as poor as you could get.

Dad was handicapped by polio, which made it nearly impossible to make a living. He'd tried numerous ventures without much success. During the Depression, even able-bodied men had no hope of an income.

One day we were down to our last tablespoon of peanut butter when a message came from the local CCC camp. The camp had a piano in its dayroom, and the instrument needed to be tuned. That was something Dad knew how to do.

**BIG JOB AHEAD.** The above photo was taken in August of 1933 in Oregon's Mt. Hood National Forest, says Oscar Perez of Chicago, Illinois. Oscar also took the picture at left. That one shows his CCC tent mates at the same site about a month or so later after cold weather had obviously come to the high country. Oscar belonged to Company #610.

Dad and I drove to the camp in our old Model T. While he worked, the CCC boys took me to the snack counter and gave me a 5¢ candy bar. It was round and filled with marshmallows— the first candy I'd ever eaten.

Dad was paid $3 for tuning that piano. It was just one of many times President Roosevelt saved the day for a common man who needed a little help to feed his family. *—Frances Sarvas Sharpsville, Pennsylvania*

## CCC Money Saved the Day

MY FATHER WAS an architect and builder. After the stock market crashed, he lost all but two homes he'd built in our community.

All we had to eat was potatoes, bread, jelly and a few vegetables from Mother's garden.

Sometimes Mother stinted on food for herself so she'd have enough to feed her husband and six children. I remember drink-

ing lots of water to keep us from being too hungry.

When the CCC camps opened, my brothers began working on a reforestation project at Babler Park near St. Louis, Missouri. They were paid $1 a day. They could keep a few dollars of their wages, but the rest had to be sent home.

By the grace of God, we somehow came through those years better and stronger. They say adversity builds character, and I've come to believe it.

*—Margaret Whitaker, Bunnell, Florida*

## Happy to Dig Ditches

THE WPA put many men back to work in my southern-Vermont hometown. It also provided our community's first public water system.

As a teenager, I benefited from the WPA, too, digging 6-foot-deep ditches from the curbs to people's houses. It was a big deal if I made $2. Those were exciting days. *—Howard Mattison Coraopolis, Pennsylvania*

# CCC Boys' Catcalls Had Horse and Rider on The Run

*By Henrietta Huffman*
*Mt. Crawford, Virginia*

**THE HORSE AND HENRIETTA.** A Morgan horse, a lovestruck teenage girl and a truckload of CCC boys spelled trouble.

THE CCC WORKED in the national forest near our home, and the crews traveled from one work site to another in large flatbed trucks.

It was so exciting for my sister and me to see these boys from faraway cities. The trucks passed our house almost daily, and we generally arranged to be in the front yard whenever one came by.

The boys would shriek and holler to us, and we'd wave and call back to them. The most they could do was throw us notes, so Mother didn't object too much. None of them had cars, and they couldn't leave the camps except in large groups for planned events.

My sister and I began to recognize some of the boys and look for them as the trucks passed. We fell in love over and over that summer, as only young girls can do. I was 16 years old, and life was full of possibilities.

## Morgan Made Up His Own Mind

Whenever we had errands to run, we saddled up "Logan". He was a Morgan horse, with a deep mahogany coat and shiny black mane and tail. He was handsome, and I think he knew it. He had a mind of his own and did our bidding only when it pleased him.

One morning Mother wanted something from the store, so I went out to catch Logan. After luring him with an ear of corn, I caught hold of his forelock and slipped on the bridle. After being curried and brushed, he was ready to saddle.

But Logan had a trick of filling up his chest with a big breath of air as he was being saddled. I forgot about that as I pulled the girth tightly under his stomach.

When I stepped up into the stirrup, the saddle turned to the side. Logan had let his breath out, and the saddle was loose. I had to saddle him all over

---

*"As soon as they saw me, they started whooping..."*

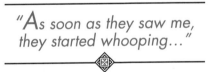

---

again, this time giving him a slap to make him exhale.

By the time I was finally ready to go, Logan was skittish. Exasperated, I slapped him with the reins and off we went.

Logan was trotting briskly down the road when we rounded a curve and saw a truckload of boys from the CCC camp coming toward us. As soon as they saw me, they started whooping, screaming and banging on the sides of the truck.

The noise scared Logan. He jumped up and down in place a couple of times, then turned and began galloping back the way we'd come. He was a runaway horse, headed for home and his stable.

To the people who lived along the road, it probably looked like I'd turned the horse around to chase the truck-load of boys!

But I had no control of that horse. I could barely hold onto the saddle and reins to keep from being thrown. Of course, the boys thought this was hilarious and screamed all the more.

## Barn or Bust

Soon the truck was out of sight in the distance, but Logan didn't slow down until he reached the barn. Somehow I held on, with a fistful of mane and a hand on the saddle. When he finally stopped, I got off, took the saddle down and put his blanket on.

Only after I'd given Logan some water and put him in his stable did I realize my knees were shaky. I could barely walk back to the house. I found Mother in the kitchen, with her back turned to me. "Well," she said, "where's the brown sugar?"

Shocked, I said, "What brown sugar?" I had completely forgotten that I'd been on my way to the store.

Something in my voice made Mother turn around. When she saw my disheveled appearance—wild hair, hat around my neck, clothes in disarray—she said, as she often did on such occasions, "Well, mercy me, what have you been up to now?"

When I explained and told her how mad I was at Logan and the CCC boys, she decided the brown sugar could wait until tomorrow. ☒

# CHAPTER THREE

# When Hoboes Rode the Rails

***NO TICKET NECESSARY.*** Hopping a freight train during the Depression was often the only way people desperate for any kind of opportunity could get from one part of the country to another. (Photo: Brown Brothers)

# From the desk of Clancy Strock

Dear Katie,

I'm sure that you've never met a hobo. In fact, I suspect you don't even know what a hobo is.

During the Great Depression, there were thousands and thousands of them in America. Some people called them bums. But a man who really was a hobo for several years explained that a bum (or "tramp") was someone who wandered around, lived by begging and had no intention of working if he could avoid it.

A hobo, on the other hand, was a person between jobs. He wanted to work and needed to work but couldn't find employment. I'm sure you've seen raggedly dressed men (and even women) standing along the street, holding up signs that say something like, "Have no money. Will work for food."

Some of them are hoboes, some are bums.

I think you'll find this chapter interesting, because it contains true stories told by former hoboes...and a few self-confessed bums. Some were desperately looking for work wherever they could find it, others simply hit the road to enjoy an adventure.

Whatever the reason, they depended heavily on the kindness of strangers. Seldom were they disappointed, because the spirit of the times was that people took care of each other. Your great-great-grandmother was a tiny lady, but she never hesitated to feed the hoboes who knocked on her door. There was no reason to fear them.

Like most people back then, she had a hard time stretching the budget to feed her own family. But she couldn't find it in her heart to turn away a hungry person. Perhaps it was because she had a son of her own who'd left home to "ride the rails" and experience life as a hobo.

(It was quite a while before Gramma discovered that hoboes had chalked a special symbol on the curb in front of her home to tell other "'bos" she was a soft touch for a handout.)

Things are different today. Imagine a ragged, unshaven stranger showing up at your back door. If you were home alone, I hope you would run and dial 911.

As you read this next chapter, you'll learn how just about every freight train back then had scores of hoboes on top of boxcars and coal cars and inside them, too. Not just men, either. Hoboing was the only way penniless families could travel to search for new opportunities.

If there was a young mother with a baby aboard, other hoboes would get off when the train stopped and beg for milk. Hoboes looked after each other. They were a remarkable fraternity and their numbers were never larger than during the Great Depression.

*Your Grandpa Clancy*

# Train's Lonesome Whistle Recalls Life on the Road

*By Bart Oxley, Belmont, California*

IN THE QUIET of the night, in the twilight between sleep and consciousness, I sometimes hear the long, mournful wail of a train whistle in the distance.

Whenever I hear that lonesome sound, my mind drifts back to the day when my world was young. I see the glistening rails, ribbons of steels stretching away until they vanish. Men emerge from the cover of a hobo jungle near the tracks and stand along the roadbed, waiting for a train.

My most vivid memory of those days is from 1939, when

> *"An empty boxcar was the way to travel..."*

thousands like me were on the road, seeking jobs. That summer, I caught a freight train out of the yards in Los Angeles and became a harvest worker.

My first job was picking plums at Healdsburg. After 2 weeks, I jumped a Northwestern Pacific flatcar to Asti, where I cut and boxed grapes at a vineyard. The money was good—$6 a day.

Riding the rails from one harvest to another entailed a variety of experiences, none of which compared to the comfort

**CLOSE CALL. Bart Oxley, shown in a relaxed moment here, nearly lost his life trying to swing on board a rumbling freight train near Salem, Oregon.**

of a Pullman car.

An empty boxcar was the best way to travel. It was noisy and bumpy, but the steady clickety-clack of wheels rolling over steel rails provided a soothing melody that often lulled me to sleep.

Other occasions weren't so pleasant. After the grape harvest, I hopped a Southern Pacific gondola to Roseville to shock hay. That ride was so bouncy I thought the train would jump the tracks.

After that, I headed for Tulelake to sack potatoes. I climbed aboard an oil tanker as the train was moving out of a side track. I had to sit on the narrow wooden platform over the couplings, holding onto the brake wheel, while the train bucked and jerked like a wild bronco.

My final trip that summer was to Salem, Oregon on the Great Northern Line. I got a job cutting wood and lived in a hobo jungle just outside town. At the end of wood-cutting, I decided to head home. I was homesick and weary of the road.

## Rumble in the Jungle

As I waited in the jungle for a southbound train, I heard a whistle wail down the line and grabbed my sleeping bag. I could see the engine coming toward me, steam shooting from its cylinders in a white cloud along the roadbed.

There were four quick blasts from the whistle. That was to alert the stationmaster, not far from the jungle, to pass a message up to the engineer on a long pole.

The train reduced speed so the engineer could reach out and grab the message. As the train began to increase speed, again a fearful thought struck. Had I waited too long? Timing was critical in catching a moving freight.

I ran alongside the train, keeping my eyes on the passing cars, grasped the rungs of a boxcar with both hands and put my feet on the bottom step of the ladder. For a panic-stricken instant, my momentum pulled me away from the car. I clung desperately to the rungs.

Slowly, like chinning a crossbar, I pulled myself against the ladder. I stayed there for a minute, breathing heavily, before climbing to the top of the car and settling on the catwalk.

I looked at my hands. My fingers were burrowed with deep grooves where I'd grasped the rungs. It hurt, but I didn't mind. I was alive, and I was going home.

Brown Brothers

**OBSERVATION DECK. The sight lines were great from the top of a railroad car—and the price was reasonable, too. Still it was not a life for the squeamish.**

# Food Was Top Priority for Pair 'on the Bum'

*By George Baker, El Dorado Springs, Missouri*

FOR THOSE WHO didn't live through it, the Depression can be hard to understand. Jobs were scarce, and the lines of applicants were long. The unemployed took whatever measures necessary to stay alive. For some of my friends and me, this included "going on the bum".

My closest buddy and I had tried this a couple of times while in high school. So when road construction came to a halt during the snowy Iowa winter of 1936-37, we didn't hesitate to take to the road.

We started with about $15 between us. By the time we reached southern Texas, we were down to a dollar each. It was imperative that we hang on to those last 2 bucks.

If a man was rousted by the yard bulls and couldn't show a dollar, he was declared vagrant and sentenced to 30 days working on the county roads. We'd heard horror stories about

---

> *"A real meal was something we only dreamed of..."*

---

these "vag camps" and had no desire to check their accuracy firsthand.

From the beginning, we'd supplemented our meager funds by bumming handouts from back doors. Now we had to live on them.

Breakfast was easy. Every little town had a bakery, and we could usually get a free bag of day-old doughnuts or rolls.

During the day, we concentrated on getting handouts at back doors. We'd learned to avoid rich neighborhoods. The affluent didn't get that way by handing out leftovers, and sometimes they called the law. We avoided shantytowns, too—the folks there likely had little enough for themselves.

## Beggars Couldn't Be Choosers

The best bet was a farmhouse or a middle-class neighborhood, where we could usually get a peanut butter sandwich or some leftovers. We appreciated every morsel. Bums are not picky eaters. We weren't starving, but our bellies were never full. A real meal was something we only dreamed of.

In midwinter, we hopped a gondola in Beaumont, Texas. Yard bulls caught us in Lake Charles, Louisiana and kicked us off the train in the middle of the night. They worked us over pretty good.

After the train pulled out, we sneaked back into the depot to wash up and nurse our bruises. We were covered with coal soot and ashes, and a trickle of cold water didn't help our appearance much.

About daylight, we hitched a ride with a trucker and arrived in New Iberia, Louisiana in late afternoon. Hoping to get something to eat before dark, we decided to hit a few houses. Our first and only stop was a farmhouse some distance back from the road.

Two dirty, disheveled bums can be intimidating, so my partner waited at the road while I knocked. A lady of about 40 answered and looked me over carefully. Then she asked, "Is that boy out at the road with you?" I said he was.

Stepping inside, she returned with soap, a basin and a couple of towels. She told me to call my friend and wash up at the pump. She'd let us know when supper was ready.

## These Were True Grits

After a while, the woman invited us into a neat, clean kitchen. Two places were set at the table. Each plate held a small piece of fried ham, which I'm sure made the family's helpings smaller. There was a loaf of homemade bread, a generous hunk of country butter, a big bowl of hominy grits and a 2-quart jar of milk.

"We don't have a lot to offer," the woman said, "but you can have all the bread, milk and grits you want."

We were from Iowa and didn't even know what grits were, but, boy, did we eat. We finished off everything that was set before us.

As we ate, we could hear whispers from the dining room. "Who's in the kitchen, Mama?" "Shh, just eat your supper."

When we finished, the lady offered to get us more, but we declined—and not out of politeness. We were stuffed!

We appreciated any handout, but this was more than we expected. This lady invited us into her kitchen, just a few steps from where her family was dining. It gave our self-respect a much-needed boost.

I'm sure that fine woman has gone to her reward, and I hope she was somehow repaid for the kindness she showed a couple of bindle stiffs during the lean Depression years. ▨

**LOUISIANA ANGEL.** Just when George Baker (below) and a buddy were really down on their luck, they ran into a kind woman who restored their faith in humanity.

# After Court-Martial From CCC, He Hit the Road

*By Jack Lingle, Parsippany, New Jersey*

I WORKED during the summer of 1938 so I could enroll at St. Thomas College in Scranton, Pennsylvania that fall. I quickly discovered I had enough money for tuition, but not room and board. That same week, my brother, who was working for the National Youth Administration, received a notice to report to a CCC camp.

He didn't want to go, so I went in his place, figuring I'd work for 6 months, return with $180 and enroll for the second semester. I was sent to a camp in Winslow, Arizona and worked as a guide in the Petrified Forest and Painted Desert. Everything went well until the captain called me to his office one afternoon.

The identity switch had been discovered, and I was to be charged with fraud. I was court-martialed by a few officers and ordered to leave camp that night.

The guys took up a collection and gave me $4. I walked about 3 miles, then caught a freight train to Phoenix and another to Albuquerque, New Mexico. I found a hobo jungle under a bridge and had my first taste of "coffee in a can". The grounds had been boiled twice, but it sure was tasty. It was there that I first heard the song *Roll Out the Barrel*.

A few days later, we were on a Southern Pacific "hotshot" steaming into Canadian, Texas when someone shouted that Canadian was hostile.

### Ran for Their Lives!

As the train slowed down before the junction, about 20 of us jumped off and rolled down the banks. The railroad bulls chased us through a tunnel, their bullets ricocheting off the tunnel walls.

We were herded into a bullpen, where we showered and got a meal. Then we were taken out of town in the back of a truck, dumped off and told to keep going.

A guy named Jack Murphy and I met in the bullpen and decided to travel together. One stormy night in Texas, we

**TURNED OUT OKAY.** After being drummed out of the CCC, Jack Lingle (in his Army uniform above and second from left in inset) "hoboed" awhile before enlisting in the service. He's second from the right with his Army buddies in the top left photo.

got off a freight in pitch dark and made our way to a barn we could barely make out in the dark.

We lay down on the floor in the dark and were just dozing off when cows came in and began stepping all over us. Poor Murphy took some real abuse that night.

We spent several days in San Antonio looking for work, hitting up bakeries and stores for handouts and spending the nights in the hobo jungle.

### "Safety Belt" Protected Them

From there, we rode through Oklahoma, Kansas and Iowa, often traveling at night. Sometimes we strapped ourselves to the catwalk with a belt or a piece of rope.

We also rode the refrigerated cars, or "reefers". To ride a reefer, you opened the trapdoor on top and climbed down into the compartment that held the ice.

When the railroad police kicked us off a reefer, we'd look for the sand pile so we could warm up. With the old steam engines, sand was funneled onto the tracks for traction, and the pile was kept warm with a steam pipe. It was a good place to sleep after sitting on a block of ice half the night.

We rode on through Indiana, Ohio, Pennsylvania and finally to Baltimore, Maryland, where we quit the freights. A trucker heading for Scranton offered us a ride if we could help with gas money. We'd spent hardly anything—we were saving our money in hopes of finding a job in New York City—so we bought him 20 gallons.

The trucker dropped us off 16 miles from my hometown of Carbondale, Pennsylvania, and we hitchhiked the rest of the way. I had never been so grateful to see the streets of my hometown as I was that sunny day in October. ⊠

# Lessons of the Road Saved His Family 25 Years Later

*By Clyde Traver, Corning, California*

I BECAME A HOBO fresh out of high school, when I couldn't even get a job for a dollar a day. So I "grabbed an armful of boxcars", as we said, and left the Mississippi Valley with 18¢ in my pocket.

It took only a few days to learn the hobo signs left on posts and building corners. There were lots of alleys and backyard gates for us to advertise on: "Bad dog". "Poor feeder". "Generous owner—be polite".

Before long, I had grown to hate sleeping in the city dump and on the tops of boxcars. On a rainy night, any available space under a bridge or vacant building was a deluxe hotel.

But those 2 years on the road were my college education, and no man ever had a finer one. It helped me get a job when other men went hungry, raise nine children and pay cash for the house I retired in.

My first lesson came in a windswept city dump in South Dakota. Four of us were sitting around a small fire, reminiscing about the last time we'd eaten and dreaming of when we might eat again, when a man walked up and asked if he could join us.

"You know the rules of a hobo jungle," someone said. "Throw a stick on the fire, and welcome."

### An Incredible Offer

Moments later, the man returned with far more wood than protocol required. Pulling up an empty 5-gallon bucket, he sat down and said, "You boys look hungry. How do hotcakes, bacon and eggs sound for breakfast?"

Teasing a hungry man is dangerous; tantalizing him with food is suicide. But the man quickly added, "If you do what I tell you, I promise you we'll dine on pancakes, bacon and eggs within the hour."

All of us knew Jesus had fed 5,000 people with a few loaves and fishes, but this guy sure didn't look like Jesus. Yet something about him made us believe.

What did we have to lose? We were all cold and hungry. Most of us hadn't eaten for at least 24 hours, and the town we were in wasn't noted for being friendly to our kind. What did he suggest?

"Look," the man said, "when most of you hit a back door at this time of day, the lady of the house has just seen her husband off to work and her children off to school. She's kicking

**JUNGLE BRUNCH. While starving in a South Dakota hobo jungle, Clyde Traver met a man who taught him positive thinking.**

back with a cup of coffee before she starts her housework—and you ask her to make a sandwich? I'd say no myself.

"But if her neighbor dropped in and asked to borrow an egg or a cup of sugar, she's more than willing to oblige. How much trouble is it to go to the refrigerator for an egg?"

"What's your point?" someone asked.

"If you ask for a couple of eggs or a few strips of bacon, most women won't refuse," the man said. "She doesn't have to stop what she's doing to make you a sandwich. Now, if each of you will go and get what I ask, we'll get those pancakes started."

"Yeah? And what are you going to cook them on, a hot rock?"

"You let me worry about that, my friend. You just get the 2 dozen eggs."

### "Scavenger Hunt" Commenced

Within minutes, each of us had set off to get the requested ingredients. My errand was to get a pound of bacon.

At the first place I stopped, the housewife wanted to know why any man without a frying pan would want four strips of raw bacon.

When I explained, she gave me nearly a quarter pound, then directed me to her friend across the street and called her to explain before I even got there.

In less time than it usually took me to get a sandwich, I was back at the hobo jungle. Even so, I was one of the last to return.

During our absence, the stranger had scoured tin cans with ashes from the fire and was heating water for coffee. For his frying pan, he nailed a short wooden handle to the lid of a 5-gallon pail, also polished shiny clean with ashes.

That morning we dined on pancakes, bacon and eggs—all because one man had the ingenuity not to ask for a banquet, but for the ingredients to make his own.

Twenty-five years later, I remembered his wisdom when I found myself in Milwaukee, Wisconsin, out of work, with six hungry children to feed.

What do you do when there's no work, no welfare and your unemployment's about to run out? You make pancakes, bacon and eggs for breakfast.

First I took the problem apart and examined it. The rent was paid for another 3 weeks. There was enough coal to keep the house warm for 2 weeks or more if the children wore sweaters and heavy wool stockings. Our groceries might hold out for 2 weeks, and my wife had enough money to buy milk for the baby for about 10 days.

I knew there was work for me in California, but I had no money for a plane ticket or even bus fare. Once in California, I'd need a car to get from job to job and carry my tools.

---

*"You look hungry...how do bacon, eggs and hotcakes sound?"*

◆

---

But I had no money to buy a car.

Then I remembered an old car sitting beside a local service station. The owner wanted $25 for it. I raised the money by making the rounds at the union hall and other places where my friends hung out. Within an hour, I'd handed out several IOUs and had $27 in my pocket.

After cleaning up the car, I used it as collateral to obtain a $300 loan. I gave half the money to my wife and took off for California. After 4 days of hard driving and 3 of job-hunting, I was working again.

I sent my wife enough money to heat the house and put decent food on the table. Then I got a room in a boardinghouse, stopped sleeping in the car and had a decent meal myself—my first in 10 days.

Five months later, I went back to Milwaukee to get my family. I was driving a big station wagon that was only 3 years old and paid for.

I had 2 months' rent paid on a house and enough furniture to start housekeeping again. And all because I wanted bacon, eggs and pancakes floating in maple syrup for breakfast. ⊠

# Water Tanks Were Core Of Communication Network

*By M.L. "Hobo Bill" Mainer, Centralia, Illinois*

BEFORE THE DAYS of diesel power, steam engines had to stop every 50 to 70 miles to replenish their water supply. Water tanks were scattered all along the railroad right-of-way, and any traveler who spotted one could be almost certain of a hobo jungle nearby.

With plenty of water available, these were ideal spots for cooking up a mulligan, making a "big pot" (tin can) of coffee, washing clothes or bathing behind a clump of bushes.

Every train had to stop at the water tank, so the hobo had ample time to eyeball the cars, looking for an empty box or someplace he could ride in relative comfort. And we were always close enough to hear the whistle of any train about to pull out.

But one of the primary reasons for "jungling up" at the water tank was information. For hoboes, the water tank was an

### Series of Symbols Made Up Rail-Riders' Grapevine

MY FATHER and his brothers owned a Ford garage in our small Indiana town. The hoboes would jump off boxcars behind the garage, walk to the end of the dead-end street, then turn and walk two blocks straight to our house.

One day my father asked a hobo in a friendly way, "Why didn't you stop at the other houses? You walked two blocks to my house. That was my wife that just fed you."

The hobo chuckled, "I learned from the rail-riders' grapevine that there was a good place to get food in this town. I read the symbols." Then he drew some of the symbols for Dad. My sister and I had fun looking for them.
—*Gloria Kendall, Palm Harbor, Florida*

Good place for a handout

Religious people

You can sleep in this farmer's barn

Dishonest man—don't ask for work

Mean bull in yard

SAM — Tells a buddy which way they're traveling

Poor water

Police officer lives here

Good jungle

Will help you if you're sick

RDA-MKE

up-to-date directory complete with yellow pages.

Most hoboes had a moniker, which might identify their nationality, trade and hometown—like "Joe the Greek from Battle Creek", "N.Y. Mike" and "IWW K.C. Bill". In addition to leaving his moniker on the tank, a tramp might include the date, with signs denoting his course of travel.

For those who knew how to decipher it, he'd also leave a message saying which part of town was best for panhandling or "begging a lump" (asking for a handout).

The water tank told hoboes whether the local bulls were "on the prod", gathering volunteers for the chain gang. In some areas this was a racket, and those who fell into the clutches of such work gangs suffered cruel treatment.

If the weather was too cold for sleeping outside, the experienced traveler could find directions to the best place for a free flop. The water tank could tell you when and where the annual harvest season would likely start as well as the date and location of the annual hobo convention.

Railroad water tanks have all but disappeared from the landscape, but for many years they were an important part of railroading—and a vital communication network for hoboes. ⊠

## Generosity Taught Children To Count Their Blessings

ONE OF MY MOST enduring memories of the Depression is the lesson my generous mother taught those of us who were less fortunate. Dad supported his family of eight by working as a traveling salesman and running a small farm outside Marshfield, Wisconsin.

Many other men were out of work. Some, beaten down by failure, felt they had no choice but to knock on doors, asking for food. They sometimes did odd jobs, but usually people expected them to eat and be on their way.

Not everyone welcomed hoboes—they were dirty and rough-looking from jumping on and off freight trains and trudging along dirt roads—but Mom did. We had so many of these visitors we were convinced one of them had marked our house.

Because we had to struggle so hard to keep food on the table, we children didn't always approve of Mom's generosity to strangers. Her response was always, "There but for the grace of God go I."

One Sunday, my oldest brother was griping because Mom had given a hobo some of the chicken we were having for dinner. Mom reached across the table, picked up Bud's

GARDEN GIRL. Mary Trimble sent this 1932 photo taken on her family's farm in Marshfield, Wisconsin. It shows a neighbor, Mary Eileen Hoag, with a garden cultivator.

dish of homemade ice cream and took it out to the porch for our current caller.

Mom's attitude made a strong impression on all of us. She made us see that we were blessed to have been born into a family that could make it on its own.   —Mary Trimble
Rogers, Arkansas

## Uncle's "Glamorous" Travels Were a Matter of Survival

UNCLE CLARENCE lived on our farm during the Depression. He was in his early 20s, and I thought he was the best uncle in the world—handsome, sophisticated and always ready to play with my brothers and me.

In late fall, after the corn was picked, Uncle Clarence and a friend would head for warmer climes. Several times each winter, he'd send me a postcard. His short messages transported me into an exciting world of imagination.

In spring, Uncle Clarence would return with some small remembrance. One year, he brought a cotton boll he'd picked. I took it to my country school to share with the students and teacher. None of us had seen a cotton boll before.

Years later, when I mentioned the exciting life I thought Uncle Clarence had led, he said he was really just trying to survive. He rode the rails, working when he could,

Brown Brothers

TRAMPIN' LIFE. Although being a hobo has been romanticized, it was not a situation most would have willingly chosen.

and returned to help out during the busy months for the little Dad could pay him. He left each winter because he knew it would help to have one less mouth to feed.

It was a far cry from the glamorous life I'd imagined.
—Betty Baldwin, Forest City, Iowa

## Children Had No Fear of Hobo Jungles

HOBOES ARRIVED in our small town on the Rock Island freight trains. They traveled in the cars, atop the cars and even on boards *under* the cars. They'd jump off before the train reached the rail yard, then hop back on at the far end of the tracks to avoid the yard bulls.

There were two hobo jungles, and my husband—then a curious young boy who lived near the tracks—loved to visit them and listen to the conversations. The men mostly talked of home, or the places they'd been or intended to go.

The hoboes brewed coffee in a tin can and started the fire with waste from a train's wheel bearings. They cooked hobo stew with food gathered from townspeople.

My husband says they picked up cigarette butts and emptied the tobacco into a Prince Albert can. When they had enough, they rolled their own and called them "hard rolls".

Mom was always a soft touch when hoboes visited our house, and I remember making many sandwiches for them. We never pointed or made fun of them. They asked for food simply because they were hungry. It was an innocent time, and there was no fear in answering the back door to feed a hungry man.
—Betty Berney, Phillipsburg, Kansas

# Foiled by Hard Times, Inventor Had to Hop a Freight Home

*By Jean Hall, Tulsa, Oklahoma*

IN THE LATE 1930s, my mother was raising five children alone on a farm in Oklahoma. My oldest brother, Jack, was in his mid-20s and had invented a dashboard-mounted gauge that would indicate when a tire was going flat. A local businessman agreed to provide financial backing so Jack could take his invention to the Ford Motor Company in Michigan.

Our family was excited, sure something big would come of this. Jack (right, in 1937) was so confident he was already promising all the wonderful things he'd buy us when his invention paid off.

Jack went to Dearborn and met with Henry Ford and some of his staff. They were interested, but some engineering problems had to be worked out first. Jack found work in Dearborn and set about perfecting his gauge. After several months, he sent for my brother Adrian to help.

But the economy caught up with them, and soon my brothers were unable to find steady work. In the end, they were washing dishes at a restaurant in exchange for meals and very low wages.

The situation was getting desperate. They'd have to come home. There wasn't much money on the farm, but at least we had plenty of food.

### One If by Bus

They had only enough money for one bus ticket, so Adrian would take the bus. Jack would catch a freight train, since he was older and had some experience at this.

Jack hopped a freight one cold day with a friend who'd lost his factory job. The trip taxed them to the limit of their endurance.

They hid in boxcars under freight cartons to avoid detection by the railroad detectives, and they wrapped themselves in paper to keep from freezing to death. They survived on occasional handouts, hot coffee and advice from more experienced hoboes.

It was late at night when their train arrived in Fletcher, a 2-mile walk from home. Their clothes were dirty and their faces were blackened with soot.

At midnight, we heard a loud knock. Mother lit the lamp and went to the door. It was common for hoboes to stop and ask for help—but not at that hour.

Jack, being a bit of a prankster, wanted to see if Mama would recognize him. Without identifying himself, he

> *"They hid under cartons to avoid the railroad detectives..."*

asked if he and his friend could eat and spend the night.

Mama told him we had company (we didn't), and suggested he try the next farmhouse. Jack insisted he wanted to stay with us. Mama was getting nervous.

"Mama, don't you know me?" Jack said. "This is Jack. Have you got anything to eat?"

I thought my mother was going to collapse. She grabbed him and covered him with hugs and kisses, soot and all. She hadn't known if she'd ever see him again.

Mama went straight to the kitchen and began cooking. Soon the house was filled with the aromas of fried meat, cream gravy and hot biscuits. We all gathered around the table into the wee hours as Jack told about his adventures.

We were pleased to have our big brothers back home, safe and sound. But we knew it was only a matter of time before the "call of the wild" took Jack on the road again. 

# Riding the Rails Helped Family Put Their Life Back on Track

*By Richard Erickson, Seattle, Washington*

AFTER MY MOTHER died, traveling the country with Dad while he looked for work became a way of life. For my brother, Harold, and me, Dad was the center of our universe.

In 1938, we were driving up California's Highway 101 in our 1929 Marquette. For two kids from the flatlands of Minnesota, the redwoods were magnificent.

Suddenly another car rounded a curve and sideswiped us. There was no guardrail between us and the steep slope to the river. Dad threw one arm around Harold and me and gripped the steering column with the other. The car tumbled down the slope like a matchbox, flipping three times before slamming into some willows at the river's edge.

Incredibly, none of us—including our dog—suffered more than a few cuts. The bad news was Dad had lost his wallet. All we had was his union card and the clothes and camping gear we'd stored in the trunk.

The car was destroyed, but Dad removed a few parts and sold them to the garage owner in Weott. Buying them had to be an act of charity. The garage owner never could've recovered what he paid for those parts.

### Options Were Limited

We camped next to the river for 2 nights while Dad pondered what to do. If we could get to San Francisco, Dad could show his card at the union office and get a loan to carry us over until he found work. But how would we get there without a car or money? The garage owner directed us to a freight train stop outside town.

We climbed onto a flatcar and waited 30 minutes. Finally the engine tooted three times and the train started to move. We were on our way. Dad smiled and said, "This isn't so bad, is it?"

Riding through the redwoods was wonderful. It was like an enthralling amusement ride at some special park. But after an hour, we realized we'd forgotten one important item—water.

When the train stopped in the small town of Fort Seward, we saw a grocery store about a block away. Figuring we'd be there awhile, Dad told Harold to run to the store for a bottle of water. "If you hear the train toot three times, run back as fast as you can," Dad said. "That will mean the train is leaving."

No sooner had Harold turned the corner than the train began to move. It hadn't tooted at all, let alone three times. So much for Dad's knowledge of trains. In later years, we kidded him about it, but it wasn't funny that day.

Dad helped me off the flatcar, then grabbed the dog and our belongings. By the time the last carton hit the ground, the train had moved several yards and was picking up speed. It was going at a good clip when Harold returned with the water bottle.

Fort Seward turned out to be mostly a ghost town. The railroad station was closed, and we were too far from the high-

**THREE FOR THE ROAD.** These photos were taken a few years before Richard Erickson, his older brother, Harold, and their dad miraculously survived a bad car accident in California. After that, they had to hop a train for San Francisco.

way to hitchhike. There was nothing to do but wait for the next train.

A couple trains passed through, but they didn't even slow down. We slept under an old loading dock that night.

The next day, three trains passed without stopping, and we spent another night under the dock. Was that first stop a fluke? The bread and bologna we'd bought at the store were running low.

On the third day, a train finally stopped and we hurried aboard. There were no flatcars or boxcars. We had to perch atop a flatcar loaded with lumber.

It was past midnight when the train crawled into Sausalito. Some of the cars would be ferried across the bay to San Francisco, and no hoboes were allowed on the ferries. Railroad bulls with nightsticks walked the length of the train, chasing everyone off.

I've often wondered what that bull thought as he

silently watched our family descend from the lumber car with our dog and belongings. Dad politely asked him how we could get to San Francisco, and the bull pointed to a bus stop.

The bus driver told us no buses or ferries ran to San Francisco at that time of night. But he could take us to the north end of the Golden Gate Bridge, and we could walk across and catch a streetcar on the other side.

It was 2 a.m. when we reached the Golden Gate, then only a year old. It

> ## "My father rarely cried, but that night was an exception..."

was shrouded in clouds, and the amber lights gave it an eerie look. The 2-mile walk across it seemed to take forever.

When we reached the other side of the bridge, we collapsed onto a bench. Then a police car pulled up. As Dad told the officer our story, another police car arrived, then a third. Harold and I were wide-eyed. Were we going to jail?

While Dad asked two officers about hotels, two others came over to Harold and me. One gave Harold an envelope and told him, "Give this to your father *after* you're on the streetcar." They wished us good luck and good night and drove away.

The streetcar soon arrived, and we all got on. After a block or two, Harold gave Dad the envelope. My father rarely cried. That night was an exception.

Inside the envelope were 10 $1 bills —and in those days, that was a lot of money for those men to kick in. Before we left town, Dad repaid this kindness by making a contribution to the policemen's relief fund.

When we got downtown, we went to a small hotel and fell into bed, exhausted. The next day, Dad found the Lathers Union hall, which loaned him some money and found him a job. The elderly couple who managed the hotel looked after Harold and me while Dad worked.

Dad bought a 1928 Chevrolet for $16.75, and by the end of the summer, he'd saved enough for us to drive back to Minnesota. It was time for Harold and me to return to school. I couldn't wait for the teacher to ask what we did on our summer vacation. ☒

# Surprised Family Learned Not All Hoboes Were Men

*By Evelyn Corzine, New Port Richey, Florida*

OUR TEXAS FARM was 18 miles from the nearest small city, so we didn't have many hoboes pass through. But occasionally we'd hear that hopeful knock on the door and find a tired, bedraggled man with all his worldly goods in a sack on his back, asking if we could spare a meal. My mother never turned one away.

We didn't suffer some of the Depression-era hardships so many others did, so there were always leftovers.

Mom would pile a plate high with good things like fried chicken, mashed potatoes and gravy, vegetables from the garden, corn bread and biscuits, and fruit cobbler, pie or cake. The men had their choice of buttermilk, sweet milk or clabber to drink.

These visitors never seemed to expect to be invited inside, knowing they were dusty and sweaty from the many miles they'd walked down unpaved

> ## "The hobo who impressed me most was a woman..."

roads. They sat under a shade tree to rest and enjoy their sumptuous meal, and they thanked Mom profusely when they returned the empty dishes.

But the hobo who impressed me the most was a woman. She knocked on our front door late one afternoon and asked Mom if she could spend the night. Mom was surprised but said she could manage. My older brother would give up his room and sleep on the couch.

Mom prepared a wonderful meal, and the woman ate with us. She was a big talker, though I can't remember what we talked about. She had all of her earthly possessions in a flour sack, and she gently removed some of her "treasures" to show us.

At bedtime, Mom and I took her to the room where she'd be sleeping. As we put clean sheets on the bed, the woman began to undress. I stood frozen in amazement as she peeled one dress after another over her head. She was wearing five or six of them.

The next morning, after a hearty breakfast and nonstop conversation, she was on her way. Only then did I ask Mom why the woman wore so many dresses at once. My wise mother said it lightened the load she had to carry by hand.

We often wonder about the final destiny of those poor souls who passed our way, whose lives we brightened for a short time. ☒

**BOUNTIFUL GARDEN.** Evelyn Corzine's mother, Alice, willingly shared vegetables from her garden and other food with a hungry stranger.

## Sticky Sandwich Left Tramp Full But Thirsty

MY GRANDMOTHER'S HOUSE was close to a main highway and she frequently had visitors asking for food or water. But one day when a tramp asked for something to eat, Grandmother had no leftovers. All she could offer was a peanut butter sandwich. The tramp accepted it, thanked her and went on his way.

That Saturday night, we visited our great-grandmother, who lived about 2 miles farther up the road. She told us a tramp had stopped by earlier in the week and asked for a drink of water. He told her a lady down the road had given him a dry peanut butter sandwich that nearly choked him to death! —*Ray Birch, Fairfax, Virginia*

## Visitors Helped Themselves To Breakfast Leftovers

ONE MORNING after we children went to school, Mother began washing clothes. She wanted to get the clothes hung out early, so she left the breakfast things to clean up later.

When Mother left the clothesline and came back inside, two hoboes were sitting at the table, eating our leftovers. Mother made them coffee and fixed some more food. She wasn't afraid.

She was happy to help them out, and they were soon on their way to hop a freight train. We never saw them again.
—*Bette Cash, Amherst, Virginia*

## Biscuits and Hard-Boiled Eggs Always on Hand for Passing Hoboes

MY MOTHER never invited hoboes in, but she always fed them. They sat on the big granite doorstep in front of the kitchen door and gladly ate biscuits, hard-boiled eggs and cold milk.

If it happened to be bread-baking day, the hobo was lucky and got hot bread with creamery butter, plus a cup of coffee that had been brewed in an open pot on the wood stove.
—*Ruth Towle, Canterbury, New Hampshire*

## Hungry Men Lined Boxcars "Like Birds on a Wire"

WHEN TRAINS came through our town, hoboes would be lined up on top of the boxcars like birds on a wire. They couldn't have gotten another man up there.

The boxcars were full inside, too—and those men were the lucky ones. If it rained, the fellows on top couldn't do anything but sit there, mile after tiresome mile. How cold they must have been!

When the train stopped, a few men would get off, only to be told there was no work anywhere. They were so disappointed to hear those words over and over. You could see the hunger in their faces.

We kids talked to many of these lonely fellows. Most of them were decent men, and they were always nice to us. We had no fear of them. They readily told us their stories, grateful that someone had taken the time to speak to them.

Mother often put some extra potatoes and gravy in a dish and had us take it to a fellow we'd told her about, or one that looked particularly hungry. The men often seemed surprised, even if we had nothing more than potatoes. It was all we had to eat ourselves, but we felt good about giving them something.

When the men returned the dish to the house, they'd thank Mother with tears running down their faces. Many said it had been a long time since someone had been so good to them.

I've always been proud of my mother for sharing what little we had with total strangers. I'm sure God rewarded her for her kindness. —*Dorothy Behringer, North Branch, Minnesota*

**FED HER BROOD—AND THEN SOME.** Dorothy Behringer (standing in the middle) posed in 1934 with her mother, her older sister and four younger brothers. Dorothy's mother took pity on the lonely, hungry wanderers that crossed her path.

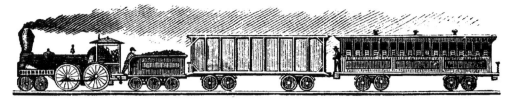

### "Bo Britt Eddie" Never Lost Love of Hobo Life

MY HUSBAND, Eddie, started hoboing when he was 17 and continued throughout the '30s.

In July of 1938, he hopped a freight to Marquette, Iowa, then boarded a flatcar that he thought was bound for the harvest fields in the Dakotas. At daylight, he jumped off the train and discovered he hadn't gotten any farther than Britt, Iowa.

Eddie found work as a carpenter in Britt and was eventually given the hobo nickname "Bo Britt Eddie". That August, he attended his first Hobo Days in Britt. The annual convention continues today, drawing hoboes from all over the country.

Hobo events were a big part of Eddie's life. At the Hobo Days in Marquette, he made hobo stew with vegetables he grew at home. The stew was served free to anyone who asked.

The hoboes also made items that they sold to raise funds for their conventions. Eddie's specialty was drinking cups made from tin cans and wire.

He and his hobo friends often visited nursing homes to talk about their experiences. Eddie read the poems he'd written about his hobo years, and his friends played instruments and sang.

When Eddie passed away, his obituary in *The Hobo Times* read, in part: "Eddie 'Bo Britt' Colsch caught the westbound May 18, 1997. Eddie was a friend to all, hobo or not, and many of us who knew him shed a tear when that final whistle blew. Bo Britt will be remembered for his uncommon kindness toward everyone he met, and his fond longing for the hobo life he once lived." —*Evelyn Colsch Caledonia, Minnesota*

**LIFE AMONG THE HOBOES.** These are some items that belonged to Eddie Colsch, better known as "Bo Britt Eddie". A cup made from wire and a tin can, a plaque and photos appear alongside Eddie's picture.

### Hobo Days' Mulligan Stew Serves a Crowd of 5,000

WANT TO MAKE a pot of hobo stew? The hoboes who attend the annual Hobo Days convention in Britt, Iowa whip up 20 pots of mulligan stew every year—enough for 5,000 8-ounce servings, according to Evelyn Colsch, who shared the recipe.

Here's the list of ingredients: 450 pounds of beef, 900 pounds of potatoes, 250 pounds of carrots, 35 pounds of green and red peppers, 300 pounds of cabbage, 100 pounds of turnips, 10 pounds of parsnips, 150 pounds of tomatoes, 20 pounds of chili peppers, 25 pounds of rice, 60 pounds of celery, 1 pound of bay leaves, 24 gallons of mixed vegetables and 10 bottles of Kitchen Bouquet.

99 LBS. NET WEIGHT WHOLE BEAN UNCOATED TABLE RICE

# College Student Thumbed Rides In Search of Work

*By Ed Decker, Overland Park, Kansas*

AFTER my sophomore year of college, summer jobs in my hometown were as scarce as a ray of sun at midnight. I decided to head west, with the vague idea of working in the wheat harvest.

With resources limited to a very few dollars, I figured the best way to get there was hopping freight trains. And so did a hundred or more other folks waiting at the rail yard. We loafed there until evening, when a long string of cars began to pull out, and everybody rushed aboard for a free ride.

We didn't get far. Three railroad detectives worked the train from engine to caboose, pushing and throwing off all the "bums". After spending the night under a tree, I decided hitchhiking would be a friendlier way to travel. It was.

A series of thumbed rides took me all the way across Kansas without even a hint of a job. Before I knew it, I was in Colorado with dozens of other wanderers.

It took a few days to get used to the footloose life, but it did become bearable. Sometimes it was even comfortable, and I felt totally free.

## His Money Melted Away

My meager stake disappeared too quickly—bread was a nickel a loaf, and cheese and bologna cost 20¢ a pound. I was miserly with my last coins, spending them on Bull Durham roll-your-own smokes. For a nickel, you got a small sack of tobacco and papers. Even a bum deserved a little luxury.

Food became a problem, until I knocked on my first back door and asked for a bite to eat. A kind housewife gave me a cold meat loaf sandwich and wished me luck. Maybe that was because I was young and tried to stay reasonably clean.

Farther along, I discovered something else: Get into a town near sundown, find the marshal or other officer of the law and ask for something to eat. You'd be steered to a hole-in-the-wall restaurant and given a sandwich and a cup of coffee, courtesy of the town fathers.

Then you were directed to shelter for the night—a shed, barn or even the town jail. These overnight stops featured a fascinating assortment of wayfarers—some friendly, some unfriendly, some silent and sullen. One night I argued religion with a ragged, bearded preacher until our fellow sufferers yelled at us to shut up and go to sleep.

At one town in Colorado, eight of us got not only sandwiches and coffee, but a breakfast of hotcakes at 4 a.m. the next day. But there was a catch. After eating, we were escorted to the firehouse and told to wash down Main Street for that day's homecoming celebration.

Did you ever tackle that kind of job, with a fire engine pumper putting out full pressure? It took two of us to hold the hose steady. If either of us let go, the nozzle would've lashed back and cracked our heads.

We survived, although we got soaked from stem to stern. When we were done, the police chief told us to get out of town and not come back. At least we had breakfast that day.

## "Hot Tip" Not So Hot

Another time, I fell in with a guy who said he knew of a ranch where we might be able to stay for a while. It wasn't the kind of ranch you'd imagine. There were no cattle, and all the work involved slopping around in irrigation ditches that didn't seem to go anywhere.

One of the two hired hands was also the cook, so we did get to eat. But some of that stuff would've been condemned elsewhere, including moldy bread and plates of greasy vittles. After a couple of days, we were told to move along.

One day while plodding along an empty road, I saw a small, placid pond and decided to take a quick bath. I stripped and jumped into the water, which was cold and refreshing. I splashed happily, until I realized I wasn't alone.

Two or three little creatures came swimming toward me, curious to see who was invading their domain. I never did discover what they were. All I could see were pointy noses and beady eyes, and the V-shaped ripples they left behind in the water. I cut my bath short and got out of there in a hurry.

One town seemed like another, and since there was no pressing reason to get anywhere, I'd go to the highway each morning and say to myself, "This way, or that?" Then I'd go the same way the first passing car was headed.

One morning, after sleeping on a counter in an empty store, I was so chilled that when the sun came up, I lay down on a blacktop road to warm myself.

It was time to go home. I abandoned the life of the open road and ended my life as a bum. ⊠

**FREE TRANSPORTATION.** These men have just hitched a ride on a tank car. If you didn't mind getting dirty and were able to dodge the yard bulls, you could travel just about anywhere you wanted.

**LURE OF THE OPEN TRACK.** The photo of the locomotive above was shared by Lorraine Lobach Kern of Leesburg, Florida (her dad was a fireman on a train like this). Louis Johnson (at left when he was about 16) had already hopped a train west when this picture was taken in 1934.

# 'Riding the Rails Provided the Best Lessons I Ever Learned'

*By Louis Johnson, Ormond Beach, Florida*

I RODE FREIGHT trains on and off from 1932 to '39. My first trip was at 15, when I hitchhiked from Memphis, Tennessee to Los Angeles, California. Two days later, I hopped my first freight and started home.

Whenever the train stopped, I'd run to the nearest house to bum food, as I had no money. I slept in "reefers", the small ice-storage compartments used for hauling produce.

On my next trip to California, I found a job picking grapes for 35¢ an hour. I slept on the railroad platform at night and lived on crackers, sardines and peanut butter from the company store.

On another trip, I hopped a freight in El Paso, Texas with at least 50 other bums, including two women. We were all riding on flatcars, and it was pretty cold. When the train made its first stop, we found empty boxcars on other trains.

The yard bulls didn't bother us much, but there were states where you had to be careful. Texas had a couple of tough bulls, and Georgia and Florida were always looking for hoboes to put on their chain gangs.

I had a couple of run-ins with the police. One night in San Antonio, Texas several of us were walking down the tracks to catch a train when a squad car pulled up. The policemen asked us what we were doing and we told them.

## Offer Hard to Refuse

The officers told us to come to the station instead. We could shower, eat and sleep, and they'd turn us loose in the morning. That sounded pretty good, so we went. Seven days later, we finally got to leave. All we had to eat for a week was molasses, bread, beans and watered-down coffee.

My next stop was Tucson, where I stayed in the hobo jungle and made mulligan stew. We all bummed meat scraps and vegetables and cooked them in a 5-gallon salad oil can.

From there, I rode to Colton, California—the end of the line. I hitch-hiked 60 miles to Hollywood. The first star I saw was Robert Young. He was in front of the CBS Radio studio, loading his friends onto a bus for the Rose Bowl. I hit him up for a cup of coffee. He gave me a quarter.

I stayed for 2 months, bumming, trying to work and sleeping in a used-car lot. One night during a rainstorm, I jumped into one of the cars. A cop found me at 3 a.m. and took me to jail. The judge gave me 24 hours to get out of Los Angeles County.

I hitchhiked back to Colton, hopped another train and arrived in Baltimore, Maryland on March 7. My hobo days were over.

Riding freights provided the best lessons I ever learned and never hurt me at all. Even though I was hungry much of the time, when I look back, I realize how much I loved it. ▨

# Mysterious Guest Vanished Without a Trace

*By Mildred Williams, North Haven, Connecticut*

IN THE 1930s, whenever someone knocked at the back door of our Connecticut home and asked for the lady of the house, we all knew the caller's purpose. These visits usually came at suppertime. The aroma of home-cooked food drew hungry guests like filings to a magnet.

Mother would glance quickly at the serving bowls to see if we could spare another dinner. There was always enough for one more. Then she'd bustle to the door, ready to welcome another stranger.

These men were quiet and polite, and we never imagined they'd rob or harm us. We were simply told to move over and place another chair at the table, as we were having guests. Mother would remind us of our blessings, and we were told to be thankful we could share our meal with these men.

### Treated with Respect

We were taught to look upon our guests with respect. Mother never called them hoboes, tramps or wanderers. They were just men in desperate straits, victims of circumstances beyond their control.

One bitterly cold day after a heavy snowfall, a man came at lunchtime. Mother gave him soap and a towel to wash his hands, then gave him a bowl of stew, bread and butter, and a piece of pie. He was so thankful.

When he was ready to leave, Mother noticed he didn't have a coat, so she gave him Dad's Sunday coat. She also

**COLD DAY, WARM GESTURE.** After a snowfall like this one, Mildred Williams' mother showered kindnesses on a man she'd never met.

gave him a clean handkerchief, 50¢ for coffee or carfare and two sandwiches to eat later. As he left, he turned to wave and give Mother his blessings.

A minute later, we realized he'd forgotten his sandwiches. My brother started out the door after him, looking for his footprints in the snow. But there were

> *"Mom gave the man Dad's Sunday coat..."*

no footprints. We ran from window to window, trying to find them, but there didn't seem to be any.

We wondered about that visitor for a long time, because he was the last

one to come to our house. Mother always said he was sent to test her compassion. She obviously passed with flying colors.

Mother's favorite saying was, "Whenever you contribute to the poor and extend a helping hand to those in need, you will be rewarded doubly."

She lived her philosophy and reaped her reward. She blessed others, and in doing so, she was blessed herself. For the rest of her 87 years, she was never without a dollar, was blessed with good health and never asked any of her children for help.

I'll never forget Mother's many kindnesses, especially to the mysterious visitor who left no footprints in the snow.

---

## Handouts Fed Spirit as Well as Body

ONE SUNDAY MORNING we were having a breakfast of buckwheat cakes, the kind made with buttermilk and yeast. We didn't have syrup, but there was plenty of homemade apple butter.

As we were eating, a hobo came to the door for a handout. My father said, "If you can eat what we eat, you are welcome." My parents never refused anyone something to eat.

The man came in and sat at the table with us. While we ate, he told us he'd gone to a house on a hill overlooking our small town of Craigsville, Pennsylvania.

When he'd asked for a handout, instead of giving him food, the lady had replied, "Seek the Lord." The man turned to my father and said, "I think I found Him." —*K. Dale Lewis Worthington, Pennsylvania*

**MEAN MONGREL?** Herbert Jelley's dog, "Mike" (that's them at left), looked menacing but didn't seem to intimidate strangers asking for food. Herbert's Swedish grandmother cooked for them in a kitchen like the one above.

# Did Grandma Miss a Date with An Angel?

*By Herbert Jelley, Cibolo, Texas*

WE LIVED WITH my grandmother in a small Minnesota town during the early '30s. Jobless young men frequently hopped off the freights and canvassed houses, asking for food.

A steady stream of wanderers found our back door. We were convinced these men had a system for identifying houses where they could get something to eat. Our dog should have scared them off. "Mike" was half-German shepherd and looked downright menacing. But the hoboes would walk right into the yard and pet him.

Our neighbors across the street greeted requests for food with a stock response: "If you're hungry, go to a restaurant." The hoboes rarely stopped at that house. I'm glad they came to ours.

We kids learned a lot from these men. In summertime, we sat with them while they ate in the backyard. One showed us a sack full of matchbooks he'd collected and told us about the cities where he'd gathered them. We enjoyed this interesting geography lesson.

Another man showed us how to carve whistles from small branches. All of them enjoyed talking with us, and most offered to work for their food.

One day I was playing alone in the backyard when a young man appeared. My Swedish grandmother was a bit out of sorts that day and said to him, "Why can't you get here close to mealtime? It's 3 in the afternoon. I've put things away."

Then she muttered a few words in Swedish and stormed back into the house. The man looked at me, shrugged and walked away.

About 10 minutes later, Grandma came out with coffee and a plate of bacon, eggs and toast. She looked around, then asked me what happened to our visitor.

"He left," I said. "I guess he thought you turned him down."

I'd never seen Grandmother so upset. She began to sob, saying over and over, "What have I done? What have I done?"

## Seized with Regret

When Mom came out to see what had happened, Grandma said she feared God had sent that man to test her. She was probably thinking about the second verse in Hebrews 13: "Do not neglect to show hospitality to strangers, for thereby some have entertained angels unawares."

Mom was usually kind and considerate, but this time she didn't let Grandma off the hook. "Well, how can you expect people to understand when you talk like that?" she scolded her. "Learn to control your tongue!"

I wanted to hug Grandma and tell her not to worry. Someone else would surely feed the guy.

I was reminded of all this not long ago, when I passed a man at a busy intersection. He was holding up a sign that said,

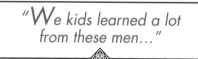

*"We kids learned a lot from these men..."*

"Homeless—will work for food". Should I have stopped and offered him at least enough money for a meal?

Partly to ease my guilt, I thought of all the programs that exist now to help such people, and the charitable groups to which I contribute that provide food and shelter. And I thought of all the jobs available today that didn't exist during the Depression.

These days we do a much better job of making sure the hungry are cared for, but there's a downside: Modern charity is impersonal. In the 1930s, people were enriched by the marvelous feeling that comes from giving directly to people in need. ▨

# Hitchhiker Glad to Spend Night in Jail

*By Bill Eberle, Highland, Indiana*

AS A COLLEGE STUDENT, I hitchhiked around the country during summers from 1930 to '32, looking for jobs. I found three. Hitchhiking is a no-no today, but in those days, it was the way to go. Drivers knew we were looking for work and wanted to help us.

One night I arrived in Topeka, Kansas around sundown. It was starting to rain, so I decided to spend the night at the jail. That was common then, and the jailers in most cities were cooperative.

Topeka's jail consisted of a large room with cells around the outer walls. About 25 men were there when I arrived, and there was no way to tell which were prisoners and which were "sleepers". All the cell doors were open, so I picked an empty one for myself.

There was a lot of conversation and idle chatter. After a while, some of the men decided to hold a kangaroo court, levying fines for imagined offenses. I told them I didn't have any money.

"Take off your shoes," one man said. I took off the shoe that had no money in it.

Then he said, "Take off the other shoe." I had a few dollars in that

---

> ## "All the cell doors were open, so I picked an empty one..."

---

one but managed to slip the bills into the first shoe when he wasn't looking.

This went on for some time, but eventually everyone settled down and we all went to sleep.

The next morning, two men came to the door and yelled, "Line up out here." They marched us a couple of blocks to a lot filled with wood and told us to start chopping. So we did.

After about half an hour, we were lined up again and marched to a building that was set up for breakfast. We sat down and had a really good meal. After we finished, the men took us outside and said, "Get on your way, and good luck."

If anyone from Topeka should read this, I want them to know that we certainly appreciated their hospitality. ▨

**JOB SEEKER. Between 1930 and 1932, Bill Eberle traveled around the country in the summer. At right is a photo of him from around that time. The middle photo is from a bit later (about 1936) when Bill was working at a gas station in East Chicago, Indiana. At far right is Bill today.**

---

## Tired Soul Checked Himself in to "The Hobo Inn"

MY GRANDPARENTS' Wisconsin farm could have been dubbed "The Hobo Inn". Their back fields and woods bordered the railroad tracks, and hoboes had marked the trees for others looking for food and a place to stay.

Grandma had the hoboes sit on the side steps to eat their meal. It was usually a dish of oatmeal with fresh cream and plenty of sugar, or homemade fried cakes (similar to today's doughnuts), with a strong cup of coffee.

If they needed a place to sleep, Grandpa let them sleep on thrashed straw in the barn, but they had to turn over their cigarettes. There was no smoking allowed in the barn. Milking by the light of kerosene lanterns was dangerous enough.

One late fall afternoon, Grandma and I went under the front porch to get the croquet set. To our surprise, we found a bed of leaves bearing the impression of a body. Some poor tired soul had gathered the leaves from under the oak tree and made himself a bed. We never even knew he was there.
—*Merrybell Seeber Delavan, Wisconsin*

# Underneath the Soot Was an Unexpected Gift

*By Margo Johnson, Two Harbors, Minnesota*

WHILE WORKING as a nurse in a Wisconsin hospital, I cared for an elderly lady who was rewarded beyond measure for feeding hoboes.

This lady lived on the edge of town near the railroad tracks during the Depression. As the trains slowed down and prepared to stop, the hoboes would jump off. They were always hungry. They'd go to the back door of one home after another, begging for food, until they found someone kind enough to slip a sandwich through the door.

This lady had many such visitors, and she never turned any of them away. She kept a table and chair on the back porch so they could sit while they ate, and she would provide a basin, towel and soap so they could wash up.

One day she heard a rap at the back door and knew it would be another poor tramp off the train. She could have reasoned, "I've fed enough of them—let this one go to the neighbor's." But she didn't.

The lady went to the door and found a sooty, bedraggled young man. He just stood there, without saying a word. She said, "You're hungry, aren't you?" The young man nodded.

She gave him the usual soap, towel and basin of warm water, then told him, "You may clean up a bit while I fix you some lunch." She prepared a tray of food and took it to the table on the porch.

When the lady turned to invite her guest to eat, she was looking into the eyes of her own son. What a happy reunion that was!

The woman hadn't seen her son for a long time and hadn't known whether he was dead or alive. He had been so dirty and sooty she hadn't recognized him.

She said she was repaid a hundredfold that day for answering all those raps at her door, feeding all who came her way, and doing a little extra by letting them wash up so they could face the public with some dignity.

This wonderful lady has now gone to her rest. But I'm sure she heard the Lord say, "If you have done it to the least of these, you have done it unto me." 

---

## Sleeping "Dragon" Put Up More Fight Than Tot Expected

MOM ALWAYS had a handout ready when hoboes knocked on our back door—but when you fed one, you got another, and another and another. Their communication setup was as good as a party line.

One morning I was out early, tilting at imaginary dragons with a willow-stick "sword", when I spied a bunch of rumpled blankets spread out in the barn. I didn't know what they were doing there, but they looked like an easy dragon to slay, and one good swat wouldn't hurt Dad's blankets. So I gave it all I had.

A hobo came roaring up out of those blankets as if the devil had him. I ran like a streak of lightning for the house, with the hobo yelling after me, "Don't be scared, kid! Don't be scared!"

I was way past scared and well into panic. When I got to the house, my words tumbled out in shattered syntax as I told Dad what I'd done.

Dad went out and calmly told the man he was worried about people starting fires in the hay, and that he should've asked permission before sleeping there. Besides, Dad said, he'd frightened the children. The hobo allowed that he'd been pretty scared himself for a few minutes.

The guy was really polite and apologized for scaring me. He just hadn't known what was happening to him. Dad realized I'd played a part in this incident, too, and made me say I was sorry. I didn't need coaxing.

—*Eldon Root, Paso Robles, California*

**DRAGON EGGS?** Eldon Root was only 5 when this 1930 Easter photograph was taken.

# Polite Travelers Were Just Trying to Survive

*By Patricia Schreiner, Grayling, Michigan*

WHEN I WAS a child, I met many "knights of the road". We lived between two sets of railroad tracks in Ypsilanti, Michigan and often had hoboes come by to beg for food.

In summer, they wore the most tattered clothes I'd ever seen, and many went barefoot. In winter, they wore jackets over sweaters or ragged overcoats with the linings hanging loose. Most had no boots, only shoes with flapping soles. If they had gloves, the fingers were usually raveled away.

These men may have been hungry and dirty, but they were never anything less than polite. All they asked for was something to eat, and my mother always provided it—even if just a sandwich.

We didn't ask these men questions, and they didn't offer information. They never asked to come inside, and most left as soon as they were given food. Mom had a bench outside the back door and encouraged them to sit down for a minute, but few did.

I especially remember a snowy, sub-zero day when a hobo came to our back door. Mother gave him a sandwich and

*"The poor man looked half frozen..."*

a bowl of soup and told him to step inside and warm up. He refused.

We all felt terrible. The poor man looked half frozen. He just stood outside, spooning up the soup and eating the sandwich.

As our visitor reached inside to put the empty bowl on the kitchen floor, he said quietly, "May God always bless you, Madam." Mom had tears in her eyes as she watched him walk down the back alley to the railroad tracks.

There was only one lady in the neighborhood who refused to feed these men. She called them "lazy bums". We had no way of knowing whether that was true, but we knew for a fact they were hungry, and they needed to know there were people who cared.

Those days taught us a lot about getting through rough times, and we survived. I like to think some of the knights of the road survived, too. Maybe one of them had something to eat at our back door. ⊠

**CIVIL SURVIVORS.** Although down on their luck, most hoboes were humble men who didn't forget their manners.

Brown Brothers

## Though Struggling Himself, Dad Shared Whatever He Had

MANY HUNGRY young men came to our back door in Mobile, Alabama, offering to work in exchange for food. But one man asked for money so he could get a bus ticket to visit his sick mother in another state.

When my father came to the door, I'm sure the young man feared Dad was going to call the police. Instead, Dad asked how much more money he needed. The man mentioned an exact amount, and Dad gave it to him. We never had any money to spare. We were struggling just to get by.

Today I wonder whether that man was just telling a sad story to get cash. If he was, he didn't "win". My father was the winner, because he always shared what he had with those who were less fortunate. —*Marge McKinsey, Miami, Florida*

## Visitor Provided Perfect Remedy For Little Bookworm's Ailing Eyes

AS A CHILD, I loved reading so much that I even propped a book over the sink when I washed dishes. At night, I read to my younger siblings, then hid under the covers and read until I could no longer see the words.

My eyes were constantly red. One morning they hurt so much I had to stay home from school.

While I was home, a knock came at the back door. A tall, thin man asked very politely for something to eat.

As my mother filled a bag with sandwiches, cake and cookies, the man looked at me. Then he asked my mother if I'd seen a doctor for pinkeye. "No," she said, startled. She didn't know anything about pinkeye.

RDA-MKE

The man told her to put a poultice of bread and warm milk on my eyes, and the redness would disappear. My mother was so struck by his concern that she gave him an extra sandwich. She also made the poultice, and my eyes cleared up completely.
—*Tressa Hamilton, Chandler, Arizona*

**ANGEL AT THE DOOR. Tressa Hamilton (left of center with her arms around the blond boy) found her life blessed by a hobo's concern.**

# Wise Father Had Hobo Perform a Task

*By Lois Bahler, Remington, Indiana*

HOMELESS, hungry hoboes often walked the railroad tracks near our small dairy farm. Sometimes I saw them jump into the boxcar of a slow-moving train, looking for a warm place to sleep and maybe catch a ride to a city with a breadline.

One evening after we finished our supper of tomato soup and corn bread, I noticed a dark figure walking toward the house. As the figure came closer, I saw it was

*"We stood in the shadows as Father opened the door..."*

a man wearing a long, dirty black coat that flapped in the cold wind. Horrified, I ran to tell my parents.

The man slowly turned into our yard, came to the door and knocked. We nine children stood back in the shadows, holding our breath, as my father calmly opened the door.

The man said, "Would you please have something for me to eat?" I glanced at the empty dishes on the table, then at Mother. Her brow was furrowed.

My father said, "We will give you something to eat, if you'd be willing to first shovel a load of cobs into the cob house." The man quickly agreed, but I felt sorry for him, having to work when he was so hungry.

My mother quickly prepared another pan of corn bread. There was nothing else to serve him except fresh milk.

When the man finished unloading the cobs, my father brought him to the kitchen table. My mother brought him milk and the whole pan of corn bread, which he devoured. Then he rose, thanked us and headed back down the road to the rails.

As I grew older and became better acquainted with the Bible, I realized my father was wise to have the man perform a task before getting something to eat.

In II Thessalonians we read, "For even when we were with you, this we commanded you, that if any would not work, neither should he eat."

# The Day God Looked in Our Window

*By Barbara Hazzard, Grafton, Massachusetts*

EASTER CAME EARLY in 1939, when I was 6 years old. Snow covered our tiny mill village of Perryville, Massachusetts. The day before Easter, Ma's head began to itch like crazy. When she asked Pa to check her scalp, he found lice.

"Cooties!" she screeched. It was unthinkable. Ma was the original Mrs. Clean, acting as if the Good Housekeeping people might come knocking any minute to confer their seal of approval. She was so ashamed I thought she'd faint.

Ma ordered Pa to go to town for a fine-toothed comb and some lice killer. But the store was already closed. "You'll have to wait until tomorrow," he told her. "Use kerosene."

Pa checked my sister and me, but we were fine. The lice must have come from the neighbor whose hair Ma had cut and styled the day before.

Ma was near tears. "How can I go to church tomorrow?" she moaned. "I'll have to stay home."

On Easter morning, Pa took the first bus to town. My sister and I stayed home and pouted, while our new Easter duds—the ones Ma had spent hours making—hung in the closet.

**TRAMPING THROUGH SNOW.** An old man who showed up in need on a snowy Easter morning was never to be forgotten by Barbara Hazzard's family.

### Strange to Be Home

Ma quietly set about preparing Easter dinner and sent me to turn on the radio. "Maybe we can get some church music," she said. "It just doesn't seem like Easter without going to church."

As I crossed the kitchen, I glanced into the parlor and saw an old man peering through the window. Long white hair hung from under a battered fedora to the shoulders of his

---

*"He was standing in the snow, sockless, in worn-out boots..."*

---

wrinkled suit coat. A flowing white beard covered the front of his vest. The man stared at me with sad eyes weighed down by dark circles and sunken cheeks.

"Ma," I whispered, "God is looking in our window."

"What are you talking about?" she scolded. "If you're lying to me, and on Easter, too..."

Ma's words were left hanging in the air when she saw the man framed in the window. She rushed to the door and flung it wide, urging the man to come in and warm himself. He was standing in the snow, sockless, in worn-out boots.

Usually, hoboes weren't allowed into our house. They always waited in the woodshed or on the stoop while Ma prepared a sandwich and coffee, plus cookies or cake for the road.

If they needed socks, she gave them a pair of Pa's. If Pa was home, he mended their shoes and boots. Ma sewed buttons on their jackets and put a dime from her rainy-day coffee can in their pocket.

Ma heaped a plate with food, filled Pa's mug with steaming coffee and shooed the old man to the table. He bowed his head and said, "This is the day which the Lord has made. Let us rejoice and be glad in it."

### Mom Went to Work

Ma disappeared upstairs. Closet doors and drawers opened and closed as she searched through Pa's clothes. She returned with an old work jacket and a pair of wool socks. She sized up his boots and cut out cardboard liners for them.

When the old man finished eating, he took a small dog-eared Bible from his jacket pocket and began to read aloud to us. Then he gently closed the Bible and rose to leave.

Ma held out the clothes and said, "These are for you. You're not dressed for the weather. Put them on."

The old man shook his head. "I can't take them," he said. "You've given me more than I asked for. I have nothing to give you in return."

Ma assured him she wanted nothing. "I have so much already," she said.

### The Only Gift He Could Give

Then the man reached into his vest pocket and removed a small wooden cross. He peered lovingly at it, then handed it to Ma. "This is the only thing of value I possess," he said. "I want you to have it, dear lady. You've been so good to me."

"I can't take it from you," Ma sobbed.

The old man pressed it into her hand. "Take it. You'll always remember me, the old man who came to you in need on Easter Sunday."

He put on the clothes, stuffed the liners into his boots and shuffled to the door. As he crossed the threshold, he turned and made the sign of the cross over Ma and said, "God bless you, good woman, for being so kind."

Ma smiled faintly as she watched him tramp through the snow to the railroad tracks down the hill. Her eyes shone through her tears as she pressed the cross to her bosom. Staying home on Easter Sunday had been a blessing after all.

The little cross was hung on the wall above our table, near a picture of The Last Supper. It became Ma's medal of honor for helping to ease, if only briefly, the misery and suffering of all those men who came to her marked door.

Ma has never forgotten that man. To this day, she believes he was sent to her by the Lord. ⊠

# CHAPTER FOUR
# Recycling's Nothing New

*WASTE NOT, WANT NOT.* Those who survived the Depression remember a time when absolutely nothing was ever thrown away. Old rags, for example, often found new life in colorful rag rugs. (Photo: J.C. Allen and Son)

# From the desk of Clancy Strock

Dear Katie,

Every now and then, our local TV station carries a public service message reminding us to recycle our trash. That's certainly a fine idea, but for those of us who lived through the Depression, it's an old, old idea.

Of course, back then, we didn't call it recycling--we called it survival. "Waste not, want not" was the motto of the day.

When you read the stories in this chapter, you'll discover how ingenious people could be when pushed into a corner by poverty and desperation. They even figured out how to save the 2¢ it cost to mail a letter!

One abiding memory I have is of my mother listening to the radio on Tuesday nights as she mended and darned and patched the clothes that'd been washed on Monday. If a garment was finally beyond repair, she snipped off the buttons and popped them into her button box while the usable remnants went into the scrap bag, destined to become part of a quilt someday.

The general feeling then was that there was no excuse for wearing ragged or dirty clothes--and no shame in wearing patched ones. Nowadays it appears we've turned that around (if the kids I see at the mall are any example).

Automobiles were perpetually "recycled". No matter how old or battered a car was, people kept it running. The windshield might be out or the tires so thin you could see the air inside, but resourceful people managed to keep their Essex or Reo or Dodge on the road.

As far as I know, my father never threw *anything* away. Maybe that's where your dad picked up his saving ways. Dad's excuse was "you never know when it might come in handy". (Come to think of it, Katie, that's what your dad says, too.)

As a result, we had ancient harnesses hanging from pegs in the barn long after the last horse was gone. We had milk cans but no milk cows...and chicken waterers but no chickens.

Wasting *anything* was not tolerated--especially electricity. Nothing drew Dad's wrath like the discovery of an empty room with a light still burning. Once he'd extracted a confession from the guilty party, he delivered his standard "you must think I'm made of money" speech, punctuated with a brisk whack on the posterior.

It must have sunk in. To this day, I can't leave a light burning in an empty room. And although I know there's absolutely nothing I can buy with a penny, if I find one in a parking lot, I still bend down to pick it up (I tell your Gramma that it's tax-free income).

I guess those Depression-era lessons aren't easily forgotten.

*Your Grandpa Clancy*

# With 'Basics' in Short Supply, Mom Made Everything Count

*By Sally De Coninck, Spencerport, New York*

WHEN MY NIECE recently began to lecture me about the need to recycle cans, bottles and newspapers to save the planet, I recalled some tricks Mom said she used in the Depression. During those years, "recycling" was a matter of survival.

She dry-cleaned old coats, then ripped out the seams and made new coats and snow pants for the little ones. Worn-out clothes were cut into children's or doll's clothes or made into braided rugs or quilts.

Mom saved old diapers for dust cloths, car polishers and cleaning rags. When sweaters were beyond mending, she unraveled them and knitted new ones.

Broken jewelry was great for child's play, costumes, mosaics and even newly designed jewelry. Mom saved worn lampshades to re-cover and used old light bulbs to darn socks. Socks that could no longer be darned were turned into scouring rags.

When Mom wrote a letter, she used both sides of the paper—never mind what Emily Post says. She saved any paper that came into our house with one clean side—a letter, homework, a greeting card—to write notes to us or herself.

The decorative portions of cards were kept for decorations and gift tags. Mom also sewed them together with bits of yarn for letter holders, fruit bowls and candy dishes.

Gift wrap and ribbons were ironed flat and stored carefully for future use. I think Mom wanted to avoid a repeat of the Christmas all our gifts were wrapped in the Sunday funnies.

Some of her methods might tempt younger folks to chuckle. But those who lived through the Depression never forgot how hard it was to obtain the basic necessities.

Next time you see an older person pick up a piece of string or save a paper clip, smile and give thanks you were born in a time when everything you need is available. ▨

**SUPER SAVER. Sally De Coninck's mother was a genius at using and reusing items, like many during the Depression.**

---

**PUNGENT MEMORY. Vern Berry (shown on early-day trip and today) recalls an aromatic evening.**

## Gasoline Fumes Marred Couple's Rare Night Out

MY YOUNG HUSBAND and I were living in a small Colorado town in the '30s that offered little in the way of recreation. When a kindly customer invited us to his home for an evening of cards, I was thrilled.

My only concern was that my one dress-up dress was soiled. It was made of wool, so I couldn't wash it. I drew a little gasoline from a pump at our repair shop and rubbed the spots, which came right out.

With that problem solved, I thought about my tacky shoes. Mom wore a larger size than I did, but I borrowed a pair from her and stuffed the toes with newspaper.

Our host was the boss of the railroad section, and one of the few people in town with a regular paycheck. Section hands lived in railroad-provided boxcars similar to today's mobile homes.

Our evening with the man and his wife was memorable—for all the wrong reasons. As the room grew warmer, I began to smell gasoline. Then my neck began to burn.

I was terrified our hosts would notice the odor and my reddened neck, but if they did, they didn't mention it. They were very hospitable and even served store-bought pickles—something I hadn't been able to buy for a long time.

We eventually moved back to Iowa, where a better job and better times provided us with all kinds of recreation. But I'll never forget that night in Colorado, when I smelled of gasoline, suffered a blistered neck and wore shoes with newspaper stuffed in the toes. —*Vern Berry, Bettendorf, Iowa*

# 'We Didn't Even Own a Trash Can'

*By Bertha Whetstone, Wetumpka, Alabama*

RECYCLING isn't new to me. As the youngest of 13 children, I grew up learning to recycle everything. There was no need for landfills or garbage dumps. We didn't even own a trash can.

**HAPPY ANYWAY. When she was a kid, Bertha Whetstone didn't realize that her family was poor.**

We bought very little canned food, but when we did, Papa saved the cans to store nails and bolts. We children used them for simple toys, too. Sometimes we'd beat a can flat, nail it to a stick and use it to push a wheel.

Table scraps were fed to the dogs and cats. Fruit and vegetable peelings were fed to the hogs. Eggshells were crushed and thrown to the chickens.

When our hand-me-down clothes wore thin, Mama cut the best material into squares for quilt tops. Buttons were cut off and stored in the button box. After picking cotton in fall, we scraped up whatever cotton was left in the fields and picked out the seeds. Mama carded it to make quilt batting.

Hickory and oak ashes from the fireplace were used to make soap. Any remaining ashes were mixed with fallen leaves and scattered around our fruit trees, flower beds and fields.

When we cleaned the barn and chicken house, we spread the manure over the fields and flower beds. Mama's roses and zinnias were bigger and more brilliant than any I see today.

Papa robbed the bees of their honey and melted the comb into beeswax, which had many uses. Mama saved the tallow from beef and shaped it into bars to soothe our chapped hands and feet.

**RAISED A BAKER'S DOZEN. Bertha's parents had their hands full bringing up 13 children with little money.**

Our shelves and dresser drawers were lined with newspaper. Iron scraps were saved to patch farm equipment. Nails were pulled from old boards, straightened, sorted by size and stored in cans. When our shoe soles wore thin, we cut inner tubes to fit the inside of the shoe to protect our feet from the hot dirt while we chopped cotton.

Yes, we were poor, but I didn't know it. We had wonderful parents, worked hard, laughed a lot and were very happy. ⊠

## Prince Albert Helped Keep Their Hair Curly

WHEN I was a young farm girl during the Great Depression, money was hard to come by—especially for things that my mother called frivolous.

Still, we country lasses were always trying to make our hair look its best. Without money for a real "machine" permanent or for aluminum rollers or wave clips, we soon learned how to make our hair curly without much effort.

First we'd find an empty Prince Albert tobacco can. We'd put it in the fire—under the wash pot on washdays or when we burned leaves—and leave it there until it turned dark and the paint flaked off.

### Tin Strips Turned into Rollers

Then we'd remove the bottom and the lid from the darkened tin, which had lost some of its strength. Next, using the only pair of scissors our mother had, we carefully cut the burned can crosswise in strips about a quarter inch wide.

Each tin strip was rolled in paper (a page torn from our Sears catalog). The ends of the paper were folded over, and the "rollers" were ready to be used.

Unlike the aluminum rollers—which had a little rubber roller on the end of the "bail" that would fit over the rolled hair and engage in the hollow form of the roller, thus holding the hair in place until it dried—the ends of our metal rollers were simply bent over the rolled-up hair.

We were always very proud of a new set of metal rollers, even if they were harder to sleep on than the rag kind. Of course, we were just as proud of our new "do" *and* we had some of the curliest hair imaginable!

*—Myrtle Beavers, Destin, Florida*

# Teen Scavenged Dump for Recyclable Treasures

*By Michael Lacivita, Youngstown, Ohio*

MY PARENTS were too proud to go on relief, so I decided to spend my summer vacation in 1937 working the dump on the east side of Youngstown, Ohio. I was 13 years old.

My goal was to find treasures—aluminum, brass, copper, iron, glass and rags—that our more affluent citizens threw out. Finding an aluminum pot or copper kettle was like hitting the jackpot.

Six days each week, I left home at dawn and pulled my wagon several blocks to the dump, which burned continuously. The smoke smelled terrible. Today I shudder to think of what we were exposed to.

Those who worked the dump had a code of honor and took turns chasing a car or truck about to unload its bounty. If an old copper washtub arrived, there was real joy in Dumpville for whoever was next in line.

In between arrivals, we would gather around Old Ned, the unofficial dumpmaster. He had a shanty at the dump and kept us entertained with his tales of the old days.

During the school year, I crossed the dump four times a day, since that was the shortest path between home and school. One day I spotted a large aluminum cooking pot being unloaded from a truck. I ran after that pot as it rolled down a hill. Ned hung on to it for safekeeping until school was out.

Payday came when the ragman came through the neighborhood, calling, "Ragman! Ragman! Any rags today?"

I loved to watch his horse eat out of a burlap sack slung over his neck. I envied him. He seemed to have more to eat than I did.

We waited eagerly at the curb while the ragman climbed off the wagon to weigh the junk we had to sell. This was *real* curbside recycling.

The ragman bought metal based on its weight, and many of us tried to outwit him by hiding a stone in an aluminum pot. It never worked, but the

> *"My goal was to find treasures the affluent threw out..."*

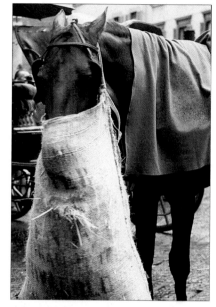

**PUTTING ON THE FEED BAG.** Although Michael Lacivita envied the ragman's horse, he was still more than happy to pocket the "dump money" the horse's owner paid him.

ragman always got a chuckle out of it.

The items we scavenged from the dump brought only a few pennies, but that was big money in those days.

---

**HE WASN'T "COOPED UP" FOR LONG.** Leonard Attisano (on the roof of his family's pigeon coop with his brother, Nicky) spent most of his free time out looking for treasures in Brooklyn.

## "Junking" Junkets Helped This Brooklyn Boy

WHENEVER school wasn't in session, I was out "junking" in Brooklyn. I'd get up at 6 a.m. and walk up and down the streets with my wagon.

I wasn't the only one doing this, and the residents were very nice to us. They even separated their trash for us. They put kitchen garbage in the trash cans and hung burlap bags containing rags and paper on the fences.

I'd finish my "route" by noon and come home to sort my items. The papers were tied into bundles and the rags sorted according to fabric. Each item sold at a different price.

In the afternoon, my brother and I would go out to pick up wood, which we cut and stored for winter. We couldn't afford to buy much coal.

Most of the wood used to heat our house came from condemned buildings being demolished by work crews. Some of these workmen were nice, but others chased us away. In hindsight, I realize they feared we'd get hurt walking around all that debris. —*Leonard Attisano Brooklyn, New York*

## Who Needed a Toy Store?

ONE OF MY favorite toys was one made by my dad, who had the ability to build, repair or draw just about anything.

He built me a wooden "pinball machine" that was about 18 inches long and 12 inches wide. The "balls" were actually marbles, and nails were used for the bumpers and scoring areas.

I was about 5 years old at the time and spent many happy hours enjoying this game and others he made for me.

—*Dolores Del Medico*
*New Hartford, New York*

## Kids' Playground Was Envy of the Neighborhood

MY DAD COULD make nearly anything out of wood and other scraps. With old wood and leather straps, he made us the best stilts in the world. When we wanted bikes and he couldn't afford any, he "made" some that were as good as new by fixing up and painting scrapped ones.

Dad made lots of playground equipment from scraps, too. He buried a car axle, topped it with a wheel hub and boards, and we had a great merry-go-round. He stood a car frame on end and anchored it in the ground for a swing frame. He built us a teeter-totter, too.

Nothing went to waste, and our backyard playground was the envy of the neighborhood kids. —*Dlores DeWitt*
*Colorado Springs, Colorado*

**A WHOLE NEW WAVE. This woman likely didn't style her hair with essence of flaxseed. But Virginia Farmer's customers did (story at right).**

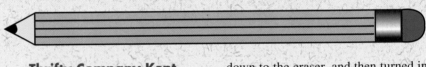

## Thrifty Company Kept An Eye on Pencils

THOSE OF US lucky enough to have jobs during the Depression often worked under the strictest of rules. One employer required us to use only pencils for reports and calculations, as they were less expensive than pens and ink.

Each pencil had to be used right

## She Waved Her Way Through High School

MY AUNT took a beauty course in a big city, and whenever she came to our little town, she'd give all us girls a finger wave. I watched closely and decided I'd like to try to do the same thing myself to earn a little extra money.

Since you couldn't buy the materials for a wave set where we lived, I made my own using flaxseed.

I'd buy 10¢ worth from the drugstore, place it in a pan, add water and then cook it. After straining it out, I'd get about a quart of wave set.

At 10¢ a finger wave, my business grew by word of mouth, and I soon had enough customers to provide me extra money for buying clothes and for the material to make my own clothes.

That flaxseed helped me a lot during school, and I'm thankful for it.

—*Virginia Farmer, Alto Vista, Virginia*

down to the eraser, and then turned in before we were issued another.

But the company's thrift didn't end there. One young man who worked beside me had an almost ludicrous job. He stayed after hours and erased everything we'd written on our scratch pads so they could be used again the following day!

—*Betty-Jane Heitz*
*Savannah, Georgia*

---

**WEAR IT OUT—THEN WEAR IT AGAIN. For families like Margie Porteus' (that's little Margie on the left), clothing that was threadbare hadn't necessarily outlived its usefulness.**

## Home Ec Skills Came in Handy

WHEN I WAS attending school in Oklahoma, my home economics teacher taught us a valuable skill. She made sure we knew not only how to make new garments, but how to "make over" old ones.

My project was a faded green tweed coat. I ripped it open, turned it inside out, then sewed it back together so the bright green lining was on the outside.

My dad, who'd grown up poor in Georgia, told me how his parents made their own buttons with oblong pieces of wood. He carved 2-inch cedar buttons for my new coat. I was very proud of them.

Mother never threw anything away, so that made-over coat finally ended up as blocks in a woolen quilt. I still have the buttons.

—*Margie Porteus*
*Paonia, Colorado*

# Family of 17 Survived Through Teamwork

*By Curtis Darkes, Hamilton, New Jersey*

FOR OUR FAMILY, home was an 84-acre farm in Lebanon County, Pennsylvania. My parents bought it for $2,700 at an auction in 1927. When the Depression hit 2 years later, they had 11 children. By 1936, there were 15.

Survival was our primary goal, and we all had to help out. We were taught to take care of whatever we had and make it last as long as we could. We had no money, so nothing was discarded as long as it had any possible future use.

On a farm with no plumbing or electricity, there was a lot of manual labor. We treasured every tool and piece of farm equipment we owned. With hard work and a few miracles, we had three meals a day, and clean clothes for school and church.

## No Need to Diet

We were well-fed, but on our diet, no one had a weight problem. Most of our food was what we raised ourselves. Any leftovers from our large garden were sold at the farmer's market. That money was used to buy whatever necessities we couldn't raise or make ourselves.

We made our own butter, cheese, cottage cheese and buttermilk. We grew our own wheat, which we had milled into flour. We roasted our field corn and had that ground into cornmeal. We ate "sun-dried" sweet corn and apples year-round.

With 15 children, we needed lots of clothes. Most were made from feed sacks. If we didn't have enough, we could buy extra sacks from other farmers at minimal cost.

Sometimes we bought a bundle of scraps for $1.25 from a clothing factory. Those scraps were priceless to us. Mother sifted through them and made whatever she could for whichever child needed it most.

There was never enough matching material for a complete garment, so most of our clothes were multicolored. Smaller scraps were saved for patchwork quilts.

## Every Day Was Washday

We did laundry every morning before school. Water was heated on the wood-burning stove and carried to the hand-agitated washer. The clothes were put through a hand-cranked wringer, then hung outside to dry in every kind of weather except rain. Sometimes the clothes froze in our hands before we could get them on the clothesline.

We all helped care for the crops and livestock, and Dad and the older boys cut down trees to provide the tons of firewood we used every winter.

Any "down time" was spent repairing and maintaining our tools and horse-drawn farm equipment. Dad was also our cobbler and barber, and he occasionally cut hair for other people for 15¢.

We knew we were poor, but that was never a problem. We were blessed with good parents, and all 15 children did whatever they could to help. It was hard work, but none of us had any regrets.

Living through the Depression may not be an experience we'd choose to repeat, but I believe it made many of us better, stronger people. I'm glad I'm still here to remember and pass on my own memories. ⊠

**SURVIVAL SCHOOL.** Like many who survived the Depression, the women in this sewing class found their skills invaluable at a time when new clothes became an unattainable luxury.

## Sewing Skills Benefited Neighborhood Children

HOME ECONOMICS courses used to be an integral part of the school curriculum. In 1930, every girl in my graduating class was required to hand-sew her own gown. This training came in handy during the Depression, when everything in my wardrobe was made by hand.

My mother-in-law always kept bolts of white linen for making sheets and pillowcases. After her death, I began using the linen to make clothes for myself and the children.

One creation was a pair of dress overalls for my son, Peter. It was so rewarding to design a garment, make a pattern from newspaper and watch the finished product emerge.

Family and friends also provided old woolen skirts, still in good repair, which I turned into overalls for the neighborhood tots. Others in our sewing circle knitted coordinating mittens, sweaters and hats. —*Sara Riola*
*Lakewood, New Jersey*

## Lettering on Flour Sacks Sometimes Left Its Mark

WHEN OUR WHEAT was milled in town, it came home in white sacks la-

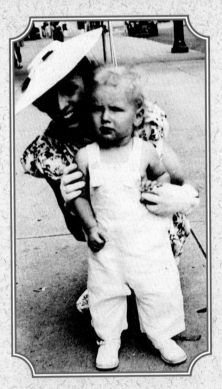

**OVERALL SUCCESS.** Sara Riola was pleased with this pair of dress overalls she made for her son, Peter.

beled with blue and red lettering. Mother used the sacks to make modest, below-the-knee bloomers for me.

She tried to bleach out the lettering with salt and sunlight, but sometimes it didn't work. Each pair of bloomers had a yoke, and one read right across my tummy: "48 lbs. when packed".
—*Arvilla Copeland, Lenexa, Kansas*

## Was Frugal Bachelor Coming or Going?

OUR CLOSEST neighbor was a man who lived three-quarters of a mile down the road. He lived alone and was very frugal—but in those Depression days, everybody had to be.

This man often wore his overalls backward, and one day when he came to our place, my dad asked him about it. "I switch them around," our neighbor said. "This way they wear evenly."

It was a little strange seeing a button fly in the back, but we got used to it.
—*Shirley Wasson, Grinnell, Iowa*

## One Size Fit All...His Children

MY FATHER owned two shoe lasts, the cobbler's forms on which shoes are built. One size was for adults, and the other for children. Each year we received a new homemade pair of shoes, regardless of how our feet grew.

In spring, when the soles wore out, my father would re-sole them. In summer, we just went barefoot.

—*Inez Beach, Montpelier, Ohio*

# Homemade Jelly Was Cornerstone Of Family's Bartering System

*By Mel Erlinger, Seminole, Florida*

WE LIVED 25 miles south of St. Louis, Missouri during the Depression. Dad had grown up across the river in Freeburg, Illinois.

In summer, Dad would convince someone who had a car and wasn't working (who was?) to drive us back to his parents' farm to pick fruit. The driver got a meal, a dollar for bridge fare, a couple gallons of 12-cent gasoline and a share of whatever we picked.

We brought home plums, peaches, cherries, grapes, blackberries and blueberries, and Mom spent most of a day making jelly, jam and preserves. Few people had telephones, so Dad would walk through the neighborhood or mail penny postcards to tell our neighbors when he'd be around with Mom's handiwork.

On the appointed night, Dad and I would load my big red wagon with as much jelly as it could hold. Then we'd hang a small lantern on the back and start out, with Dad coughing all the way from his World War I disability.

### I'll Trade You!

After a few blocks, we'd make our first stop. On one trip I remember, we traded seven or eight glasses of jelly for a half dozen eggs, a bundle of kindling, a pound of sugar and a pair of gloves a child in the family had outgrown.

At our next stop, we traded for homemade soap and candy, a pair of pillowcases and more kindling. Another stop brought 2 pounds of flour, a roll of toilet tissue, a can of corn and another half dozen eggs.

When we got home, we unloaded the wagon, put the wood in the coal shed, extinguished the lantern and carried our bartered goods up the 39 steps to our second-floor flat.

This process was repeated every few weeks until there was no fruit left to pick. In the meantime, other people would stop by our house to do some bartering of their own.

It's difficult to imagine doing this today, but bartering worked back then. People were all in pretty much the same boat, trying to survive—but still making an effort to help each other out. ▣

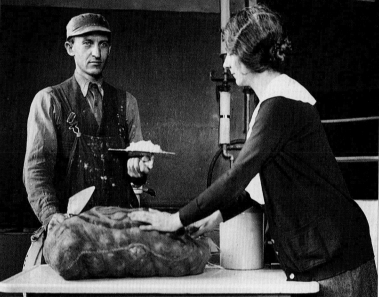

**BERRY-BASED ECONOMY.** Mel Erlinger (at top right) tells how his family used fruit to get them through the Depression. Looks like the workman above is trading his furnace-plastering labor for a big bag of onions.

---

**MONEY? WHAT'S THAT?** Lucile Good (in 1935 photo) and her family met their needs by trading for them.

### Bartering Helped Cash-Poor Families

BARTERING was a must during the Depression.

Daddy got a car in exchange for a bushel of potatoes. Mother spent a day working for a neighbor and was given a cut-glass cracker bowl that I still have today.

When Mother couldn't sell her watermelons and cantaloupes, she traded them for sugar, coffee and other staples.

She traded chicken, eggs and butter for whatever we needed, too.

My brother, Richard, and I helped get our sugarcane ready to go the mill, where we traded it for sorghum molasses. We took sacks of wheat to a grain company and got flour in return.

Daddy traded for lots of horses, but the one I remember best was an old white one that turned out to be very lazy. Daddy realized right away why that horse had been such a bargain!

*—Lucile Good, Tucson, Arizona*

REVERSE, RESTITCH, RENEW. Like this woman, Mary Sudy's mother knew how to use a sewing machine to make clothes last a bit longer.

## Mom Stitched and Dad Tacked To Keep Family Clothed

WHEN MY SHOES became victims of sidewalk hopscotch, Dad repaired them for me on a shoemaker's anvil. He repaired my brothers' shoes, too, changing the anvil's heavy metal foot according to the size needed.

Dad would pop some tacks in his mouth, then take out one at a time as he pounded them in around the edge of the sole. I wondered how many tacks his cheeks could hold...and whether he ever swallowed any.

Ma did her part with her pedal sewing machine. She took apart the boys' worn shirt collars and reversed and restitched them for longer wear.

Little girls always wore dresses, and I especially remember two that Ma made on her Singer. They had the same plain pattern, with round necklines, puffy sleeves and gathered skirts, but matching bloomers transformed them into very pretty outfits. —*Mary Sudy Mt. Clemens, Michigan*

## Unable to Maintain Cars, Owners Made "Hoovercarts"

"HOOVERCARTS" weren't built in Detroit, but in our community in Florida's panhandle, they were the main mode of transportation during the '30s.

Many people had bought Chevrolets, Fords and Studebakers during the boom years of the '20s. When the Depression hit, and gasoline and repairs got expensive, only two people in our town could afford to continue using their cars—the proprietor of the company store and the letter carrier.

Everyone else used the chassis and wheels on their cars to make Hoovercarts. The metal body was removed and replaced with a homemade wooden one. A tongue, made from a white oak pole, was attached to the front of this contraption so two mules could be hitched up to pull it.

I especially remember riding to church on summer nights. Quilts were spread over the floor of the wagon for a softer ride. We looked for the Big Dipper, caught fireflies and sang hymns as the rubber tires bounced along the rutted, sandy road to our church in the pines. —*Baron Conaway State University, Arkansas*

## Youngster Got Skunked With Money-Making Scheme

IN 1930, I was 11 years old and didn't know the Great Depression had arrived. But I soon found out.

During the '20s, my older brothers had sold skunk pelts for as much as $5. That sounded good to me. A farm boy with $5 felt like he owned half the world.

My brother Albert showed me how to skin my first skunk. We turned the hide inside out, stuck a shingle in it and hung it in the corncrib to dry. Then I wrapped it in waxed paper, tied it in a shoe box and took it to the post office to ship to a Chicago fur company.

The clerk asked if I wanted the package insured. "I guess so," I said.

"For how much?" the clerk asked.

"Five dollars," I proudly announced. The postage and insurance cost me all of 35¢.

I ran to the mailbox every day, hoping for my check. A week went by, and I found a letter from Chicago. With great anticipation, I excitedly opened the envelope and looked at the check. It was for 30¢.

I had been skunked by my first skunk—and smelled like one, too.

—*Emerson Riggs Farmington Hills, Michigan*

## Inner Tube Lining Was Easier on the Feet

WHEN OUR school shoes got holes in them, Dad would line them with cardboard. But that didn't last very long on the gravel schoolyard, and if it wore through, we'd come home with blisters on our feet.

Then Dad came up with a better idea—lining our shoes with strips from old inner tubes. Those strips lasted much longer than cardboard—and felt better, too! —*Patsy Gwinn Wichita Falls, Texas*

ROLL REVERSAL. Eleanor Scott (with her family above) says her mother's baking skills helped keep food on the table. See the story below.

## Mother's Dinner Rolls Kept Them Off the Dole

MY FATHER could no longer find work in 1938, but he wouldn't even consider welfare. He believed families should take care of themselves.

My mother baked very good dinner rolls, and several people encouraged her to sell them. She started out with friends and relatives as customers, rising at 5 a.m. every Saturday to set yeast. Before long, our home was filled with the aroma of baking rolls.

By 9 a.m., the first rolls were out of the oven and cool enough to place in baskets with fresh linens so my brother, Fred, and I could deliver them.

We each had regular customers who paid 15¢ for a 9-inch pan of dinner rolls or 25¢ for cinnamon-nut rolls. We always took extra rolls in case we found a new customer.

By late afternoon, we'd sold at least $5 worth of rolls. That was enough to buy the ingredients for the following Saturday's baking, plus our own food for the week.  —*Eleanor Scott*
*Clarence Center, New York*

## Sturdy Wooden Boxes Had Multitude of Uses

WOODEN BOXES helped my family make do with what we had. The boxes were available at the grocery and other stores, and adults and children alike used them for everything you can think of.

Mom used orange boxes for nightstands and kitchen cabinets. To dress them up, she covered the front with old dress material.

We children used orange boxes for "jigs", the same thing kids call go-karts today. If we were lucky enough to find an old ironing board, we'd put the box on top and attach wagon wheels or old roller skates.

Shotgun shell crates were especially heavy and well-made. Dad used two of them to make a box with a lid, then attached a latch and lock for storing anything he didn't want us kids to fool with.

Apple boxes were used for storage, stacked sideways in the basement for shelving, or used for woodworking projects and kindling. My folks also nailed one outside the kitchen and used it in winter for an icebox.  —*Ward Elliott*
*Boscawen, New Hampshire*

## Two-Room Shack Was Home for Six

IN THE 1930s, my three siblings and I lived in a two-room shack in the mountains near Shouns, Tennessee.

Our father was usually off looking for work and was seldom home. Mom sometimes got work doing other people's laundry on washboards. It paid little but helped feed us.

Once when Dad was away, Mom had to walk 4 miles to the relief office in the nearest big town. She walked all the way home with a 25-pound bag of flour sitting on her shoulder.

I remember one winter when Dad was gone, none of us had any shoes, and there was snow on the ground. A friend who lived farther up the mountain with his family came down to get us and take us back to his house.

He brought a pair of his son's tennis shoes for my brother to wear and wrapped the rest of our feet in gunnysacks. We stayed at his house for about 3 weeks. I've often thought about the kindness that man showed us.

Soon after that, we went to live with my mother's brother until we could move into a house of our own.

I'll never forget those days. Times were really tough, but we made it.

—*Nola Sherrill*
*Jacksonville, Florida*

FANCY TOGS. The Depression was on, but you would not know it by this 1929 photo, shared by John Doll, of Fillmore, California. "My older brother, George, and I were two of the best-dressed kids in one of the toughest neighborhoods in Chicago," John says. "Our family was on welfare, but The Good Fellows were a charitable group that kept the poor clothed. Their contacts for used clothing were the Chicago wealthy. Though secondhand, our clothes were of such high quality I doubt you could buy their equal even today. The fancy clothes didn't make our lives easy on the street, but we looked good!"

## Bad Times
## Waxed and Waned

A GOOD FRIEND and I both grew up in Arizona during the '30s, and she recalls that when times were really tough, her mother would wrap her school lunch in some pages from an old Sears catalog.

At school, when lunchtime arrived, she'd plunge her hand deep into the bucket and unwrap her biscuit sandwich inside before pulling it out.

That way, the other kids wouldn't know her family was too poor to afford waxed paper. (Of course, it didn't dawn on her that many of the other kids were just as busy with their sleight-of-hand tricks.)

Later, when things got better and the family could afford waxed paper again, my friend says she felt so euphoric that she wrapped *everything* in waxed paper—her biscuit sandwich, her cookies and even her banana!

To this day, she uses those times as a mental measuring stick. If something really wonderful happens in her life, she can be heard to exclaim, "My, that's as good as a banana wrapped in waxed paper!"
—*Madeline McVey*
*Kingman, Arizona*

## Small-Town Football Team
## Had No Money for a Ball

IN THE EARLY 1930s, everyone in my hometown of Watertown, Minnesota was so poor that my high school football team couldn't even afford a football!

The business community came to our rescue, donating the huge sum of $11.75—enough to purchase *two* footballs. The local paper published the names of all the businessmen who'd been generous enough to chip in a quarter or 50¢.

Since we couldn't even afford a football, you might wonder how we managed to get things like shoulder pads and helmets. One player's brother just happened to be equipment manager for the University of Minnesota's team and passed on all their discarded gear.

Few of our players weighed more than 150 pounds dripping wet. So you can probably imagine how ridiculous they looked trying to fill a pair of shoulder pads designed for someone who weighed over 200 pounds!
—*Loren Thorson*
*Green Valley, Arizona*

**BIRTHDAY GIRL.** Although Clara Strelow (shown here on her 18th birthday) and her family worked two farms during the Depression, they still had to struggle to pay the bills. Fortunately, sharing with neighbors and friends got them through.

J.C. Allen and Son

## Even with Two Farms, It Was
## Hard to Make Ends Meet

WHEN OUR FAMILY of nine moved to a farm north of Oklahoma City in the early '30s, we weren't prepared for the drought or the Depression.

Although we were working two farms, we couldn't get ahead. Sometimes we had to sell a cow for only $9 to buy sugar, flour and other necessities.

I had no good shoes to wear to my high school graduation, so we drove to the Salvation Army store in Oklahoma City. I was fortunate to find a nice pair of gray pumps, which matched my robe, for 60¢. I was very proud of them.

To help pay for college tuition, I worked in the National Youth Administration program for 12-1/2¢ an hour. My older brother and I took some of the same classes so we could share books. We also searched the library for textbooks we could borrow.

Those times taught everyone to share. A gentleman from church gave us his surplus turnips. During the week, we took any extra eggs and milk to our minister, as there was little money for tithes.

I wouldn't want to go back to those days, but I'm thankful we got through them with God's help.
—*Clara Strelow*
*Edmond, Oklahoma*

**DEPRESSION 101.** As Harrell McCullough relates below, hard times hit college campuses just like everywhere else. And being a poor college student was no fun at all.

# Poor College Boys' Experiences Prepared Them for A Tough World

*By Harrell McCullough, Oklahoma City, Oklahoma*

WHEN I HEAR university students complain today about the lack of jobs, I think back to the early days of the Depression, when I attended the University of Oklahoma.

The university was much more status-conscious then. If you didn't belong to a fraternity or sorority, you were a "barb" or second-class citizen. If you were poor, you were just a bum. Sorority girls did not date bums.

But it was the boys who came to the university with no money who had real drive and ability.

Having a poor boy as a member gave a fraternity added prestige. The boy would be given a job in the kitchen so he could afford to join. That was about the only upward social mobility available to him.

These young men worked for their room and board, but no money changed hands. All payment was "in kind". The established rate was 1 hour's work per day for a room, and 2 hours' work for each meal. If you complained, someone else was waiting for your job. Working 7 hours a day left little time for attending classes or studying, so many boys ate only once a day. The trick was to get a job in the kitchen so you could eat as much as you could hold at that one meal. You can survive that way, but you're hungry most of the day.

If a poor boy got a seat in the hole of his only pair of pants, he wore the pants from his ROTC uniform. When he wore a hole in the heel of a sock, he pulled the hole down and turned the toe under. He did his laundry in the bathroom and put his pants under his mattress to crease them.

## Returned to "Sender"

He saved the 2¢ to mail a letter by putting a random name and address on the envelope with the recipient's name in the upper left corner. Without a stamp, the post office would return the letter to the "sender"—the intended recipient.

A Coke in the union cost a nickel. Any coed who ordered a 10¢ drink was blackballed by the boys on campus.

That wasn't fair, but then, nothing made sense in those days. Farmers were foreclosed upon because they couldn't sell their crops. Meanwhile, many went hungry because they couldn't buy the farmer's crops. Sellers were desperate to sell land, and buyers were desperate to buy. No one could do either, and nobody understood why. There was infinite fallout—like the girl who ordered a 10¢ drink.

After graduating, the poor boy went job-hunting in a very depressed world. Many job openings occurred only when the previous employee died.

But the poor boy had an advantage—his experiences had made him tougher and smarter. When he finally got a job, he didn't dare ask what it paid. He found that out when he got his first paycheck. ▨

# Newlyweds Counted on Cotton Crop to Pay Grocery Bill

*By Lorene Kossey, Fritch, Texas*

WHEN I FINISHED high school in 1932, I had to borrow $10 from an elderly couple to buy a dress and shoes for graduation. To repay the loan, I worked in the cotton fields of the Texas panhandle for 50¢ a day.

In 1933, I met the man who would become my husband. Leonard and I courted by walking everywhere—church, Sunday school and parties. We enjoyed it, and most of our friends were in the same boat.

On Saturdays, we sometimes walked to town and bought a hamburger for a nickel, followed by a big dish of nickel ice cream.

We sat at a little wrought-iron table and felt just as rich as anybody. We could also go to a Saturday matinee for a nickel, or join our friends on horse-drawn hayrides.

We were married September 28, 1934 and bought groceries on credit until we gathered our cotton crop. Our first bale brought enough to repay the grocery bill, and we had enough left over to buy a secondhand Model T Ford roadster for $25.

I made everything we wore. When our first child was born, in 1935, I sewed all his little clothes from shirttails, the backs of pant legs and skirts from worn-out dresses.

Everyone was going broke, and we couldn't find work anywhere. Leonard had relatives in Borger, Texas, so he hopped a freight train to look for a job there. He found a few weeks' work building a bridge over the Canadian River.

But when that job ended, he couldn't find another. He sent all his money home and hopped a freight with 50¢ in his pocket. He rode the train almost to Abilene, then hitchhiked the rest of the way. He still had the 50¢ when he got home, but he was hungry.

Every time it seemed we just couldn't go any further, something would happen and we were able to make it. We had faith that God would see us through, and He did.

We finally moved to Borger, where Leonard landed a job with Phillips Petroleum. We felt it was heaven-sent. Now we could have an indoor bathroom, electric lights and gas heat.

Leonard stayed with Phillips for over 18 years. We were always grateful for that job, and happy that we'd put our trust in God. ⊠

**THIRTIES WERE NO PICNIC.** When Lorene and Leonard Kossey were dating and went to Abilene Lake for a picnic in 1933 (inset), the Depression was on. Despite that, they married a year later. Their cotton crop and trust in God helped pull them through.

Ewing Galloway

**COUNTING THEIR BLESSINGS.** Chances are that the table pictured above was a lot more bountiful than the one where Era Bonds and her family ate their meals (see story at right). But according to Era, they did not feel any less blessed.

## "I Always Thought We Were Rich"

WE HAD 11 mouths to feed in our household, so nothing went to waste. Mother saved everything, including buttons, string, paper and sacks. She made a lot of our toys, like tops fashioned from sharpened wooden spools.

Mother turned sugar sacks into towels, blouses, underwear and curtains. She used the printed sacks from chicken feed to make shirts and dresses.

Daddy always wore a blue serge suit. When the seat became thin and slick, Mother cut off the legs to make me a skirt that I was very proud of.

When we got meat from the butcher, Mother saved the wrapping paper and string. When washed and dried, the paper could be used to line cake pans. Mother used the string to knit and crochet hats, gloves and doilies.

Both parents taught us to be thankful for what we had. I always thought we were rich. It was only later that I realized we were poor.
—*Era Bonds*
*Simpsonville, South Carolina*

## Her Dad Invented "Bingo Machine"

IN THE 1930s, my father, John Reider, called bingo games at St. David Church in Detroit, Michigan.

The numbers were printed on disks and put in a cigar box, which Dad shook by hand. Then he'd reach in without looking and pull out a number.

The players paid 25¢ a card, but they never played for

## BINGO!

money. First prize was a basket of groceries or a bag of sugar or flour. Second prize was a pound of bacon or a variety of canned fruits and vegetables. Sometimes the prizes were linens—sheets for first prize, pillowcases for second.

One evening Dad announced there'd be a surprise at the next bingo game and encouraged the players to invite all their friends. He spent a lot of time in the basement that week, and he remained quite secretive about what he was doing.

At the next game, Dad unveiled his invention. He'd put a metal cigar can on a stand, then welded on a handle and clamped the whole works to a table. The cylinder revolved when the handle was turned. When word got around, people came from all over to see Dad's "bingo machine".

An added benefit was that nobody had to yell, "Shake 'em up!" anymore.
—*Marian Brennan*
*Alamogordo, New Mexico*

## Cardboard Boxes Cut Into Makeshift Soles

THERE WERE nine children in our family, and each morning before school, we all went on a hunt for cardboard boxes. We'd lay the cardboard on the floor and trace around the outsides of our shoes. When the cardboard was cut out, we had "soles" for the day.
—*Eleanor Swanson*
*Farmington, Connecticut*

## Kids Collected Coal At Train Stop

DURING the Depression, a New York-to-Florida train used to stop for refueling near our house, about midpoint on their trip. My brothers, friends and I often went to meet it.

We'd stand on the bank and look at the "rich Yankees" inside—especially in the dining car, with its white tablecloths and fine silverware.

Some of the men would come to the door and throw money out to us, and we'd scramble in the dirt for it. A nickel, dime or quarter was really something.

After the train left, we'd take our buckets and walk down the tracks, picking up any coal that had dropped from the coal car. Our parents were very glad to get this fuel for our small grate.

How grateful we were for the warmth as we sat around this small fireplace—even if it only kept our front sides warm, and not our backs.

—*Louise Farmer*
*Cayce, South Carolina*

*"YANKEE DOLLARS" AND CAST-OFF COAL.* Trains bound for Florida and New York often passed by the home of Louise Farmer. She and her brothers would go down to watch them refuel and, with any luck, pick up a lot of coal and a little money.

## Arrival of "The Box" Filled Sisters with Anticipation

MY SISTER and I got lots of our clothes by way of "the box". That was our term for the packages my aunt sent with clothes our cousins had outgrown.

The mailman would leave a notice in our apartment mailbox to pick up a package at the post office. The anticipation was wonderful. "The box" would contain new clothes! (Well, they were new to us.)

Years later, when a longtime friend got married, my sister and I went through the reception line and exclaimed, "Jane, your dress is beautiful! Did it come in *the box*?"

My sister and I knew what her sudden burst of laughter meant, but her confused husband had no idea what was so funny.
—*Irene Slyter*
*Longview, Washington*

## Mom's Quick Thinking Stalled Gas Shutoff

MY FATHER was a successful young stockbroker in 1932 and '33. Then his business failed. My parents lost their pretty home and car and had to rent a small house.

Dad became a traveling salesman, leaving Mother home with three small children. She was so frustrated with bill collectors that when the gas man appeared at our door to turn off the gas, she let him into the basement—then locked him in until he promised to leave our gas on until Dad returned.

Mother had us pick dandelions for making wine. We wore hand-me-down clothes and ate a lot of meatless spaghetti.

Our Christmas gifts were refurbished toys our parents had owned. But we weren't aware of "doing without".

We had a great family, and our parents made it all fun.
—*Nancy O'Keefe*
*Edina, Minnesota*

NOTHING WENT TO waste at our house during the 1930s. We recycled everything over and over, until there was nothing left to recycle!

We learned to reuse items out of plain necessity. If something broke, we didn't buy a new one—we fixed the old one so it would work again.

Paper sacks were always saved for Halloween bags and masks, drawing paper and gift wrap. If we received presents wrapped in store-bought gift wrap, we pressed and saved it to use again.

Mother would use the brown paper bags for lamp shade covers, window blinds and sewing patterns. They were also handy for draining foods and baking.

**ROLE MODELS.** Lois Curnutt's parents (shown here with her brother) taught their children how to be self-sufficient.

# With Little Cash, Nothing Went to Waste

*By Lois Curnutt, Odessa, Texas*

ing and used them as buffers when pulling something behind the truck or tractor.

Rubber inner tubes were saved to make slingshots, propellers, shoe patches and house slipper soles. We inflated them for swimming and attached strips under rugs to keep them from slipping.

A strip of inner tube made the best jar opener ever—I wish I had one now!

We made flowers, jewelry and other decorative items out of old silk hosiery and the fine wires from old electric cords. Hosiery was used to stuff quilts, pillows and toys, and to strain juice, fruit puree and cheese.

We bound tin cans together, then covered them with gunnysacks or fabric scraps for footstools. Individual cans covered with fabric made building blocks or holders for kitchen tools, pencils and sewing notions.

Many food items came in tin buckets, which we decorated for Easter baskets and kitchen canisters. Some were painted and turned into planters. An empty bucket was perfect for hooking over the bibs of our coveralls for berry-picking.

Our clothes were recycled many times. Any usable fabric was turned into a new item of clothing. We salvaged pockets, collars, snaps, hooks, buttons, lace trim, cuffs and zippers for other uses. Scraps were used for quilts, pot holders, place

Boxes and crates had endless uses. We used cardboard to line our shoes, insulate the walls of our house and keep the chicken house warm. Apple and fruit crates made fine cupboards and shelving, tables, toys, desks, chairs and stools.

We needed to be self-sufficient in those days. We didn't have the cash to buy much, but we knew how to make what we needed. ⊠

---

*"Wood scraps were never burned—they had too many other uses..."*

---

mats and floor mats. Smaller scraps became stuffing for pillows, cushions and toys.

Nothing became a rag until it was really a *rag*. Then we fit them onto a metal mop head for cleaning the floor, or used them to dust furniture.

Wood scraps were never burned—they had too many other uses, including toys, lamp bases, ladles, spoons and rug hooks. Our best hooks were carved from wood scraps and polished like glass.

Sawdust left over from woodworking projects was sprinkled on flower beds, used in a cleaning compound for hardwood floors or stuffed into soft toys.

We turned rubber tires into flower beds, rope swings and forts. Dad piled them on the disk for extra weight when till-

**THREE-WHEELED WONDER.** Lea Pinto of Ukiah, California was raised on a farm by her grandmother and uncle during the Depression. Presents were hard to come by in those years, Lea recalls, so she was particularly delighted when her uncle made her this nifty tricycle.

# 'Pounding the Preacher' Paid for His Services

*By Lois Mize, Akron, Ohio*

I GREW UP in a farming community in St. Clair County, Alabama. Almost everyone was poor during the 1930s. We struggled along and managed to get by, except for one problem. No one had the money to pay the preacher at our Methodist church.

Members of the congregation got together and decided, after lengthy discussion, that the only solution was to "pound him". This practice originated with early settlers, who helped needy neighbors by giving them a pound of whatever they could spare, such as seeds or sugar.

The preacher's pounding was set for harvesttime in early fall. On the chosen evening, everyone drove horse- or mule-

> *"The only solution was to 'pound him'..."*

drawn wagons to the preacher's house. My father took a bushel of sweet potatoes.

Everyone was very generous with non-perishable foods like cornmeal and cane syrup. Some gave winter apples, potatoes, pumpkins and squash. Others gave home-canned vegetables and fruits. There was a great variety of dried fruits and beans.

The pastor and his family received us graciously. The evening was like a party. The children played in the yard, and the young people were pleased at the opportunity to visit. The older people sat on the porch, discussing the harvest and community problems. It was a nice respite from our everyday chores on the farm.

Before we left for home, the pastor gave a prayer of thanks for the food and the people who had given it.

Looking back, I think those were among the best of times. We were all bound together by our needs. ⊠

---

## "Radio Minister" Filled Church's Temporary Vacancy

THE MINISTER of our small Baptist church near Pittsburgh, Pennsylvania was long overdue for a vacation, but we couldn't afford to pay a substitute. We came up with a solution that worked well for everyone.

The First Baptist Church of Pittsburgh had an outstanding minister, Bernard Clausen, whose 11 a.m. service was broadcast on KDKA radio each Sunday. With his office's cooperation, we learned what scripture he'd use the next Sunday and the exact time his sermon would air.

We set up a good radio on the platform next to the pulpit and proceeded with our service as usual—hymns, announcements, offering and scripture reading. At the appointed time, we turned on the radio for Dr. Clausen's sermon. Afterward, we had our own benediction, and the service was complete.

It didn't cost our church one red cent for this "visiting minister", and our regular minister had his well-deserved vacation.

—*Dwight Waltz*
*Williamsport, Pennsylvania*

# CHAPTER FIVE

# You Could Depend On Family

***SHARE AND SHARE ALIKE.*** With so many of the nation's institutions collapsing under the economic strain, folks turned to those nearest and dearest to them to find the strength to go on. Together, they survived the worst. (Photo: J.C. Allen and Son)

# From the desk of Clancy Strock

Dear Katie,

Sometimes I'm not sure whether to envy you or feel sorry for you. I envy you because you've never had to go without life's necessities.

When you've needed new clothes, Mom and Dad have been able to get them for you. You haven't had to get a job to help buy the family groceries. And, goodness knows, there are lots and lots of presents with your name on them every Christmas.

Can you imagine coming downstairs on Christmas morning and finding nothing but last year's doll, in new clothes your mother made? Or just a new hair ribbon and a book of Bible stories?

People with exactly those memories tell their stories in this next chapter. What I think will surprise you is why they think of them as *good* memories.

And I'm glad you didn't have to work under the hot summer sun to pick beans for *a penny a pound*! I can't imagine harder work for a kid, but a person who did it is proud of the memory and tells why in this chapter.

As the saying goes, you had to be there to understand.

There were no welfare programs. When you needed help, you turned to relatives, friends or the church. My grandparents' home at times housed a married son and his wife and two kids, a married daughter and her husband and two children plus an unmarried daughter. Imagine--11 people in a four-bedroom house!

Years later, I asked Gramma how she had managed. After all, she was well into her 60s at that time. She sighed and said, "It certainly taught me patience." Indeed. That's what families did in the Depression. They helped each other.

Our farm was a popular place for my mother's family to convene on Sundays. After all, we had plenty of sweet corn, chickens, eggs and garden veggies to feed the crowd. And, regardless of the season, we always churned up a big batch of homemade ice cream with rich milk from our own cows.

Dad sometimes grumbled about the "7-day locusts," mostly because of the way they depleted our flock of egg-producing hens. But memories of those gatherings that brought together my grandparents, aunts, uncles and cousins are some of the best I have.

Christmas was always at the grandparents' home. The highlight was the gift exchange--25¢ a present during the worst of the Depression. Can you imagine it!

Today Christmas is about the only time most families get together. Katie, you are lucky that the Nelson side of your family is so close-knit and gathers more often than most. You may not suspect it, but you, too, are accumulating some fine memories that you'll treasure many years from now.

*Your Grandpa Clancy*

# 'Rubber House' Stretched to Hold Extended Family

*By Mary Duggan, San Jose, California*

OUR FAMILY lived in my grandparents' "rubber house" during the Depression.

My grandfather called it that because the walls of his two-bedroom bungalow in Denver, Colorado seemed to stretch beyond their capacity, embracing anyone who needed a place to stay.

Daddy, my little sister and I moved in after my mother died in November of 1932. A year later, Grandma told us, "Uncle Jack and his family will be living with us for a while." No explanation was offered, and none was necessary.

Five adults and the baby lived upstairs, and the five older children settled in the half-finished basement. There were two double beds for the four girls, and my 13-year-old cousin, Allan, slept on a cot under the clothes chute.

### An Entertaining Cousin

An old bedspread hung from a clothesline between one of the beds and Allan's cot, which inspired us to dress in silly outfits and put on shows. Allan entertained us nonstop. In summer, we were drawn to the cool of the basement to play school, church, Old Maid and Authors.

That winter, Uncle Jack made us a dollhouse. We helped a little by eating penny suckers so he could use the wooden sticks to make a staircase.

When he was finished with it, the house was a real showpiece, complete with electric Christmas lights. The schoolteacher across the street was so impressed that she gave me

her doll furniture to put in the house and play with.

During the year and a half we all shared that house, I discovered the deep love shared by the remarkable adults who lived upstairs. In today's world, they'd be considered saints.

We six children are still alive and well, and we remember those days fondly. Grandpa's rubber house left us with more memories than a mansion could ever hold. ⊠

**EXPANSION PLANS.** Mary Duggan (top left) recalls that there was always room for more at her Grandpa Lavelle's little "cabin" in Denver, Colorado (above). That's Grandpa at top right. Although space was limited, Mary and her relatives have few regrets.

◆ ◆ ◆ ◆ ◆ ◆ ◆ ◆ ◆ ◆ ◆ ◆ ◆

## Families Doubled Up When Times Got Tough

MY DAD WAS an office worker at a barrel factory in New Hampshire. When his job was eliminated, he took any work he could find to put food on the table. One job I remember was shoveling gravel to cover tar on the roads.

When my mother's family in Maine lost their jobs, they moved in with us. Somehow Dad managed to provide for all of us until our relatives found small jobs.

After a time, we moved in with Dad's parents on their farm. It was a big adjustment—no electricity, no running water, no telephone. But we were never hungry, and our homemade clothes kept us warm.

My sister and I worked in the kitchen and helped care for the animals. Our school day ended at 4 p.m., and we always had chores waiting for us when we got home.

As I look back on those rich years, I realize the role they played in my development. Though I went on to become a registered nurse and never returned to farm life, the knowledge I gained was invaluable.

—*Elizabeth Coffed, Greensboro, Georgia*

WE HAD 11 PEOPLE living in our house in 1935. Four children were still living at home. My oldest sister moved home with her baby in May. Then my oldest brother moved back in with his wife, who had a baby in September.

Although the house was crowded, we all pitched in with cooking, cleaning and laundry, and everyone got along. We thought those two babies were the greatest thing that ever happened.

My dad was one of the fortunate men who kept his job on the railroad, and Mom had three meals on the table every day. Dad helped ease our washboard duties by buying a Maytag electric washer for all those diapers.

*—Verda Findley*
*Oklahoma City, Oklahoma*

**DOUBLE DUTY.** Washers like the Maytag at left got a real workout—especially with diapers—when grown children with babies moved back home to ride out the Depression, as in Verda Findley's family.

# Aunt Ethel Took in Laundry to Meet Family Expenses

*By Cliff Towner, Fountain, Florida*

"LAUNDRY, machine-washed, 10¢ a basket. Ironing, 5¢ extra."

That was the hand-printed card Aunt Ethel pinned to the community bulletin board at the local A&P. Many such cards offered goods and services for cash or barter during summer of 1935.

Aunt Ethel and her daughter, Ruthie, had moved in with my parents, older brother and me because they were family and they had nowhere else to go.

There wasn't any Aid to Families with Dependent Children, Social Security or Supplemental Security Income to assist people through hard times. There was only family, and the generosity of equally hard-pressed neighbors.

Aunt Ethel would get up before dawn and go to the cellar to start the ancient wringer washer and set up three large rinse tubs, which had to be filled by hand. Each load was hand-fed through the wringer, then through the series of rinse tubs.

After the final rinse, the clothes were fed through the wringer into a large wicker basket. Then Aunt Ethel struggled up the steep cellar steps to the clothesline outside.

Meanwhile, Mom was hard at work

in her beauty shop upstairs, giving a finger wave, shampoo and wave or henna rinse for 50¢ each, or a marcel for 75¢.

Occasionally, Mom gave a permanent wave, using an octopus-like machine with dangling wires and clips. Permanents were few and far between, because they took most of the day and cost a whopping $5.

My dad and older brother were usually outside washing and Simonizing a car, perhaps a big sedan from the affluent part of town. It might take 3 or 4 hours, but their efforts would bring in another $2 for food.

When the clothes were dry, cousin Ruthie and I put the baskets in my Rocket Express wagon and delivered the orders, hurrying to get back in time to gather with the family to listen to our favorite radio programs.

Hard times? On the contrary. To a 6-year-old in 1935, they were the best of times.

# Faith and Friends Helped Widow Survive Tough Years

*By Dolores Eggener, Marinette, Wisconsin*

FOR OUR FAMILY, the Depression began early. My parents married in 1922 and were very happy, especially after my brother, Jack, was born. They loved children.

But unemployment soon struck our area, and one man after another found himself out of work. Just as my parents began looking forward to my arrival, my father lost his job.

Months went by, and the future looked bleak. Insurance policies were canceled, and an already frugal existence had to be trimmed even more.

Just when all seemed hopeless, my father was called back to work. But after 1 week on the job, he caught a cold, which turned into pneumonia. He died at age 25. I was born 3 months later.

From my birth in 1926 until the mid-'30s, life was very difficult. All our friends and relatives were hurting, too, but we leaned on one another and took turns helping when we could. Happiness prevailed despite our troubles.

### Everyone Helped Out

Jack and I became "latchkey kids" at a very young age. Friends, neighbors and the nuns at our parochial school kept an eye on us until Mom came home from work. Widows didn't get much assistance back then, and Mom was too proud not to work.

There are so many dear people to whom we owe our thanks. One particular day stands out in my mind. Mom had been laid off from her factory job, and we had no food. Mom often fried a simple bread dough and sprinkled it with a little sugar

HAD TO GO IT ALONE. When Dolores Eggener's father died 3 months before her birth, her mother had to raise and support two children all by herself. That's little Dolores above with her brother, Jack, and her mother. The photo below was taken at a circus in 1936 and, as you can see, despite all the hardships they endured, there were plenty of smiles, too.

*"Now there was absolutely nothing on the pantry shelves..."*

for our meal, but now there was absolutely nothing on the pantry shelves. I can still see Mom pacing the floor and praying.

As Mom and I stood looking out the kitchen window, we saw the daughters of a widowed friend walking toward our house. They came to the door with a covered dish. "My mother sent this because she made too much," one of the girls said. Mom blessed and thanked them profusely.

Later that day, our aunt's mother-in-law came by and gave Mom a dollar. That was a fortune, considering what a dollar would buy. Milk was 8¢ a quart, eggs 13¢ to 15¢ a dozen, small yeast cakes 3¢ and a meaty soup bone 10¢ or less.

Through the kindness of others, we overcame that particular hurdle, and many more. In time, life got easier, but those with whom we shared the hard times are embedded in our hearts forever. ⊠

# Uncle Steve's Kindness Enriched Many Childhoods

*By Jean Marion, Goodland, Indiana*

THE GOOD PART of growing up during the Depression in Goodland, Indiana was that nearly everybody was poor, so we didn't notice.

Our recreation was backyard games, the standard snack was popcorn and Kool-Aid and a dime movie was a once-a-year treat. But the kids in my neighborhood had more fun than most, thanks to my Uncle Steve.

He was a retired widower with the time and patience to fix a broken toy or invent a new one, catch a snake for us to pet, and listen to our problems and dreams.

Uncle Steve drove us to school when the weather was bad and gave us first aid when someone got hurt. No one went to the doctor unless it was very serious. He was our main "fixer-upper".

Uncle Steve bought a bike, taught all of us to ride it, then settled endless arguments about whose turn it was. He bought lots of Christmas candy and sorted it in bags so each child received the same amount.

On the Fourth of July, he let us choose fireworks but kept us away and safe while he set them off. That holiday was a real occasion, complete with watermelon.

## Uncle's Shopping Service

At Christmas and Easter, my girlfriends and I enjoyed a little more attention than the boys, because Uncle Steve would take us shopping.

In Goodland, shopping was limited to one store or the Sears catalog, but there were lots of stores in Lafayette. We seldom had money to buy anything, but it was such a pleasure to see all the lovely things, and the decorations alone were worth the trip.

In the summer, Uncle Steve would take us swimming—first to small pools in neighboring towns and later to Lake Michigan. The latter was an all-day trip...2 to 3 hours with a car full of giggling girls and all their junk, picnic lunches, and sand and sunburns on the way home. He tried to prevent our burns by stopping at JCPenney and buying robes for us to wear.

They were just small things—a used bike, a bag of candy, a ride to school on a rainy day (no school buses for us), watermelon and fireworks. It's hard to convince younger people these days that anything so simple could be special, but to us, those pleasures meant everything.

Growing up in an era when fun and funds were limited wasn't so bad after all, at least for us kids from the west end of Goodland, Indiana. ⊠

**COURTESY OF UNCLE STEVE.** Jean Marion (third from right) enjoyed a day at the beach with her girlfriends. Chances are, Jean's Uncle Steve provided the transportation for their 2- to 3-hour trip to Dunes Park on Lake Michigan.

## Grandma's Stylish Outfit Just the Thing For a Poor Farm Girl

MY PARENTS WERE having a rough time on our farm outside Giltner, Nebraska in 1934. We were lucky to have enough food for me and my four younger brothers, but there was no money for anything else, like a new dress for my senior picture.

So Grandma, who was my size and always very stylish, loaned me one of her dresses and a pair of pumps. The dress was black georgette with velvet cape sleeves, and Grandma added a white pique collar. As you can probably tell from this photo (at left), I felt elegant in that outfit!

This wasn't the first time Grandma had come to my rescue. Four years earlier, she'd bought a pony and paid to board it at a barn so I could ride the 5 miles to Giltner and finish school.

It didn't take much to make us happy in those days, and we appreciated everything we had. I never felt sorry for myself or wished for more. I was just thankful for my loving grandma.
—*Eileen Chaney, Aurora, Nebraska*

# A Story from Papa Was The Greatest Gift of All

*By Louis Tucciarone, Oneonta, New York*

GROWING UP in Brooklyn, New York during the Depression took a lot of courage and determination. Our family of 11 was on home relief. Breadlines were part of every neighborhood. Hustlers sold make-believe jobs, sending desperate men to addresses that didn't exist.

Mama started each day by making the beds and washing clothes on a scrub board in a large tub. Her hands were constantly chapped, the bones of her knuckles almost piercing her tender skin. She'd rub them with olive oil, praying "Jesu Christi", then make the sign of the cross and kiss her fingers to complete her prayer.

No matter how bad things were, we knew we'd find Mama at home with something special for us. After school, if we were quiet, she'd fry us a piece of bread dough and sprinkle it with powdered sugar. This was the best of all treats. Fried dough and a smile from Mama always made us feel special.

## The Saga of Uncle Pasqualle

In the evenings, before our bedtime, we'd gather around Papa for a story about the Old Country. The one we all loved best was about his Uncle Pasqualle, who they thought was dying of pneumonia.

Papa began every story with, "You no gonna believe what I'm a-gonna tell you." We'd laugh and say, "Yes, we will, Papa."

Mama would be sitting across the room in her rocker, crocheting doilies under a dangling light bulb and winking at Papa with approval.

"One day my Uncle Pasqualle, he's a-callin' me," Papa would begin. "He say to me, 'Harry, call-a the doctor. I'm-a no feelin' so good.' I call-a the doctor, and he say to my uncle, he say, 'Pasqualle, you gotta pneumonia, and you gonna die.'

"Uncle Pasqualle, he say to him, 'Doctor, if I'm a-gonna die, then I'm a-wanna eat what I wanna eat.' Now Uncle Pasqualle, he say to me, 'Harry, get me a quart of wine and a quart of hot cherry peppers.'

"The doctor, he say to him, 'What's a-matter, you crazy? You eat that and you gonna die for sure.' Uncle Pasqualle, he say to him, 'I'm a-gonna die anyway, so what's-a the difference?'

### Would He Recover?

"Well, you know what happens? You no gonna believe what I'm a-gonna tell you. Uncle Pasqualle, when he finish the hot peppers and all the wine, he fall asleep. The wine and the hot peppers burn the pneumonia out of him. And you know what, Uncle Pasqualle, he lived another 50 years. The stupid doctor, he died 2 months later."

Every time Papa told this story, it would go from a quart of wine to a gallon of wine and a gallon of cherry peppers. And of course he'd add another 10 years to Uncle Pasqualle's life.

Then Papa would reach for his pipe, which my brother Donald and I scurried to light. He'd take a couple of puffs, look at his watch and say, "Twenty-three skidoo".

We'd kneel next to Papa, make the sign of the cross, say our prayers and give Papa a kiss. Then we'd dash to Mama and kiss her. There was no fuss, no stamping of feet. It was a happy time—a time when a story from Papa was always the greatest gift of all. ☒

## Crafty Idea Kept Family Warm for the Holidays

ONE DECEMBER, we realized we'd need coal for our furnace before Christmas. Money was so scarce that we couldn't afford it, even though coal was only $12.50 a ton.

One day I collected 12 old-fashioned milk bottles with the "cream tops" and crafted snowmen out of them. My two children went door-to-door in the neighborhood and sold them for $1 each, and we had a warm and happy holiday.

—M.G. Leborgne, Laguna Hills, California

**EMPTIES WARMED THEIR WINTER.** Unable to afford the money for coal to keep the family warm, M.G. Leborgne found a way to make milk bottles like these supply all the heat they needed (see story above).

## Christmas Disappointment Turned to Deep Appreciation

CHRISTMAS was the highlight of the year for us, in spite of the Depression. Every December, Dad went to the pasture to cut down a native cedar, which we adorned with our time-worn decorations.

On Christmas Eve, anticipation rose to a fever pitch. Our eyes refused to stay closed, even after the kerosene lamp was blown out. Every sound was *surely* Santa landing on the rooftop with everything we'd dreamed of all year. The faith of a child never waxes stronger than on Christmas Eve.

The Christmas that I was 7 will always remain vivid in my memory. The year was 1935, and the morning dawned bright and brimming with expectation. My younger brother and I sped to the tree, blissfully unaware of the cold plank floor beneath our bare feet.

Under a slightly lopsided tree, we found four small gifts, two for each of us. I enthused over my presents and urged my 4-year-old brother to do the same.

I pray my parents never knew that I later slipped away to cry in disappointment. All I'd received was a yard of blue hair ribbon and a colorful Bible story booklet about Esther.

As I've grown older, I've learned to appreciate every gift, no matter its size. That bright blue ribbon binds the festivities with the beauty of a Christmas long past. The book on Esther remains one of my dearest treasures.

The greatest value is not in the gift itself, but in the spirit in which it's given—and received.

—Mildred Wickson, Menard, Texas

## Vanishing Doll Buggy Made Memorable Christmas Day Return

ABOUT 2 WEEKS before Christmas in 1932, I realized my doll buggy was missing. It was an old wicker model with cracked green paint. I looked and looked but couldn't find it.

I asked my mother what had happened to it. She said she didn't know, but she'd heard sleigh bells the night before. Maybe that had been Santa Claus—maybe he'd taken my buggy. We'd just have to wait and see.

Well, 2 weeks was a long time for a 4-year-old to wait, but wait I did. When I went to bed on Christmas Eve, I heard sleigh bells ringing. To this day, I'm sure I heard them.

The next morning, there under the tree was my buggy, with a fresh coat of orchid paint. What a beautiful sight!

When I got older, I found out Dad had painted the buggy out in the barn, but to me, that gift will always be the work of Santa Claus. That Depression-era Christmas remains the most joyous of my life.

—Elaine Eagon, Waukegan, Illinois

**DADDY'S LITTLE GIRLS.** Charles Manzke pulled a wagon with some very precious cargo—his daughters, Elaine and Lila.

# Dolls Thrilled Sisters for Three Christmases

*By Joyce Henceroth, Ravenna, Ohio*

IN OUR CITY, the year 1934 seemed to be the peak of the Depression. Long breadlines were common, and men sold apples on street corners to earn a few pennies.

We were fortunate, because my father worked 2 or 3 days a week at Goodyear in Akron, Ohio. We lived on a farm with our grandparents, so we always had ample food.

That Christmas, my sister and I enjoyed the usual stocking full of oranges, walnuts and candy canes. But we also found some special gifts.

Each of us received a 20-inch rubber baby doll dressed in a diaper and shirt and wrapped in a blanket. We named our babies Nancy and Polly and took very good care of them.

### A Dollnapping?

The following year, several days before Christmas, the dolls mysteriously disappeared. My sister and I searched frantically for Nancy and Polly but couldn't find them.

They reappeared under the tree on Christmas morning, their smudged faces freshly scrubbed and wearing completely new outfits.

My doll wore a lovely green print I recognized from the latest bag of horse feed. She also had a long green cape and matching bonnet, and Mother and Grandma had even fashioned a tiny fur muff. Her shoes were handmade, with cardboard soles and green cloth uppers.

Before Christmas in 1936, the dolls disappeared again, but this time we weren't worried. Instead, we shivered with

---

> *"Real babies couldn't have had more tender care..."*

❖

---

anticipation. But we never imagined anything as grand as what awaited us Christmas morning.

Nancy and Polly were clean and shiny again...but they were each sitting in a new white wicker carriage. They wore long flannel nighties trimmed with lace, just like ours! Handmade patchwork quilts were tucked snugly around their toes.

I remember the thrill as if it were yesterday. Nancy and

**DELIGHT RAN DEEP.** These two little girls couldn't have been any happier with their dolls than Joyce Henceroth and her sister were with theirs. Though the family had very little money, Joyce's parents saw to it that their daughters experienced true joy at Christmastime, while teaching some lasting lessons about sacrifice.

Polly traveled *miles* in those prams. Real babies couldn't have had more tender care.

### Even More to the Story

A few years ago, my father and I were discussing the Depression, laughing about the feed sack shirts and aprons, and how grateful we were to get two coordinating bags for a complete outfit. Dad's wages of 20¢ an hour had to stretch a long way.

When I recalled our Christmas dolls, Dad told me a story I'd never heard before.

"You know," he said, "not even your mother knew I was going to buy those dolls. I'd been thinking it over for several days. I waited until Christmas Eve, when I knew toys would be marked down as low as possible. Then, on the way home from work, I went shopping. Those dolls cost me the last $5 I had in my pocket."

Could any two little girls have been more blessed? ▨

# Teenager Tapped Savings to Make Mortgage Payment

*By Helga Swanson, Stuart, Florida*

PAPA WAS A BUILDER of fine homes, but there was no building going on during the Depression. I suppose we were considered poor during those years, but Mother was an excellent cook and we always had good meals.

I'll never forget the day a lady came to our home on Long Island to collect the mortgage payment. Mother, then carrying her fourth child, met the woman at the door but didn't invite her in. "I'm sorry," Mother said with genuine regret. "I just don't have the money."

But I did.

I'd been saving every penny I'd earned as a baby-sitter. I sat for a neighbor boy for 25¢ an evening, and my piano teacher paid me $1 to care for his daughters while he and his wife attended choir concerts.

This job paid more because I had to spend the night at their home—they didn't return until 2 a.m.—and I washed their boarders' dinner dishes.

My savings went into a little metal bank shaped like a cash register. Sometimes I'd bring it out when we had company, and the guests would give me a dime or more to add to my savings. Mother disapproved, but the guests insisted.

## She Was Proud to Help

It had taken many years of saving, but now those dimes, quarters and dollars were enough to make the quarterly mortgage payment of $179. I was so proud to be able to help!

After paying the mortgage, I had $11 left over to buy a winter coat. I found a beautiful one at a department store—dark red wool with a satin lining and a white fox collar. How I

*IT ALL ADDED UP.* **Like the cash drawer on the old register at left, Helga Swanson's baby-sitting income eventually accumulated to quite a bit of money. That's Helga standing on the right with her family above.**

longed to have it! But the price tag was $16. Finally the saleslady said, "Oh, well, you can have the coat for $11."

A couple of years later, with my life savings gone, there were no other resources to pay the mortgage. The bank foreclosed on the house my father had built 10 years before. We moved to a rented house, but then the economy began to improve.

In the late 1930s, Papa began to work steadily, supervising the construction of 500-seat churches on Army bases. Although he was often far from home, life was a little easier. Finally in the early '40s, he managed to build us a house even finer than the one we'd lost during the Depression. ⊠

---

## Grandmothers Taught Her Lessons in Thrift

MY GRANDMOTHERS were widows and often came to visit or live with us. Both taught me many lessons about making things last until they were worn out.

As the youngest in the family, I had the job of cutting the buttons off clothes before they became cleaning rags. I stored the buttons in an old tin and had the fun of digging through them for just the right buttons when it was time to make something new.

When we ate chicken or turkey, we always kept the bones to make soup or stock—something I still do.

This habit is so ingrained that I even have a hard time leaving good bones on my plate in a restaurant!

Sunday night was a fun time at our house. After a simple meal of cereal, or bread or crackers with milk, we'd snack on popcorn and chocolate fudge and listen to our favorite radio programs.

Mother spent her radio time mending stockings or knitting us another pair of mittens for the cold Maine winters. One year it snowed early and we had no snowsuits to wear to school the next day.

Mother sat up all night, making suits to keep my sister and me warm on the 1-mile walk to school.

—*Virginia Huntington, Thunderbolt, Georgia*

# Children Learned to Share And Pull Their Own Weight

*By Myrtle Brown, Delavan, Wisconsin*

FAMILIES WERE close-knit during the '30s, and children did what they could to help out. We were taught everyone had to pull their own weight.

If we earned 50¢ or $1 doing some job in the neighborhood, we brought it home to put in the sugar bowl for food or coal. Two of my brothers and I went fishing a lot, and we sometimes caught enough to make supper for our family of 10.

To make extra money, Dad would use a maul to bust up scrap iron at the junkyards. Around home, he'd spade gardens for people and dig holes for outhouses. There was always a way to make a dollar.

Dad never had a car, so we walked everywhere, whether it was two blocks or 2 miles. We had one pair of shoes for school and went barefoot all summer. How we hated putting shoes on again in fall!

It seemed everyone had a garden, and we all shared what we grew. If one neighbor had too much of one thing, he traded it for something he didn't have. Mom baked 10 to 12 loaves of bread every few days. All the kids in the neighborhood would smell it and come over. We'd pour Karo syrup over the warm bread until it ran through our fingers. Simple things meant a lot to us.

On Saturdays, there was free entertainment in the town parks. Sometimes there were Chautauquas, with actors performing on homemade stages. Other times we'd sit on blankets on the grass to watch free movies and eat popcorn.

## They Focused on Giving

Every Labor Day weekend, Dad would find someone to drive us to our grandparents' farm, about 30 miles away. Sometimes we rode in the back of a farm truck. Those 3 days were great fun for us kids. Grandma would pile the threshing table with chicken, mashed potatoes and home-grown watermelon and muskmelon. It was all so good.

Our uncle usually brought us home. He carried his guitar everywhere he went, and we enjoyed hearing him play and sing. There was always something we could do to forget our miseries.

At Christmas, the older children performed in a program at church. Each child got a little box of hard candies plus a paper sack containing an apple, an orange and some peanuts. We'd run all the way home to share our treats with the smaller ones.

If we were lucky, Mom might be able to save enough to buy each child a 10¢ Christmas gift. Those were happy times, and we never thought too much about receiving. We were more focused on sharing and giving and what we could do for others. ☒

**SUPPER ON THE LINE?** During the Depression, a good fisherman could really make a difference at the family dinner table. Myrtle Brown and her brothers did their part.

**WOULD GET WORSE FIRST.** In 1925, Julia Snyder (left) posed with her sister and brother. A few years later, their parents had to temporarily place them in an orphanage.

## Desperate Parents Had to Take Desperate Measures

I'LL NEVER FORGET that heartbreaking time. My carpenter father couldn't find any work in our Pennsylvania coal-mining town, and Mom had never worked outside the home. Our usual supper was three cans of beans mixed with three cans of water to make a big pot of soup.

One day when I was 11, I realized something was very wrong. The landlady was at our house, and my mother was crying. The situation had become quite desperate.

Soon after that, my brother, sister and I were placed in an orphanage. I felt my world had ended. Mom sold our belongings and went to New York City to look for work. The only job she could find was working as a maid.

Eventually, Mom found Dad a job as superintendent of an apartment building. Then came the glorious day when were all together again as a family.

As I got older, I realized how hard it must have been for our parents to put us in an orphanage and how brave my mother was to go to a strange city and start over. —*Julia Snyder* *Philadelphia, Pennsylvania*

# Farm Families Made the Most of Difficult Years

*By Charlotte Andersen, Sioux City, Iowa*

MY FATHER was considered well-to-do before the Depression. He owned three farms in central Iowa, including the beautiful home place of 190 acres. It was one of the best farms around, and Papa always got excellent yields.

Then the Depression came and settled over the land like a heavy blanket. Produce prices tumbled, the bottom dropped out of land values and we were in trouble. We sold corn for 7¢ a bushel and hogs at 3¢ a pound.

Violence erupted in many rural areas. Farmers gathered on courthouse lawns to disrupt sheriff's sales of neighbors' farms. Milk was dumped into ditches and baby pigs were killed. We even burned corn for fuel. Mama objected, saying it was a sin to burn food. But it was awfully hard to find money for coal.

Many nights Papa couldn't sleep for the worry of losing his farms. He'd get up, pull on his overalls, light the lamp and read. Usually it was the Bible.

Mama tried to comfort him. "We have our health, the children are well, we have enough to eat and a roof over our heads," she'd say. "Let us count our blessings."

But Papa couldn't help it. He was responsible for his family.

The winter of 1935-36 was one of the worst on record, with numbing cold and mountains of snow. A Rock Island passenger train got stuck in a huge snowbank in our little town.

## Situation Didn't Improve

A terrible summer followed, with extreme heat, drought and dust storms. High winds carried clouds of dirt that drifted in the ditches. We always had enough rain, so Papa never had a crop failure, but he certainly came close to one in 1936.

Music added pleasure to our lives. Mama played the piano, and we liked to gather around it to sing favorite hymns. A relative who played the fiddle joined in for oldies like *The Irish Washerwoman*, *Red Wing* and *When Irish Eyes Are Smiling*.

In the dead of winter, we could dip into our store of good things in the cellar. Canned meat, smoked hams and bacon, canned tomatoes and corn, beet and cucumber pickles, and a variety of jams, jellies and preserves were ours for the taking.

Potatoes, carrots and parsnips waited in their bins, and barrels of apples stood nearby. Milk, cream and butter cooled on the concrete floor. We even had our own honey.

## Comfy and Cozy Indoors

When the cruel winter winds whistled and shrieked around our farmhouse, we were warm and snug inside. The heater in the front room and the cookstove in the kitchen radiated warmth and security.

Neighbors and friends came by often. The coffeepot bubbled on the kitchen range, and everyone shared a bountiful meal of sandwiches, cookies or doughnuts, cakes and pies. The kids played, the older folks visited, and babies were put on the bed to sleep until it was time for everyone to bundle up and head for home.

Times were hard and money was scarce, but we had the bounty of farm and garden. Crime in our county was almost unheard-of, and our citizens loved God and country.

We made our own fun, and the farm, church and school kept us busy and happy. We loved one another and didn't miss what we'd never had. ⊠

**THE LAND PROVIDED.** While farmers were just as poor as everyone else when it came to money, they usually could grow enough to eat. Most farm families survived by working hard.

# Parents' Sacrifices Shielded Children from Depression's Sting

*By Nora Yarborough, Stella, North Carolina*

BOTH MY PARENTS worked in a North Carolina cotton mill until Daddy broke his back at work and lost his job. Despite the difficult times, our parents made those years pleasant. They were protective of their four children, and I know now they sacrificed a great deal for us.

One of my sweetest memories is of Daddy gathering us

**SMART CAT. Nora Yarborough named "Solomon" after a one-eyed cat in a book.**

together to read us the library books we brought home. He was a great storyteller and really brought the classics alive. One book was about a cat named Solomon. When we later took in a one-eyed stray cat, we named it after the cat in the book.

Christmases were always special. Each year, our parents said they couldn't afford what I wanted, but Santa Claus would manage to bring it. Instead of hanging stockings, each of us set out a plate, which our parents filled with nuts, fruit and candy. One year Daddy took us to the movies to see *Rebecca of Sunnybrook Farm*—a real treat.

Each child was given 50¢ to buy presents for the other family members. I could buy five presents and still have a nickel left over for candy. One year we knew Mama really wanted a wire dish drainer, so my two brothers and I pooled our money and bought one for a quarter. Our young hearts were thrilled when we saw how pleased Mama was. That made our Christmas. Many years later, after my own children were grown, I asked Mama if she was really as proud of that drainer as we thought. Tears came to her eyes, and she said

## Expectant Daughter Depended On Mom as Her Midwife

ONE COLD January dawn in 1933, my sister Lillian came to our house with her son, Jimmy. Mother told Jimmy and me that we'd have to go to school early because Lillian was sick. We were too naive to realize it, but Lillian was about to have a baby.

Lillian and her husband didn't have the money for a hospital, so the baby was born at our house, with Mother as midwife. Lillian stayed with us until she was able to return to her own home down the street. Mother cooked for Jimmy and his father to help out.

Today, some families expect the government to take care of them. Our family took pride in doing for ourselves.
—*Margie Porteus*
*Paonia, Colorado*

**DEPRESSION REMEDY. Attendance at movies like *Rebecca of Sunnybrook Farm* soared during the '30s. Nora's family was among those who enjoyed escaping reality for a couple of hours.**

she certainly was. That gave me an extra blessing.

When the circus came to town, we couldn't afford to go, but Daddy would take us to watch them set up and see the animals. The circus parade was exciting, too.

We didn't own a sled, but we had a good substitute—the long slick bench from our dinner table. When it snowed, we

*"I didn't know we were poor until fourth grade..."*

took it to the hill behind the house, turned it upside down and piled on. It was perfect.

I didn't even know we were poor until fourth grade, when the teacher asked the children from wealthy families to donate clothes for the poor ones. I'd always been a proud little girl, and when the teacher gave me one of those hand-me-down dresses, I was highly insulted.

Today, all these memories are precious to me. After I had children of my own, I could appreciate all the sacrifices my parents had made and what a loving family we had.

Everyone is in Heaven now except for one brother and me, but we look forward to having a reunion one of these days. In the meantime, they still live in my heart and seem so close when I reminisce.

# Thoughtful Neighbors Extended a Helping Hand to Family in Dire Straits

*By Marie Cini, Howell, Michigan*

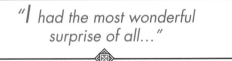

**GRATEFUL GIRL. Marie Cini, shown here in her Communion dress in 1931, had many wonderful friends and relatives who did their best to see that her family's desperate situation didn't get worse.**

MY FATHER WAS an electrician in Philadelphia, but his business went bankrupt in 1930. He started doing electrical work just for leftover food.

He trudged after a horse and wagon in the snow, with no galoshes, to deliver circulars 1 or 2 days a week. He left in the morning while it was still dark and returned after sunset. It was hard work for a dollar a day, but that was enough to buy some food.

There was no money to buy coal, which we needed for both cooking and heat. My father, brother Bud and I began taking a coaster wagon loaded with jute bags to pick up coal off of the railroad tracks.

Sometimes the railroad detectives chased us off, saying the coal was railroad property—although I never saw the companies make any attempt to collect it.

There were many people whose kindness helped us through those difficult times. When I couldn't go to school because the cardboard liners kept slipping through the large holes in my shoes, a neighbor gave me a pair his child had outgrown.

Sister Laurentina, who ran a day nursery around the corner from our house, made huge pots of soup for the poor and distributed blankets and clothes. You could only get the soup 1 day a week, but it was enough to feed a family, and we deeply appreciated it.

My sister Helen was born in January 1931 and died of malnutrition the following November. Our grief made the approaching Christmas season seem even bleaker. We had nothing...not even food.

We didn't expect our neighbors to help. Many of them were only working a couple of days a week themselves. But they made sure we had enough to eat.

An uncle who worked for Sunshine Biscuit Co. brought us cardboard trucks filled with cookies. When the cookies were gone, the trucks became our toys. Such memories still warm our hearts. There were so many people who helped out.

My father had applied for work everywhere, but after Helen's death, he was desperate. He applied for home relief,

---

### "I had the most wonderful surprise of all..."

---

which provided $1 a week for each family member, plus coupons for lard, flour and canned mutton. Aid recipients weren't allowed to earn any money, but Dad did electrical work for our landladies in lieu of paying rent.

After 6 months on home relief, Dad was offered a job at the quartermaster depot in South Philadelphia for $24 a week. We thought we were in heaven. But the birth of another child had left my mother very weak. She developed pneumonia and had to be hospitalized.

Sister Laurentina again came to our rescue. My father dropped off the younger children at the day nursery before work, and the older ones went there after school. Dad tried to find extra jobs to pay the hospital bills, but such work was scarce, and his pay from the depot was stretched thin.

### They Came Through Again

We knew there'd be no money for toys that Christmas, but the neighbors made our holiday special. One bought Bud a pedal car and brother Joe a pedal airplane, and another bought gifts for my other two brothers.

I got the most wonderful surprise of all—a brand-new doll in a trunk, given by a widowed neighbor. Even after all these years, I still recall these kindnesses with deep appreciation.

Though we had little money, our family enjoyed many happy times. We often gathered with the families of my dad's eight siblings for picnics, fishing or crabbing. Those who had cars took those who didn't. Everyone brought something to eat, and we all shared expenses. These wonderful outings left us with many pleasant memories.

After about 2 years at the quartermaster depot, Dad started working at the naval shipyard for $32 a week. After a year, he was able to buy his first car, a 1929 Pierce Arrow.

Yes, the Depression was a bad time. But people survived, and most remember the better things that happened. Adversity seems to pull people together, making us more thoughtful, kind and considerate.

It's a lesson for all of us to remember.

**HER STRENGTH ENDURED.** Vada York (far left and above) set a good example for her children, including daughter Zada and the youngsters shown in these photos.

# Mother's Determination Helped Her Clan Survive

By Zada Hutsell, Carlsbad, New Mexico

THE NINTH CHILD in our family was born October 28, 1929, a day before the stock market crashed. We'd always been poor and didn't have anything to lose, but it was a bad time.

We would've suffered more if it had not been for Mother's good sense and determination. If she worried about anything, and I'm sure she did, she never showed it.

We lived in Rule, Texas and did day labor on area farms, hoeing weeds and chopping or picking cotton.

We had a garden, and Mother's chickens supplied us with eggs, fryers and an occasional fat hen cooked with dumplings. We had a cow that gave plenty of milk, but with no refrigeration, the milk was always sour. We didn't mind. Sour milk with soda made good bread.

### "Milk Machine" Was Gone

The time came when we didn't have a cow, and we had to drink water at mealtime. We seldom had meat, but sometimes the boys went rabbit hunting and got lucky. We always had salt meat for cooking vegetables. Sometimes Mother sliced the meat, boiled it to remove the salt and then fried it. We liked it that way.

Winters were hard to endure, and it's surprising to me we weren't sick more often. Mother's medicine cabinet contained only three things—Vicks VapoRub, Black Draught and castor oil. I think we were *afraid* to get sick!

In time we moved to Jud, where two of my married sisters had settled. We were still working for farmers but no longer had a garden, cow or chickens. Then we ran out of farms to hire us.

Dad hit the road looking for work and found a little in Carlsbad, New Mexico. He never lived with us again. Our older brother left often, finding work for a while, then coming home.

I married in 1933, but my husband passed away the following year and I ended up back home with Mother, expecting a baby. When things got really

---

*"I think we were afraid to get sick..."*

◆

---

bad, we moved to a mesquite pasture. Nothing would grow but mesquite, but the house was better than some we'd lived in.

Finally things began to look up. My baby girl was born. Our older brother came home to stay and was doing farm work. Another brother joined the CCC in Las Cruces, New Mexico.

In 1936, our mother passed away. It was the saddest day of our lives. After the funeral, our three married sisters divided the rest of the family up and took

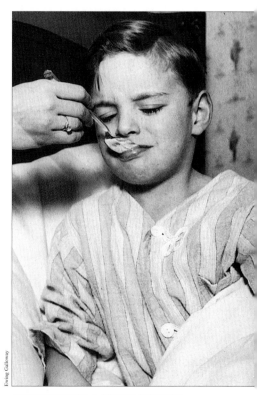

**WORSE THAN A BITTER PILL!** This young man doesn't seem to be enjoying his dose of castor oil. Zada Hutsell felt the same way.

us to live with them. In time, we all moved to Carlsbad, and all our brothers and brothers-in-law found work in the potash mines. May God help us to never have another Depression. ⊠

# 'Back to the Farm' Existence Had Advantages

*By Hazel Miller, Terre Haute, Indiana*

MY FAMILY was fortunate during the Depression—we had my great-grandfather's northern-Indiana farmhouse to live in. It was old and had no modern conveniences, but we were comfortable.

Water came from an outside pump, which had to be primed on cold days. We had kerosene lamps to read by and one old battery-operated radio.

A big coal- and wood-burning stove stood in the living room, with a hole cut in the ceiling so warm air could rise to the room above, where we slept. Mom and Dad sawed wood with an old

---

*"The Depression was hard, but kind to our family..."*

◆

---

crosscut saw, and we picked up coal from the railroad tracks after the coal cars rattled by.

My great-grandfather had planted a large orchard, so we had apples, peaches, pears, mulberries, plums and grapes to barter for other supplies. Mom canned fruit and dried apples on gauze in the sun. Wild blackberries, blueberries, strawberries and raspberries were picked for jelly and jam. Mom also made jelly from chokecherry and grape juice.

A large garden provided tomatoes, green beans and corn, which Mom and Dad canned over an open fire outside. When the coals died down, potatoes or unhusked ears of corn were placed in the coals to bake. Even hot coals weren't wasted in those days.

## Chickens Too Valuable to Eat

Most of our meat came from the rabbits Dad and my brother hunted. Mom would kill a chicken once in a while, but not often. We needed them for eggs.

Though the Depression years were hard, they were kind to my family. We didn't have a lot of material things, but we did get new clothes for school and a new coat every other year. Coats were bought a size too big so we could get 2 years' wear out of them before handing them down.

We were lucky. Our family had shelter, plenty of food and an ample supply of wood. We had a Huckleberry Finn life, full of hunting and fishing and wholesome adventures. I thank God for what He bestowed on us during those years. ⊠

**NATURE GIRL. When Hazel Miller (left) and her family moved into her great-grandfather's old farmhouse during the Depression, she still enjoyed being able to fish, pick berries and play outdoors.**

# Grandma's Pewter Pitcher Had a Secret Function

*By Louise Kohr, Olympia, Washington*

THE DEPRESSION was a time for sharing and understanding, for everyone to make the most of what he had. Everyone had a garden. We had a cow and shared milk with our neighbor. They had an orchard, so we had applesauce.

And we had God. If He allowed things to be hard for us, it was for our own good. It was a time to appreciate small blessings.

And there was Grandma's pewter pitcher. It had come with her from Sweden, on a boat full of half-starved immigrants. It occupied a special place on the top shelf of her cupboard. Now and then we'd hear the tinkle of a coin dropped into it, a reassuring sound that made us feel secure.

There were times when we could've used some help from Grandma's pitcher, but she never took any money out of it. She just spoke confidently of better times to come.

There were times when we had no bread to go with our milk, but the pitcher was never raided. It was always there on the shelf, a backup resource for whatever might lie ahead.

Slowly the economy righted itself. We grew up, and Grandma grew old. And then one day she was gone. Our assurance about her future was as solid as the rolling hills that surrounded her resting place.

The day finally came when we took Grandma's pitcher down from the shelf. We had no big expectations about what it would hold, but we certainly weren't prepared to find it all but empty.

Yes, we'd heard tinkling as coins were being dropped into the pitcher. But it had been the same half dozen small coins, dropped again and again.

Grandma left us nothing but a pewter pitcher full of hope. But it had been enough. ⊠

# CHAPTER SIX

# We Called the Orphanage 'Home'

***SISTERS' SAFETY NET.*** With many families unable to feed or clothe their children, nuns were often called on to help raise kids. As you'll see, many orphanages did a great job. (Photo: SuperStock)

# From the desk of Clancy Strock

Dear Katie,

When you hear the word "orphanage", you probably think of a place
for kids who have no mother or father. Orphans. But during the Depression, some parents were too poor to feed or clothe their own
children.

It came down to a choice between starving or finding a place
that would care for the kids. For many, that meant an orphanage.

Katie, just imagine how desperate your mother and father would
have to be before they put you and Bryan and Jenna into an orphanage. Just think how it would break their hearts--and what a frightening thing it would be for the three of you.

As you read these stories, try to put yourself in the shoes of
the people telling about their experiences. It's the 1930s. Things
at home are bad, really bad. Maybe one meal a day, ragged clothes,
no money for doctors or dentists, no heat in the winter.

Then along comes someone who says he's taking you to an orphanage. Away you go, scared to death and shedding lots of tears. Soon
you are in a whole new world full of strangers. A smiling lady wel-
comes you and shows you around the orphanage. Everything is a blur.

But you're in for a happy surprise. Because you discover you are
in a place that has hot water and indoor toilets and three really
good meals a day. You don't have to share a bed with three or four
brothers and sisters, and you have decent clothing, shoes without
holes in the soles and a warm winter coat. Talk about heaven!

However, you soon learn that even heaven comes with a price.
Many orphanages were operated by church groups and supported by donations. But during the Depression, even the most generous-hearted
people barely had enough to take care of themselves, much less give
to the church.

In order to get by, children in orphanages had lots of chores to
do, in addition to attending school. They worked in the kitchen,
took care of the vegetable gardens and operated the laundry. Imagine helping to make bread and desserts for 1,000 people every day!
Or imagine milking 200 cows. Some orphanages operated large farms
with chickens, pigs and milk cows. They butchered their own meat,
produced their own eggs, made their own butter.

Some of the children who were put in orphanages never saw their
parents again. But most were reunited with their families when
things got better toward the end of the decade.

Most of the people I've talked to who lived in Depression-era
orphanages say it was the luckiest thing that could have happened
to them. They remember orphanages as places where people truly did
open their hearts to children in desperate need.

*Your Grandpa Clancy*

# Methodist Home Came to Rescue Of Struggling Mother's Children

*By Willie Blackman, Dothan, Alabama*

WE WERE LIVING in Dale County, Alabama when my father died in 1934. Mother was temporarily handicapped and unable to care for her three children, so we were sent to live with our grandparents.

Grandfather was very poor, trying to farm without the benefit of fertilizer and using two bull steers to pull his plows.

Grandmother did her best, but it wasn't easy caring for three small children in a home where there was often no food. Breakfast usually consisted of a biscuit with black coffee, which was not a very hearty meal for children *or* adults.

Eventually someone realized something had to be done. One day a nice lady named Mrs. Espy drove up in a Model A Ford. Our belongings were placed in a box, and Mrs. Espy drove us to the Methodist Children's Home in Selma.

### Strange New World

The first 2 weeks were very frustrating. We were in a totally new environment with lots of new faces. But those other children soon became playmates, and our new world included three balanced meals a day. We were also introduced to prunes on a regular schedule.

The home had indoor toilets, showers, bathtubs and lots of hot water—things we hadn't even known existed.

We were sent to the public school with a brown-bag lunch of two peanut butter and raisin sandwiches. It's not much by today's standards, but to Depression-era orphans, it was a gift from heaven.

For as long as they lived, my sisters had nothing but praise for the Children's Home. Each child was assigned chores, and we were taught to do things for ourselves.

In spring, the larger boys were paired off to push the manual reel-type mower, but that was fun. All our chores were fun. Surely the right atmosphere had much to do with that.

During the warm months of summer, the bigger boys pulled weekly kitchen duty, which brought special favors for them, like extra helpings of cake and ice cream.

The kitchen crew made ice cream once a week, and we enjoyed it so much we made a game out of eating it as slowly as possible. The last kid with ice cream in his dish was declared the winner.

### Found Treasure in Clover

At Easter, the large lawns of beautiful grass and clover hid colorful Easter eggs. Christmas was great, too, with clothes, toys, nuts and fruits provided by the various Methodist churches. We didn't get many things that were new, but everything we received was precious.

After a few years, Mother married a gentleman farmer, and we left the home to live with them in Danville, Virginia. Our stepfather taught us to raise a garden, care for livestock, milk a cow and fish. There were so many fun things in those years! At 72, I still appreciate the many things that I learned from him.

And yet today, I remain grateful for all I learned at the orphanage, too. Although I'm no longer able to attend its homecoming celebrations, I still have a very special place in my heart and prayers for the Methodist Children's Home in Selma, Alabama. ⊠

**PEANUT BUTTER AND RAISINS.** When Willie Blackman's father (left) died, Willie and his sisters (below) wound up in an orphanage in Selma, Alabama. There they were introduced to unimagined wonders like indoor toilets, showers and peanut butter and raisin sandwiches.

**LOVE THAT CHARLIE!** This 1941 photo of Charlie Johnson and some high school friends was taken as they walked to class at the state orphanage in Corsicana, Texas.

# 'The Home' Produced Happy, Hardworking Citizens

*By Charlie Johnson, Dunnellon, Florida*

MY MOTHER was widowed by the influenza epidemic in the late 1920s, leaving her to raise four little children alone. Social Security didn't exist, and there were no widow's or children's benefits. She had no choice but to place the three oldest children in the State Orphans Home at Corsicana, Texas.

My sisters and I entered "the home" on December 29, 1929 and remained there throughout the Depression. It was a place to learn and grow, and we loved the employees, our matrons and especially the teachers. We had our own school, with classes through 12th grade, plus vocational education.

We slept between clean pressed sheets in steam-heated buildings and ate three meals a day. Excellent dental and medical care were provided. We watched movies in the auditorium on Saturday nights and returned on Sunday for church services.

In summer, we boys picked okra and black-eyed peas and baled hay on "halves" on neighboring farms. The hay was fed to our herd of 100 dairy cows, which we milked twice a day.

Later in the Depression, the home had its own pasteurization plant, brought about primarily because of a polio epidemic in Corsicana. None of the kids at the home ever caught polio.

All the children had duties in the laundry and kitchen. Some were assigned to the bakery, where we made bread and desserts for about 1,000 orphans and staff.

We had a beautiful orchard of figs, peaches and plums and large patches of blackberries and dewberries. We also raised our own vegetables, chickens and pigs.

### "Cracklin' Good"

In fall, we helped with hog butchering. After we finished, we were allowed to cook cracklings and parch corn in a big black pot over an open fire.

WPA crews did a lot of street work on our campus. One time a worker who was earning $1 a day told me how difficult things were for his family. The next day, I carefully wrapped some peanut butter from our lunch in newspaper and gave it to him. It had newsprint all over it, but he ate it.

My sisters and I benefited from our stay at the home. Jewell was class valedictorian in 1940 and went to college on a scholarship. Amalene graduated in 1942 and bucked rivets on bombers during the war.

I graduated in 1943, spent 3 years at the Naval Air Station in Pearl Harbor and then worked for the Postal Service for 30 years.

We spent the entire Depression as wards of the State of Texas, and the experience taught us to work hard, study hard, play and save our money. The State Orphans Home helped us grow into happy, self-reliant citizens. ⊠

---

### Nine Years at Orphange Taught Valuable Lessons

MY TWIN SISTER and I were born May 28, 1920, the youngest of six children. In September 1921, our father died in a car accident. He'd been laid off from the steel mill and there was no life insurance.

Mom couldn't afford to care for all six of us, so Martha and I were sent to the Baptist Orphanage in Castle Shannon, Pennsylvania with our brothers Paul and Eddie. The Shriners were our Santa Claus at Christmas and took us to the circus in summers.

In 1930, Mom got a widow's pension and was able to bring us home. I have no regrets about those years at the orphanage. I learned to not be selfish, to love God and to help the needy. —*Mary Roller Kentwood, Michigan*

# Oklahoma School Taught the Value Of Self-Reliance

*By Joan Clevenger, Hart, Texas*

MY BROTHERS and I were placed in the Tipton Orphans Home in Tipton, Oklahoma in September 1937. I was 9, and my brothers were 5 and 7. I remained there until I graduated from high school in 1947.

Times were hard during the early years, and money was tight. But we were fed well with plain, simple food. We ate a lot of potatoes, dried beans, biscuits, corn bread and molasses. We had adequate clothes, everyone had coats and shoes in winter, and we slept warm and dry.

More than 200 children lived at the home, and we all had jobs to do. The girls prepared the food and did the laundry and housecleaning with adult supervision.

The boys milked the cows, maintained the yard and buildings, cared for the livestock and did the farm work. Everyone was expected to work and care for themselves.

The Tipton Home was funded through donations from the Church of Christ and many individuals throughout the Southwest. We were taught that people helped us because they loved us, that no one owed us anything and that we'd be responsible for ourselves when we were able. Those beliefs have always worked for me.

After I graduated and entered Abilene Christian College, I was still considered a Tipton resident. The home paid for my school bills and also took care of any financial needs I couldn't cover with a part-time job, just as a parent would do for a child.

Even after 50 years, I still visit the home at least once a year and keep in close touch with more than a dozen friends from those days. For most of the people I knew, living in a children's home was a very positive experience. ☒

## "P.O." Children Forged Lifelong Friendships

I STAYED at the San Francisco Protestant Orphanage from April 1924 to December 1933. It was the best thing that could've happened to me and my brother, Thomas.

Most of the kids at the public school were jealous of us. We ate better and always had close friends to play with. If somebody wanted to pick a fight, they didn't dare pick on a "P.O." kid. We had too many friends to back us up.

When summer vacation started, we were off to the home's camp for 3 months. We remember those days with great joy.

The orphanage treated us fairly, but we had rules to follow, too. About 90% of us went on to do very well in the job world, and many served in the military. Thomas and I joined the Navy in 1937 and remained until retirement.

Many of us still get together at least twice a year and are closer than some brothers and sisters.

—*Cecil Malmin, Roseville, California*

**A "FAMILY" OF 200.** Joan Clevenger and the other children who grew up at the orphanage in Tipton, Oklahoma aways had someone to play with. Joan received these rare color photographs from an elderly photographer, who knew she'd enjoy them as mementos of a place where she and her siblings spent so much time.

# Despite Sock-Darning Days, Dad Loved His Orphanage Stay

*By Rosaline Ann Baldwin, Monroe, Michigan*

THROUGHOUT my childhood, Dad said many times that if anything ever happened to him and Mother, he'd want us six kids raised in the same orphanage he was. We've heard stories about the orphanage all our lives, and Dad is still telling them today. We never tire of hearing them.

Leslie Lee Messenger was placed in the Ebenezer Orphan Home in Flat Rock, Ohio in 1936, when he was 8 years old. The home was run by the Evangelical Church and included nearly 500 acres of farmland and orchards.

The children played a large part in maintaining the farm. They milked cows and butchered hogs, picked apples and gathered eggs. They kept the lawns mowed and the fields planted. The girls helped make clothes for all the children and took part in preparing the meals.

The chores were unending, but I've never heard Dad complain about how hard he had to work. He loved being at the orphanage and remembers everything about it as part of a wonderful childhood.

The only chore Dad didn't enjoy was darning socks. All the socks were placed on a large table, and each child had to mend a certain number. He'd scramble through the pile, looking for socks with the smallest holes.

"I'd go off into a corner to do my darning, thinking it wouldn't take long at all," he says. "Upon closer inspection, I'd discover the heel had a hole three times the size of the one

**FOND MEMORIES OF FLAT ROCK.** Leslie Lee Messenger (in inset below left and with his wife above) truly enjoyed his stay at the Ebenezer Orphan Home from 1936 'til about 1942. Although, as you'll learn in his story, young Leslie left his mark on the home, it's safe to say that the orphanage also left an indelible impression on him.

in the toe. I thought I'd be there all day darning socks."

But it didn't do any good to rush through the work. Every sock was inspected, and when his work was torn out and he was told do it over, he learned to do it right the first time.

Studies were very important, and all school-age children had to attend classes. Each morning, they'd wash, dress, eat breakfast and head out the door. But they didn't have far to go—the school was just across the yard.

### Church Was a Must

Sunday-morning and Wednesday-evening church services were a must. Everyone had the opportunity to take part in various church programs or sing in the choir, but the children were free to make their own choices.

Dad always emphasizes that there was plenty of good food. When the dinner bell rang, the children dropped whatever they were doing and came running from all directions, because they knew a hot meal was waiting. For dessert, there would be a warm slice of apple pie and a tall glass of ice-cold milk.

The kids were never bored, and there was no shortage of playmates. There were bikes and scooters to ride and games to play—marbles, kick-the-can, hide-and-seek or baseball. Sometimes they'd fling crab apples off the end of a switch to see who cold sail them the farthest.

The rules were strict, and those who violated them had to pay the consequences. The older boys liked to climb the 100-

foot water tower and carve their initials on it. Though Dad was small, he decided he wanted to "leave his mark", too.

He'd carved his initials and was just about to climb back down the ladder when someone spotted him. He was caught! Before long, everyone from the orphanage was standing at the bottom of the tower, trying to coax him down.

Dad decided he wasn't coming down at all. If he didn't come down, he couldn't be punished. But he finally realized he couldn't stay there forever and slowly climbed down. As soon as his legs were within reach, someone grabbed him. "I never got so many hugs in my life," he recalls. Of course, once the hugging ended, he got a memorable licking.

I've heard Dad say many times that he wouldn't trade his 6 years at the orphanage for anything. Our entire family has come to treasure his stories about that time, and I'm sure we'll share them for many generations to come. ⊠

# It Was Home Away from Home

*By Francis Mahoney, Casselberry, Florida*

IN SPRING of 1928, my brother, sister and I were placed in St. Pauls Orphanage in Crafton, Pennsylvania. We remained there 8 years, until August 1936.

A widower with three small children (ages 4, 6 and 8), my father knew it would not be possible for him to find work and also care for us. He could visit us, and he did every Sunday for all those years.

He also took us on extended family visits each year, always working toward the day he could make a home for us. At the orphanage, we were separated by age and gender and assigned to a dormitory with other children our age.

To family and friends, we were "poor orphan kids" living in a home. Fortunately for me, I didn't think that way. I accepted the conditions at the orphanage and enjoyed my life there and my many friends.

A typical day started at 6:30 a.m. After washing up, we got dressed, made our beds and marched to breakfast. Normally it was oatmeal with sugar and cream or pancakes, plus lots of donated bread and butter.

After breakfast, it was back to the dorm to check our homework and wait for the school bell. The orphanage had as many as 750 children. Many were wards of the court, from broken homes or had lost one or both parents.

The entire complex was funded by private donations from Pittsburgh businesses and churches. Discipline was strict but fair, and peer pressure was a strong deterrent.

Still, when it was necessary, backsides were "tanned" by the prefect (who was also the coach). Punishment was administered with a leather strap in full view of your pals and—as I can personally attest—was usually warranted.

On Saturdays, depending on our age, we had our work assignments. We cleaned our quarters and the grounds, worked on the farm and, in general, learned a "work ethic" early on.

One highlight of those years was the "auto ride". That was the day the

**ALL SHINED UP.** Francis Mahoney (at left with his siblings, his dad and a nun) was all dressed up for his Confirmation when this 1933 photo was taken.

Shriners and Knights of Columbus organized a fleet of cars to take us to Kennywood Park, the largest amusement park in the area. On the morning they were to arrive, anticipation was high as we crowded against the third-floor windows of our dormitory to watch the line of cars moving slowly down the lane at the orphanage's entrance.

Back then, cars were not as commonplace, but we'd learned to identify many models on sight. None of us had ever seen the variety of cars assembled that morning.

When it was time to go, we formed several lines and, as the cars came by, three or four children were placed in each. Mine was a spotless 1932 Ford that even smelled brand-new.

It turned out to be my lucky day as I was assigned to sit next to the driver. I watched with fascination as he went through the gearshift changes and even let me steer for a bit. From that day on, I was positive I could drive a car—once my legs grew long enough!

Upon our arrival at Kennywood, we discovered the entire park was reserved for us. We spent a wonderful day on the roller coasters and all the other rides.

We also had a great picnic lunch that our "foster parents" for the day provided as part of the generous sacrifice they'd made on our behalf.

In retrospect, I'm grateful that orphanage was available at the time of our greatest need. The discipline I learned there, coupled with the spiritual and moral foundation I received, carried me through the war years and gave me the foundation to raise five children of my own.

Although other people called St. Pauls an orphanage, there was a good reason I always called it "home". ⊠

## Santa Made Repeat Appearance At This Indiana Orphanage

CHRISTMAS AT St. Vincent Villa in Fort Wayne, Indiana was a very special time. The nuns impressed upon us that we were to prepare for Jesus' birth all through Advent. They suggested actions we could perform or items we could give up to make a soft, warm crib for the Christ child.

We started our letters to Santa in mid-November. A lot of thought went into those letters, because the toy you asked for would probably be the only one you received all year. We also could ask for two more small items like socks, handkerchiefs, bobby pins or hair bows.

Every year, we were visited by two Santas—one who gave us the gifts from Catholic Charities, and a man named Mr. Muhn, who was the most beautiful Santa anyone could behold. He is deceased now, but I'll never forget his unselfish gift to us at Christmastime.    —*Mary Deck*
*Churubusco, Indiana*

**HAPPY REUNION.** Mary Deck (third from the left) was reunited with some of her classmates from St. Vincent Villa in Fort Wayne (below) a few years ago.

# Holiday Contentment Defied Depression Blues

*By Mary Van Boxel, Williamsfield, Ohio*

I REMEMBER those long-ago Christmases at the orphanage in Cleveland, Ohio. We'd hurry through our Christmas Eve supper—creamed eggs on toast, and maybe a dollop of Jell-O—and quickly tear into our evening chores.

**OH HAPPY DAY!** When Christmas Eve finally came, Mary Van Boxel (at left and with her brothers below) shared in the excitement with the whole orphanage.

No shortcuts were permitted on this grand day. The tables had to be cleared, dusted of crumbs and reset for breakfast. The dishes were washed and dried, and the floors swept and mopped.

Then we dashed back to our living quarters, washed up and changed into our school clothes. Each child had three sets of clothes—one for school, one for play and our Sunday best, which we hung up immediately after church.

When everyone was ready, we gathered in the auditorium for a program performed by some of the more talented children. Every year there was some fiasco caused by the performers' youthful enthusiasm. One year the boy playing Scrooge allowed his foot to protrude from his makeshift grave. Another time, a shepherd tripped over his crook and fell off the stage.

At the end of the program, Santa arrived to distribute presents. All the gifts had been received earlier, opened by the staff, then rewrapped, as we were allowed to receive only certain items.

The boys got things like games, socks, underwear and gloves. Girls' gifts included stationery, pen sets, pajamas and certain books—*Gone with the Wind*, maybe; *Forever Amber*, no.

On Christmas Day, we rose early, made our beds and put our largest gifts on display. Whatever Depression-era grief and sorrow existed beyond those walls, our little hearts were happy and at peace. ▨

# CHAPTER SEVEN

# Making Food Stretch

**KITCHEN INGENUITY.** Keeping a family fed during the worst days of the Depression was truly a challenge—a challenge that, as you'll soon see, was met with some very creative solutions. (Photo: J.C. Allen and Son)

# From the desk of Clancy Strock

Dear Katie,

Millions of people learned for the first time what it was like to wake up hungry and go to bed hungry during the Depression.

Even living on a farm, as I did, our Sunday night meal often was bread and milk--a slice of bread torn into little pieces and dropped into a big glass of milk. You ate it with a spoon. Yes, it sounds awful, but it was filling. A variation was "milk toast"--hot milk in a soup bowl, with a slice of cinnamon toast floating in it.

Every November we took several bushels of corn to a nearby gristmill, where it was ground into cornmeal. That cornmeal fed us all through the winter. Your great-grandmother turned it into corn bread, cornmeal mush (sort of a thick soup) and fried cornmeal mush that we covered with syrup and ate just like pancakes. Delicious!

With our herd of milk cows, a big flock of chickens, fruit orchard and huge garden, we didn't need much from the grocery store except flour, sugar, salt, soap and butter.

But people living in big cities had a much tougher time of it. There's no such thing as a garden in a fifth-floor New York City walk-up apartment or a Philadelphia row house.

So homemakers became creative in turning bread, beans, rice, potatoes, cabbage and cheap cuts of meat into tasty but economical meals. Just check out some of the recipes on the following pages. And before you say "Yuck!", remember that it was "Eat your potato water gravy or go to bed hungry." Again.

In some areas, charitable groups opened "soup kitchens". You walked for blocks and blocks to stand in a long line with your tin bucket. Eventually someone ladled hot soup into your pail, which you took home to the family.

Some perfectly decent people became so desperate that they were forced to steal. An acquaintance of mine was a hobo during the Depression. He and a friend hopped off a slow freight going through Georgia next to a huge field of watermelons.

Surely the farmer wouldn't miss just one. And they hadn't eaten in 2 days. As they finished eating, a voice behind them said, "You boys get your fill?"

There was the farmer, shotgun pointed at them. My friend jumped up and said, "We sure did, and we're just leaving."

"I don't reckon you are," said the farmer. "Sit down and have some more." The farmer forced them to eat six more melons before they could stagger away!

"I've never again been able to eat a slice of watermelon," my friend said. "And I never stole food again, either."

*Your Grandpa Clancy*

# Feeding a Family Posed Different Challenges for City Dwellers

*By June Hurlow, Fairborn, Ohio*

IT'S BEEN SAID that over 70% of Americans lived on farms during the Depression years. These families didn't have much money, but they always ate well. Our family was part of the other 30%, and for us, "making do" was quite different.

We lived in Dayton, Ohio, and most families in our neighborhood were on relief. Those were lean years, but their lessons of thrift and innovation have been a great advantage in my life.

There were no supermarkets in those days, but there were tiny family-run groceries every few blocks. The working people bought the best cuts of meat, and the grocers gave the

---

### "Sometimes dinner was the only meal of the day..."

---

rest away rather than see it spoil. The butcher would wrap a variety of bones, scraps and organ meats for needy families. Mother ground the liver we received and used it to stretch meat loaf.

Soup bones or scraps went into a pot with home-canned vegetables and simmered on the wood-burning stove all day. At lunchtime, the broth was skimmed off the top and ladled over dry bread. The rest of the soup made our supper.

Sometimes, dinner was the only meal of the day, and it was usually a single item—beans, rice, fried potatoes. Mother made frittatas with diced potatoes, onions, as many eggs as she could spare, and bacon bits or meat scraps. She used a 15-inch skillet that my father, an iron molder, made especially for her.

We ate a lot of cabbage soup, which was like stone soup. Mother chopped up a head of cabbage and cooked it in tomato juice or broth with any other vegetables we had.

### Saved Corncobs for Syrup

When we had fresh sweet corn, we saved the cobs and dried them, then chopped and cooked them in water and sugar. When the broth was amber, we drained it off and boiled it down to make syrup.

Once a month, my brother and I would pull our wagon 2 miles to a warehouse at Fourth and St. Clair to pick up government surplus food. There was flour, sugar, canned meat, dry milk, rice, cocoa, tea, coffee, rolled oats, cornmeal and sometimes fresh vegetables and oranges. It looked like a lot, but with 10 people to feed, it went fast.

**CREATIVE IN THE KITCHEN.** June Hurlow (the tallest child on the right) recalls her mother boiled corncobs for syrup and made stone soup from cabbage.

We also received some help from a local farmer. Two winters in a row, he gave us a 50-pound bag of flour and a 50-pound can of lard. With just those two ingredients and water, Mother made biscuits and very tasty gravy.

Despite the hardships, the holidays were always rich with goodwill and compassion. I especially remember Thanksgiving 1935, a time that we later referred to as "the depths of the Depression". Our food allotment was almost gone, and Mother planned to make a pot of vegetable soup for our holiday meal.

At 9 a.m. Thanksgiving Day, there was a knock at the door. Two men stood there with two large food baskets our church had gathered for us—home-canned vegetables and fruit, chickens to roast and pies baked especially for us.

Fifty years later, I am still moved by the fact that these people, in their own poverty, shared so much with us.

While I wouldn't want to live those years over, I thank God that I grew up during the Depression. I learned early that happiness doesn't come from getting my own way, but from doing what I know is right and serving others.

# Call for a Pizza? Not with Mom Around!

*By Michael Lacivita*
*Youngstown, Ohio*

THESE DAYS, pizza is likely the most popular food in North America. Back during the 1930s, few Americans even knew about this delectable dish…unless they happened to be of Italian ancestry.

Our family enjoyed pizza often during the Depression, thanks to our garden and trusty basement oven.

Some of our friends and neighbors had wood-fired ovens made of brick and stone. They were called *fornos*, and these outdoor ovens made the most wonderful homemade pizzas.

### Stone-Baked Pizza

After the wood was burned, the ashes were removed and the pizza was slid inside. That hot stone baked a pizza in minutes.

We didn't have an outdoor stone oven, but the gas-fired Magic Chef in our cellar was just as dependable.

Our regular kitchen was in the basement of our home, because it was warm in winter and cool in summer. Here,

**PIZZA PROS. Michael Lacivita's parents grew their own ingredients to make pizza and other dishes.**

Mother made her pizza every Friday the whole year-round.

Our regular pizza was simple—topped only with homegrown tomatoes, "goat horn" Italian frying peppers and a sprinkling of grated cheese.

From age 8 on, I helped my father plant our "survival garden". In spring each year, we filled it with 300 plum tomato plants and 100 pepper plants. Pizza was only one dish we enjoyed from our garden's bounty.

### A Dish with Personality

Mother also made a plain kind of pizza, which consisted of a thick dimpled crust. Covered in oil and sprinkled with salt, this chewy delight was a real jaw-strengthener.

For dessert, she often made a small fried dish called *pizza fritta*. She placed dough into a small fry pan sizzling with oil.

**HOME DELIVERY. In the Lacivita household, a basement oven like this one got a workout every Friday.**

Out would pop a pancake-like delicacy. Sprinkled with sugar, it was a delicious dessert.

Today, it seems amazing when I hear my 10-year-old grandson, Jeffrey, order a pizza over the telephone. The toppings are limitless, available in any quantity a crust can hold.

"Heavy on the cheese, heavy on the pepperoni," Jeffrey commands, "and light on the sauce."

Pizza making has come a long way since the Depression. ⊠

---

### Naive Boys Made Sport Of "Depression Shrimp"

THE DEPRESSION was worse on some families than others. My mother's family of 15 always managed to have enough food to eat, while Daddy's family of eight nearly starved to death several times.

While reminiscing about those tough years, Mother said that her father hunted squirrels and other wild game to feed his family. Daddy was appalled. To him, squirrels were nothing more than rodents and unfit to eat. *His* family would never have eaten anything like that!

Then Daddy began telling about the time he and a friend caught a bucketful of crawdads in the creek. They discovered that if they threw the crawdads on the road, they made a delightful "splat" when cars ran over them.

Finally, one motorist stopped and offered to buy the rest of the crawdads in the bucket, and the boys eagerly sold them.

"I can't imagine what he wanted with all those crawdads," Daddy mused. "Maybe he wanted to *eat* them, I don't know. We were just glad to get the money."

Now it was Mother's turn to be appalled. "Of course he wanted to eat them!" she blurted.

"They were a delicacy—the shrimp of the Depression. Your family wouldn't eat squirrels, and you let cars splat crawdads. No wonder you nearly starved to death!"

—*Sheila Bender*
*Las Cruces, New Mexico*

**GROCERY GOODIES.** Fortunately for Hazel Kemp, her dad (at left and above) worked where food could be brought home.

MY FATHER'S JOB at the A&P grocery store provided our family with food the store would have thrown out otherwise—bruised produce, dented cans and broken boxes. Mother often said her home canning would never win any prizes because we carved all the bruises out of the fruit first.

When we got vegetables that had begun to rot, we trimmed the bad parts away and used the rest in soups and stews. We became adept at opening dented cans.

Dad made sure the store gave needy customers trimmed bones and edible rinds from the meat counter, as well as cracked eggs (if the membrane was intact), broken cookies, mashed loaves of bread and rolls with torn cellophane covers.

When these customers got home, they often found extra cans of sugar, flour, coffee or oatmeal. My father paid for these items out of his own pocket.

Almost everyone had a garden and canned the produce. Any extra food was given to neighbors or needy families. Nothing was wasted. A rat would have starved to death in most garbage cans.

—*Hazel Kemp, Forestville, California*

**WELL-FED GROUP.** In these family photos, Hazel is on left above and second from left in front, above right.

# $ Financial Burdens Took Toll on Friendship $

*By Charles Martin, Bartlesville, Oklahoma*

MY FATHER lost his job in the early 1930s, and other employment was almost impossible to find. It wasn't easy to raise seven children on a meager income in those dark days.

Longtime friends of my parents operated the small grocery store in our neighborhood. Many afternoons when I came home from school, Mother would send me to the store with a small sealed envelope. I thought the envelope contained money and a grocery list.

### What Note Really Said

I ran this errand many times before I learned the envelope contained a note saying the requested groceries would be paid for as soon as my father found work.

These trips continued, and they began to embarrass me. I'm sure they embarrassed my mother, too. She had no idea when we'd be able to pay off our growing debt.

One afternoon, the store owners greeted me politely and handed me a sealed envelope to give to my mother. I left feeling dejected and confused, not knowing why I hadn't been given the groceries that I had come for.

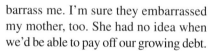

*Grocer*

As soon as I handed the envelope to my mother, I saw the disappointment and hurt in her face. She didn't need to open it to know what the message inside would be.

That's when I realized our credit had been cut off. Though I was only 8 or 9, I began to worry about what we would do. Yet I knew that we'd survive somehow.

A few dollars here and there began to reduce the debt, but I never knew whether it was completely paid. Years later, when my mother's friend passed away, Mother couldn't bring herself to attend the funeral. She wanted to, but that embarrassing memory of long ago kept her away.

### Couldn't Turn Back the Clock

In later years, I would have been more than willing to pay off any remaining debt if it would have brought peace of mind to anyone. But I always felt my mother's friend understood, and that she, too, felt some guilt about what had happened.

Nothing more was ever said about this event, and perhaps we should consider it a closed chapter in our lives. But it's the kind of Depression memory that lingers with many of us. ⊠

# Enjoy a Taste of the Good Old Days with These Depression-Era Recipes

*Just for fun, here are some 1930s' favorites to try.*

**DEPRESSION DELIGHT.** Jeanie Qualliotine (on Mom's lap and in inset) and her family enjoyed her mother's butterless, eggless cake.

## Cake Fed a Crowd— Without Eggs or Butter

WE HAD no butter or eggs and were always short on milk, but that didn't stop Mom from making her famous Depression Cake. It was delicious and went a long way toward feeding the relatives who often visited. Here's the recipe:

### Depression Cake

**1-1/2 cups sugar**
**2-2/3 cups flour**
   **2 teaspoons salt**
   **2/3 cup cocoa**
   **2 tablespoons vinegar**
   **2/3 cup vegetable oil**
   **2 cups hot water**
**FROSTING**
   **3 ounces cream cheese**
   **2 cups powdered sugar**
   **6 to 8 tablespoons condensed milk**

Combine the first seven ingredients in a bowl; mix well. Pour batter into two greased and floured 9-in. pans or one 13-in. x 9-in. pan. Bake at 350° for 40 minutes or until cake tests done. Combine frosting ingredients; spread over cake.
   —Jeanie Qualliotine
   Greenville, North Carolina

## Thrifty Homemakers Let No Food Go to Waste

MY DEAR MOTHER raised nine children almost single-handedly and knew how to stretch everything. These tips for "using *all* of the vegetable" came from one of her cookbooks.

**Cauliflower leaves:** Ask for untrimmed cauliflower. Save leaves nearest head. Trim off lower tough parts. Cook in boiling water for 15 minutes. Drain. Season and butter, or chop and add white sauce.

**Outer lettuce leaves:** Use for wilted lettuce or when cooking peas.

**Outer celery stalks:** Use for creamed or braised celery.

**Celery leaves:** Use in green salads, bread stuffings, stews and soups. Use with roasts and for garnish.

**Carrot tops:** Use for garnish.

The cookbook also had this unusual recipe for pancakes:

### Pancakes

  **1/2 medium onion**
   **2 medium potatoes**
   **3 carrots**
   **2 cups fresh spinach**
**1/4 head lettuce**
**2 eggs, beaten**
**1 cup flour**
**1 teaspoon baking powder**
**1-1/2 teaspoons salt**
  **1/8 teaspoon pepper**
**Fat for frying**

Put vegetables through the fine blade of a food chopper. (Save juice for gravy.) Blend in eggs. Sift flour, baking powder, salt and pepper; stir into vegetables, mixing well. Drop by spoonfuls into hot fat in a skillet. Fry on both sides until golden brown.
   —Laura Rakickas
   Newtown Square, Pennsylvania

## Poor Man's Cake Was Her Family's Favorite

ONE OF OUR favorite desserts was Poor Man's Cake, which Mother made often. Here's her recipe:

### Poor Man's Cake

**1/2 cup shortening**
**1/4 teaspoon salt**
  **1 cup water**
  **1 cup sugar**
  **1 cup raisins**
  **1 teaspoon cloves**

1 teaspoon cinnamon
1 teaspoon nutmeg
2 cups flour
1 teaspoon baking soda

Place shortening in a saucepan and bring to a boil. Add the next seven ingredients; boil for 3 minutes. Cool. Add flour and baking soda. Pour batter into a 9-in. square pan. Bake at 375° for 30-35 minutes.

—Dorothy Davis, Naples, Florida

## Red Flannel Hash Was Served Often on Farm

RED FLANNEL HASH was a staple for dinner on our farm. It was great served with hot biscuits and butter. Here's the recipe:

### Red Flannel Hash

6 potatoes, peeled and boiled
6 medium beets, boiled, peeled and diced
1 onion, diced and boiled
1/2 pound lean salt pork, cut into 1/2-inch pieces, fried and drained

Combine all ingredients in a large frying pan and chop by hand with a potato masher. Fry slowly over medium heat until browned. Turn with a spatula; brown again. —Ruth Towle Canterbury, New Hampshire

**COUNTRY COUSINS.** Ruth Towle (left) and cousin Claribel learned to like hash made of salt pork, beets and potatoes.

# Ingenious Cooks Made Much from Little

*By Lois Curnutt, Odessa, Texas*

DURING the 1930s, we had no regular shopping day. We went to the store only when we had spare money, which wasn't often. On those trips we bought the bare minimum of staples…flour, salt, pepper, seasonings and spices, cornstarch, corn syrup, rice and raisins.

We grew, picked or made everything else and learned to make do with what we had.

For breakfast, we sometimes ate Pap Soup—dampened flour cooked in milk with a dash of salt, then sprinkled with sugar and cinnamon. Mother served it with toast on the side. It was delicious.

Bacon was added to many dishes —beans, soups, vegetables, even lettuce salad. The drippings were saved for seasoning, frying and baking bread.

Leftovers were never wasted. Bread was used for pudding, stuffing, crumbs for breading and snacks. Cooked cornmeal was chilled, sliced, fried in butter and served with syrup for the next morning's breakfast.

Rice could be reused for pudding or Spanish rice. Mashed potatoes were turned into potato cakes or added to cream soups and cake batter. Leftover vegetables went into casseroles and soups. Sweet potatoes made a tasty mock pumpkin pie.

Here are some of the recipes we used during those years:

### Pap Soup

1 cup flour
3 to 4 cups milk
2 tablespoons butter
Salt
Sugar
Cinnamon

Place flour in a bowl and pour in a tiny bit of milk. With fingers, work milk into flour until all the flour is crumbled and stringy. In a skillet, scald the remaining milk medium-low heat (do not boil). Add butter and salt to taste. Slowly drop in crumbled flour, stirring constantly. Cook for 2-3 minutes or until dough is cooked through. Spoon onto plate. Sprinkle with sugar and cinnamon.

### Eggless Chocolate Cake

1-1/2 cups sugar
2 cups flour
1/2 cup cocoa
1 teaspoon baking soda
1/2 teaspoon salt
1 cup sour milk
1/2 cup shortening, melted
1-1/2 teaspoons vanilla

Sift together dry ingredients; place in a bowl. Add remaining ingredients and stir until smooth. Spread into a greased and floured 13-in. x 9-in. pan. Bake at 375° for 30 minutes.

### Mock Apple Pie

Pastry for double-crust pie
12 crackers
1-1/2 teaspoons cinnamon
1-1/2 cups sugar
1-1/2 cups water
1-1/2 teaspoons cream of tartar
1 tablespoon butter

Line pie plate with pastry. Break crackers over pastry; sprinkle with cinnamon. Combine remaining ingredients in a saucepan; bring to a boil. Pour over crackers. Cover with the top pastry. Bake at 450° until browned.

### Potato Water Gravy

2 to 3 tablespoons cooking oil, meat drippings *or* butter
2 to 3 tablespoons flour
Salt
Pepper
Water reserved from boiling potatoes

Heat oil in a skillet over medium heat. Add flour, salt and pepper; stir slowly until flour is browned. Add potato water, stirring constantly until gravy thickens slightly.

# Dad Built Bread Oven with Salvaged Bricks

*By Tony Kostreba, Portales, New Mexico*

IN THE MIDDLE of the Depression, the grocery stores in central New Jersey were selling loaves of bread for a nickel. But even at that terrific price, store-bought bread was out of reach for our family of eight.

Dad solved our bread problem when a local chemical factory burned to the ground. All the area residents were scavenging the site for any materials they could use. Dad loaded our Model T truck with loose, clean bricks and a big sheet of light steel. The next day, he started building Mom an oven.

Dad used heavy timbers to build an 8- x 10-foot platform about 30 inches off the ground. Fire bricks from the factory were placed around the edge, held in place with a mortar of mud and straw.

Once the base was finished, Dad curved the steel plate into a semicircle, covered it with more bricks

---

*"Store-bought bread was out of reach for our family..."*

---

and mud, then enclosed both ends. He added an opening in front that measured 2 x 3 feet, and he built a 6-inch chimney on the back.

Every other week, I'd pull my wagon 4 miles to pick up our 50-pound bag of Red Cross flour. On the way home, I'd stop at the bakery to buy 1/4 pound of yeast for 10¢. That evening, Mom would set up the large wooden tub used only for baking. By bedtime, the dough was ready to rise.

When we got up the next morning, Dad would have a roaring fire going in the oven. After several hours, the embers and ashes were cleaned out, and the brick floor was mopped. A bucket was put over the chimney, and the front opening was closed to keep the heat inside.

Meanwhile, Mom had the dough rising in large boxes that held four big round loaves each. We put the loaves in the oven with a long pole that had a wide, flat board at one end. After an hour or so, the whole neighborhood could smell Mom's bread. The loaves baked very evenly and never burned.

When we came home from school for lunch, a huge loaf still warm from the oven would be on the table. Many times, that bread was all I had to eat. ▨

FACTORY FRESH. Like this woman, Tony Kostreba's mom spent plenty of time in the kitchen. But she baked with a homemade oven that was once part of a chemical factory.

BACKYARD BARBECUE. The Kostreba family was lucky to have a pig to roast this day, but sometimes all they had to eat was bread. Tony is turning the spit; his parents are standing at left and third from left.

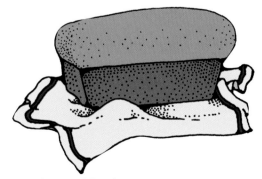

# His Stint on 'Meat Wagon' Made Mom Sing Again

*By W. Ray Skiles, Weirton, West Virginia*

TIMES WERE HARD in the coal-mining town of Leisenring, Pennsylvania in 1931. Fathers were hard-pressed to bring food home to their families, and mothers were frustrated trying to stretch what little they had.

In our house, "Mom's apple pie" had long ago been replaced by "Mom's stew pot". She kept it simmering on her coal-fired stove around the clock, always searching for anything edible to add to it. For the seven of us, that stew pot was the main source of our daily meals.

We always had some down-and-out relatives living with us, too, often bringing the household count to 11 or 12 for several days at a time. It was a heavy strain on Mom's stew pot. She had a worried expression every time she checked inside it.

### Empty Stomach Didn't Help

I often pretended not to be hungry and ate as sparingly as I could, hoping that would help stretch our food supply. This only made Mom worry more, since I was skinny to begin with.

At night, I'd fall asleep wondering how I could help. But what could a 7-year-old do that grown-ups couldn't?

That summer, a solution came in an unexpected way. A farm family several miles outside town started a butcher shop, using a horse-drawn wagon to deliver the meat.

The wagon had a small step on the back. The kids would wait for the wagon at the edge of town and hitch a ride on the step—until the driver got to his first stop and chased them off.

The step was big enough for only one person, so the first kid on the scene

**SKINNY BUT STRONG.** Shown here the summer he worked on a butcher's wagon, W. Ray Skiles helped his family survive.

*"I ran around to the front before the driver could chase me..."*

was the one who got to ride. I was always too late. One day, I decided to walk farther out of town so I could be first. It worked.

As soon as the driver made his first stop and before he could chase me, I ran around to the front of the wagon and offered to deliver his package and bring back the customer's payment and the next day's order. He liked this arrange-

ment and let me ride up front with him until he finished his route around noon.

### Paid in Pork

Then the driver gave me several pounds of the meat that he hadn't been able to sell. My mom was more than pleased to add it to her stew pot. My appetite picked right up once I heard Mom singing again.

When the other kids caught on to what I was doing, they tried to cut me off at the pass. But after dealing out a few bloody noses, I had the "job" all to myself.

I rode the meat wagon for 6 days a week the entire summer and never tired of it. I enjoyed riding around town and getting to know all the customers. I glowed from the praise I received for my contributions to Mom's stew pot.

But my greatest pleasure was in knowing I'd been able to help out in my family's time of need. ◙

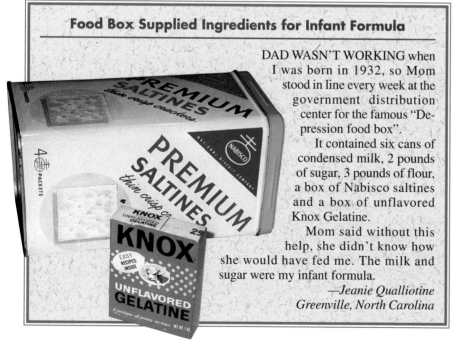

## Food Box Supplied Ingredients for Infant Formula

DAD WASN'T WORKING when I was born in 1932, so Mom stood in line every week at the government distribution center for the famous "Depression food box".

It contained six cans of condensed milk, 2 pounds of sugar, 3 pounds of flour, a box of Nabisco saltines and a box of unflavored Knox Gelatine.

Mom said without this help, she didn't know how she would have fed me. The milk and sugar were my infant formula.

—*Jeanie Qualliotine*
*Greenville, North Carolina*

### Egg Money Bought Week's "Groceries"

I REMEMBER well the day Mother sent my twin brother and me to town with the wagon and horses to buy our week's groceries. We took along 3 dozen eggs to pay for our purchases.

Our grocery list consisted of a box of matches, a gallon of kerosene and—if we had any money left—sugar. The eggs brought 5¢ a dozen. We spent a nickel for matches, a dime for kerosene and did without sugar that week.

—*Averill Hudnall*
*Imperial, Nebraska*

### "Applenapper" Learned Lesson the Hard Way

LIFE IN THE 1930s was a true learning experience, and I will always remember those days fondly. It was a time when families and neighbors pulled together, and everybody shared.

Our Aunt Edna and Uncle Add came over on Saturdays and brought their small radio. Then we'd all listen to the *Grand Ole Opry* after dinner—which consisted of cornmeal mush and a cinnamon roll. And you only got the roll if you ate all your mush!

It really wasn't so bad—some people had less. But I often think of the hurt my parents suffered trying to feed five hungry children.

One day I went to the store with Mother. We got our usual nickel loaf of bread, a nickel jar of relish and a nickel's worth of pinto beans. While Mother and the clerk were tending to business, I was able to sneak a big, shiny red apple into my coat pocket.

About half a block from the store, I took the apple out and said to Mother, "Look what I got!" She grabbed me by the ear, dragged me back to the store and made me confess to the manager and apologize.

I thought the manager would forgive me and say I could keep the apple. Instead, he lectured me about what would happen if he called the police.

I stood about a quarter inch tall that day, but I eventually loved Mother more for teaching me that lesson. Times were hard, and everybody did the best they could. Stealing was not an option.

—*Raymond Tallent, Macon, Georgia*

### Precious Eggs Saved for Recipes and Trading

MY MOTHER became an expert at "making do". Eggs from our henhouse were reserved for trading at the grocery store for items like sugar and coffee, or for using in recipes. We seldom had eggs for breakfast unless we had company.

We raised most of our food and adjusted our taste buds to fit the fare of the season. Sometimes Mom would fry side meat, or fatback, then sprinkle flour over the grease, add a little water and milk and make a nice bowl of "rabbit gravy".

We usually had a pitcher of homemade molasses on hand and biscuits made from scratch. My brother and I liked to mix the rabbit gravy with molasses and sop it up with our biscuits.

After topping that off with several glasses of fresh milk, we were ready for anything the day had to offer.

—*Gene Sellers*
*Mt. Croghan, South Carolina*

---

## Cabbage and Dressing Made a Delectable Meal

WHEN WE couldn't have chicken and dressing, Mama made cabbage and dressing—and it was so good!

She cut a head of cabbage in half and cooked it in water with salt, pepper and butter until tender. She made sage dressing from leftover biscuits and corn bread, then served it with the cabbage on top.

—*Minnie Flaherty*
*Magnolia, Arkansas*

**CABBAGE-FED CUTIES.** Fannie and Minnie Flaherty smiled for the camera in the '30s.

**WELFARE WAS NOT AN OPTION.** Evelyn Robinson's parents were determined not to go "on the dole" when her dad lost his job.

## They Saw Humor in Monotonous Meal, Thanks to Dad

IN A TIME when most people were just trying to survive, our dad's wonderful sense of humor got us through.

When Dad was laid off, Mom found work, but the meager pay left little money for food. Dad was determined not to go on welfare, and Mom agreed. He did all the cooking. Once we had potatoes three days in a row.

While setting the table, I put out a bowl for the potatoes, but Dad told me to put out two more. I excitedly told my brother, "We're going to have more than potatoes tonight. Dad told me to put out three bowls!" We could hardly wait for Mom to get home so we could eat.

But when we sat down, each bowl was filled with potatoes. Dad passed one around, saying, "Have some roast beef." Then he passed another, saying, "Try some of these delicious string beans. Would you like some corn? Oh, yes...and do have some potatoes."

We all got to laughing and joined in the game, passing bowls back and forth, pretending each one held a different food.

—*Evelyn Robinson*
*South Bend, Indiana*

# Soup Kitchen Incident Taught Him Valuable Lesson

*By Charles Martin, Bartlesville, Oklahoma*

IN THE EARLY 1930s, when I was about 10 and living in Des Moines, Iowa, a friend asked me to accompany him on an errand. This turned out to be a trip to the soup kitchen about 2 miles away.

My friend gave his name to the attendant and handed her an empty 1-gallon lard pail. The pail was filled with hot vegetable soup, and my friend was given a loaf of day-old bread.

I asked the attendant who was eligible for such wonderful donations. My family might, the attendant said, if we met certain qualifications. I thought we would, even though my father was working and we weren't yet desperate.

I filled out an application, the attendant approved it and I was given a gallon pail of that spicy-smelling soup and a loaf of bread.

I arrived home smiling and excited as I handed Mother this great treasure. I thought it was a thoughtful gesture on my part. How wrong I was!

Mother told me to sit down and began to explain how much this would embarrass my father. He wouldn't admit we needed a handout from anyone. Furthermore, he'd be fu-

**EAGER HELPER.** Charles Martin (shown at left in 1931) was only trying to be a good son.

rious his name was now listed on government welfare records.

Mother realized I was just trying to help but said I was never to do such a thing again.

My father wouldn't be home for hours. The wait seemed endless and I worried about the consequences of my actions. The razor strop that hung from a nail near the kitchen door had been used more than once.

### They Shared a Secret

But when my father got home, there was no mention of what I had done. When Mother called us in to supper, there was a steaming bowl of vegetable soup and a slice of bread at each plate. We talked about the events of the day, then enjoyed our meal without further comment.

When Mother looked across the table at me with a faint smile, I knew the soup kitchen incident would be our secret for many years to come.

I'd learned my lesson about using my father's name without his knowledge. And I learned that anticipating punishment can be much worse than the real thing. ▨

# 'Relief Box' Held Promise For Kids in Chicago

*By Leonard Peterson, Holiday, Florida*

TO HUNGRY CHILDREN in the early years of the Depression, the monthly box of relief food was a cornucopia of delights. In winter, we'd press our noses against the frosted windows, watching intently for the familiar truck to pull up in front of our apartment building on Chicago's north side.

We'd eagerly unpack the square carton, filled with generic packages with unpretentious white labels. Then we'd stack the assorted cans, bags, jars and boxes on the kitchen table.

Among other things, the box held lima beans, prunes, raisins, flour, powdered milk and oatmeal. Also included were several oblong cans of Argentine roast beef, for which Mother had concocted a dozen different recipes.

The local joke was that the plenitude of this canned meat had a lot to do with the superabundance of wild horses on the Argentine pampas. We paid no attention…we were thankful to have it.

Our favorite items were the peanut butter and sugar, which my sister Ruth turned into the most succulent fudge imaginable. We kids gorged ourselves on it.

## Survival Certificate

Besides the box, we received a green sheet of paper that looked like a diploma. This sheet entitled us to buy exactly $20 in groceries per month.

With careful spending, Mother made this last until the third week of the month. We'd just tighten our belts a notch or two for the final week.

Dad's monthly WPA salary of $55 was used mostly for rent and utility bills. Occasionally there was enough left over to squander on some lard and potatoes, and Mother would make us a rare treat—French fries.

To supplement our meager food supply, we sometimes hiked from our home near Wrigley Field all the way to Erie Street, only a few blocks north of the Loop. For a spindly legged boy of 9, this was like walking the Great Wall of China, but Dad explained that walking one way saved 7¢ in carfare.

After standing in line to receive free bags of onions and potatoes, we'd ride home on a swaying Clark Street trolley, much to the relief of my aching feet and legs.

Oatmeal, farina and Cream of Wheat were our breakfast staples. But what we really enjoyed was the leftovers. Mother would let the cereal harden overnight, then slice it and drop it into a sizzling frying pan for a golden-crusted, mouthwatering treat. ▨

## Leftovers Went into Savory Potato Dumplings

MY MOTHER was a very frugal cook and could make a dinner out of leftovers if necessary. One entree I really liked was potato dumplings made from leftover mashed potatoes, a couple of eggs, baking powder and flour.

Mother spooned the boiled dumplings into a bowl with hot water in the bottom, and topped them with sauteed onions. I can still taste them.

In the morning, Mother would bake big loaves of bread. Just as she was taking them out of the oven, Dad would bring in fresh green onions from his garden. Our lunch would be hot bread with butter and sliced green onions. What a treat! —*Margaret Kloepfel, Canton, Ohio*

**MOM MADE DO.** Times might have been tough, but Margaret Kloepfel's mother (shown at far left with a plate of homemade rolls and at left on a picnic with Margaret and her dad) knew how to serve delicious meals using simple ingredients.

*LINE 'EM UP. Madonna Christensen (third from the right) posed with her siblings outside their home in Ashton, Iowa.*

# Christmas Food Box Brought Joy To Struggling Family

*By Madonna Christensen*
*Sarasota, Florida*

LIKE MANY families during the Depression, ours had little money. At Christmastime, we received a food box from our town's Community Chest. My parents didn't like accepting charity, but they put those feelings aside so our large family could enjoy a traditional holiday dinner.

On Christmas Eve, we kids would pace the floor all afternoon, asking Ma, "When will the box come?"

"It'll come when it comes," she'd answer.

We'd stand at the window and worry aloud: "They're usually here by this time. The roads are icy. Maybe they won't make it this year."

Ma would come to the window and peer into the growing darkness. She smelled good, like the sage stuffing she'd made and stored in the unheated washroom that served as an extra icebox. "They'll be here soon," she'd say.

In time, the delivery vehicle would lumber around the corner, its chains rattling and squeaking on the packed snow. Our neighbor the grocer would come inside and visit with Ma for a moment. Then she'd thank him and they'd wish each other a Merry Christmas as he left to continue his rounds.

We kids would gather around the table to watch Ma unpack the box. There was a fresh turkey, a pound of butter (a glorious treat for oleomargarine users), dinner rolls, whipping cream, coffee, pimiento-stuffed olives, jellied cranberry sauce, yams, a clump of celery that smelled like spring, plus cans of mincemeat and pumpkin for pies.

"That's everything," Ma would say as she whisked the box away. We knew that wasn't everything. Hidden in the bottom of the box were goodies for our Christmas stockings—assorted nuts, hard candies and sweet oranges. Fresh fruit during an Iowa winter was almost as miraculous as St. Nick himself.

Memories of that time, when a simple box of groceries was an exciting gift, are still important to me—especially at Christmas. I focus on them

## Kids Could Hardly Wait For Mama's Squirrel Stew

MY PARENTS were tenant farmers in southwestern Kentucky. We didn't have a big variety of food in winter, but we never went hungry.

In summer, when it was too wet to work in the fields, Papa went to the woods to hunt squirrels.

Sometimes Mama cooked the squirrel in a big kettle on her wood-burning range with an assortment of fresh garden vegetables—onions, tomatoes, potatoes, okra, beans, corn and anything else that was in season.

Long before the meal was ready, wonderful aromas would drift from the kitchen. We could hardly wait to eat. Squirrel stew, a big pan of corn bread, sliced ripe tomatoes and cold buttermilk made a wonderful meal.

Mama made her own hominy, too. As it simmered for hours, the fragrance was mouth-watering. Before it was fully cooked, we children would be eating it out of the kettle—and so would Mama.

A few years ago, I followed her recipe and made hominy on my modern stove. The aroma was so wonderful I could almost feel Mama's presence. —*Faye Edmunds*
*Hopkinsville, Kentucky*

*NATURE PROVIDED. Faye Edmunds (at right below with her family) doesn't recall eating a lot of store-bought food.*

when I weary of today's emphasis on expensive gifts.

In my parents' name, I donate to the Sharing Christmas program in the little community that once nurtured me and my family. I do it for the children who might be waiting at the window, wondering when Santa will come.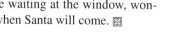

## Salt Pork and Smoked Jowl Were Family's Only Meat

WE HAD very little meat—just a little salt pork or smoked jowl. Salt pork was side meat from a fat hog, preserved with coarse white salt.

Salt pork was too salty to fry, so Mom would cut thick slices and soak them in water overnight. The next morning, she'd dry off the meat, roll it in flour, sprinkle it with pepper and fry it. She served it with biscuits and gravy made with water or Milnot.

We "buttered" our biscuits with oleo, a white substance that came in 1-pound packages with a capsule of yellow coloring to mix in. I don't know if the capsule changed the taste, but it made the oleo *look* more like butter.

—Ruth Lindsey, Jerseyville, Illinois

## Paid in Food, He Earned Enough to Share with Neighbors

MY FATHER was a millwright at the Buick Motor Co. in Flint, Michigan when the Depression came. He was working only 1 or 2 days a week but was lucky to do that.

The farmers ran help-wanted ads in the Flint newspaper and paid their workers in produce. Dad was glad for the opportunity. He worked from daylight until dark and brought home the Model T loaded with produce. "Look, Ma," he'd say with pride. "You couldn't buy all that for $5."

Our next-door neighbors were on welfare, and we always

*FROM LIZZIE TO THE LARDER. Otto Jebavy's dad (driving above) worked on the farm and then was paid in pork and produce.*

shared this bounty with them.

Once in a while, Dad would bring home half a pig. There were no freezers, so we'd be up half the night canning the meat. Not one speck went to waste.

I wouldn't want to go through that again, but it was a million-dollar experience. —Otto Jebavy, Ludington, Michigan

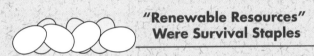

## "Renewable Resources" Were Survival Staples

NOBODY ATE high on the hog during the Depression. We ate lots of mush. Man, was that good fried and covered with syrup. Oatmeal was a big item, too. Add some homemade scrapple and eggs, and that was living.

If my family hadn't had chickens and eggs, we wouldn't have made it.

—Nelson Tash
*Egg Harbor Township, New Jersey*

## She Was "Cracklin' Good" At Rendering Bacon Rinds

OUR NEIGHBOR was a meat cutter. Whenever a customer had him cut the rind off an order of bacon, he asked permission to bring it home to share with us.

I rolled up the rinds, stood them in a deep pan and put them in the oven to render. When they were done, we had bacon grease for cooking as well as cracklin's to eat. The grease made very good gravy.

Sugar was scarce, so we used light syrup to sweeten everything. It was okay for pies, but I never had any luck using it for cakes.

—Georgie McDaniel
*Charleston, West Virginia*

*FSCC SPELLED "RELIEF". One of the programs instituted by the Roosevelt Administration was the Federal Surplus Commodities Corporation. Its purpose was to buy up items like those shown above and distribute them to needy families all over the country. Previously, the food was destroyed by farmers to maintain high price levels.*

## Quail and Hotcakes Made a Meal to Remember

MY SISTERS, mother and I ate hotcakes morning, noon and night. Mother flavored them differently for each meal. First she used grated orange peel, then vanilla. Finally the exotic aroma of cinnamon—my favorite—would waft through the house. We grew tired of hotcakes but were thankful for what we had.

One afternoon our neighbor knocked on the door. He'd shot a covey of quail in his backyard and made a deal with Mother. If she'd clean them, he'd share. That night we ate quail—with big cinnamon hotcakes on top.

*—Donna Shepherd, Anderson, California*

**HOUSE OF PANCAKES.** Donna Shepherd (at left with the curl) is shown with her mother and sisters.

## One-Bowl Meal Was One of Her Favorites

ON OUR Iowa farm, one of Mother's easy, economical suppers was a meal in a bowl. She'd toast and butter a thick slice of homemade bread, top it with one or two poached eggs, then pour warm milk over the top.

There were no limits on seconds. I still like this dish.

*—Betty Gillespie, Hillsdale, Illinois*

**FIZZ BIZ.** Mary Ann Kunselman (seated) enjoyed her mom's "pop".

## Vim and Vinegar Were a Fizzy Summer Treat

WE RARELY had soda pop to drink, but sometimes in summer Mother would let us make vinegar pop. We'd pump fresh cold water and add vinegar and sugar to each glass, mixing it well. Then we'd add a little baking soda and get ready to gulp it down while it fizzed.

We'd shut our eyes and feel all those tiny bubbles hitting our faces as we drank. That was half the fun. It tasted better that way, too—when it stopped fizzing, it was a little flat. But it was always a special treat.

*—Mary Ann Kunselman, Longmont, Colorado*

## "Pennies from Heaven" Was Depression-Era Favorite

"PENNIES FROM HEAVEN" was a very popular main dish and simple to make. We heated home-canned tomatoes until thickened, added a little sugar, butter and milk, then sliced wieners into the pot. This was served over a big pile of mashed potatoes. It was a good, tasty dish.

I still make it sometimes, and almost everyone enjoys it.

*—Maxine Kaufman, Salem, Ohio*

## Rabbits Helped Dust Bowl Families Survive Winter

WE LIVED through the Dust Bowl years in Nebraska, and we were hungry a lot. We got through one winter by eating meat from a rabbit hunt. Some of the hunters' families weren't as bad off as ours, but they participated to help their neighbors.

The neighbors gathered with their shotguns, decided how many miles to cover, then divided into teams and went to their starting points. As the men walked toward the center of the hunting area, the rabbits would jump up and run ahead of them.

Eventually, the men had hundreds of rabbits surrounded. When the shooting was over, the rabbits were counted and divided among those who needed them.

In our house, the rabbits were cleaned and salted down in a 20-gallon crock. It was the only meat we had that winter. Mom fried them until she ran out of lard, and then she baked them.

Along with the grapefruit juice, split beans and oatmeal we occasionally got at the courthouse, those rabbits enabled us to survive.

*—Arlene Nelson Norfolk, Virginia*

Rabbit Season

## Egg-Gathering Pup Took Task One Step Too Far

IN 1931, when I was 6, my Uncle Ray visited a chicken farm where the owner's dog was trained to help him gather eggs.

Uncle Ray watched, fascinated, as the smooth-haired Eskimo spitz picked up each egg in her mouth and gently placed it in a basket. The dog's 7-month-old puppy was also trained to gather eggs.

Uncle Ray talked the owner into giving him the pup and brought it home as a gift for me. The puppy was so well-behaved that I named her "Lady".

Those were lean years, and Uncle Ray and Aunt Estelle had moved in with us. We were all hungry for something to eat besides beans and potatoes. One day Mom told Aunt Estelle that if she only had an egg, she could make a one-egg cake and top it with cornstarch pudding.

Not long after, by an odd coincidence, she heard a noise at the screen door. There stood Lady, with an egg in her mouth! Lady wagged her tail and laid the egg at Mom's feet. Mom happily patted Lady and went off to bake her cake.

When it was done, Mom put it on a stool on the porch to cool while she made the pudding. But when she went outside to get the cake, she started screaming.

I ran to see what was wrong. There stood Lady on the porch with a mouth full of cake!

Mom started chasing the dog with

a broom, but Aunt Estelle couldn't stop laughing. "Let her go, Marge," she chuckled. "After all, she did furnish the egg."

Soon Mom was laughing, too, and pushed the rest of the cake toward Lady, telling her, "You may as well finish it." Our dessert that night was pudding, but Lady took the cake. —*W. Ray Skiles*
*Weirton, West Virginia*

## "Naked" Chicken Escaped Dog...and Dinner

MY PARENTS kept a vegetable garden and a few chickens at my grandmother's home 45 miles away. We tended the garden on weekends and canned the produce as soon as we got home. Sometimes we'd bring home a chicken, which we kept in a crate in the basement until it became Sunday dinner.

One day while we were out, our Boston bulldog managed to get into the basement and release the chicken. When we came home, there were feathers all over the house—and in the dog's mouth. We found the chicken, "naked" and humiliated, sitting on top of the upright piano.

Mother felt the poor chicken had suffered enough and returned it to the farm on our next trip.

Our Sunday dinner turned out to be meat loaf, as I recall. —*Kitty Marsett*
*Lebanon Church, Virginia*

**BOY'S BEST FRIEND.** While W. Ray Skiles and his puppy enjoyed each other's company as much as the boy and dog at left, Ray's dog had also been taught an unusual skill.

## Mother Turned to Surgery To Save Prized Egg-Layer

MOTHER'S 25 to 30 chickens kept us supplied with lots of fresh eggs during the lean Depression years. Dad built a small chicken house for them to roost in at night, but during the day, they roamed all over the yard and the nearby fields.

Mother had a speckled hen that was a particularly prolific layer. One day, Mother noticed this hen's craw had swollen to the size of a baseball. She was determined not to lose that good egg-layer—so she decided to operate!

While I held the hen's wings and legs, Mother delicately opened the craw with a knife. She found it was packed with tiny pebbles and slivers of glass.

Mother carefully removed the glass, sewed the chicken up with needle and thread, then dressed the wound with iodine. For the next few days, she kept the hen in a straw-filled cardboard box behind the stove.

When the hen recovered, she went right back to laying eggs and never had any other problems. —*Joseph Galinis*
*North Royalton, Ohio*

**THE IODINE TREATMENT.** Joseph Galinis (leaving for school with his brother at top left) assisted his mother (with Joseph's father in inset) with a "delicate operation" on a hen.

# Students Awaited Rare Treat with Hungry Eyes

*By Rosemary Lynch-Kirsch*
*Pahrump, Nevada*

IT WAS a warm Indian summer day in October 1936, and I was tempted to play hooky. It would probably be one of the last beautiful autumn days that year in Minnesota. But I resisted the urge and trudged up the stairs to my third-grade classroom. The last bell rang just as I slid into my seat.

Mrs. Arne took roll call and read some announcements, then stood up with an air of mystery. With hands held

> "Was anyone even breathing?"

tightly together, she paused and looked around the room to be sure she had everyone's attention.

"Children," she announced, "the apple growers in the state of Washington have large crops this year and want to share their apples with the children of America. The apples will be handed out

before lunch. You are to clasp your hands on your desks, not touching them, until each child has one."

What a morning! It was impossible to concentrate. We fidgeted in our seats, stealing glances at each other. My classmates' eyes looked different that day— wide with hunger and anticipation. Most of us were lucky enough to eat regularly, but fruit of any kind was rare. The most we could hope for was an orange or banana on our birthdays.

At last, the door opened and a man came in with a bushel basket of this precious cargo. How quiet it was as he passed out the apples. Was anyone even breathing?

Hands clasped, I looked around the room, trying not to stare at my apple. Everyone was waiting, waiting for that first bite, and watching with hungry eyes.

Finally the last apple was handed out. "Children," Mrs. Arne said, "you may eat your apples now." For a few seconds, we all felt timid. None of us wanted to lose our pride by appearing hungry.

Then I heard the delicious sound of everyone munching apples. At that, Mrs. Arne turned away from us. Her head and shoulders dropped as she sobbed in silence.

---

## Fishing Put Food On the Table

WE WERE LUCKY to live on Long Island, with access to the local creeks and bays. There was no pollution then, and the waterfront was not as popular. Anyone who was ambitious could find plenty of clams, eels, mussels, scallops and crabs.

Digging for clams was an all-day job if you had the right equipment, but few of us had anything fancy. We had to wait for the tide to go out, when the sandbars were bare. Almost all our fishing was done by hand or with nets.

We caught eels mostly at night, using spears. It was hard work, but fulfilling if you liked eels. Fishing wasn't a pastime for us—it was food on the table.

On Sundays, we'd drive to farms on the island to stock up on vegetables. With plenty of food from the farms and the bay, we didn't need much money. We worked hard, but we enjoyed life, too.

—Mabel Zelenka
*Griffin, Georgia*

**INDUSTRIOUS ISLANDER.** Mabel Zelenka (at left) and fellow Long Islanders harvested clams, eels, mussels and more from creeks and bays. Many of her neighbors lived in beachfront cottages like the one above.

# Cherry-Picking Thieves Got Their Just Desserts

*By Clinton Griffith, Fallowfield Township, Pennsylvania*

THE AVERAGE DIET during the Depression offered little variety. When dinner was announced with "Come and get it", you knew what "it" was …beans. Pie, cake and ice cream just didn't exist.

One late-summer day in 1932, my friend Bill told me about a fabulous cherry tree he'd seen in Farmer Renald's backyard. It was just loaded with big cherries.

Opportunity only knocks once. We immediately started planning how to get some of those cherries.

I asked Minnie, a good lady who'd come to help us after my mom died, if she knew how to make a cherry pie. "You get the cherries," she said, "and I'll bake you a pie."

We needed a bag for the cherries, and I knew where to find one. Minnie had a bag over her pillow that served no purpose

---

*"I didn't even plan to eat it—
I was just going to look at it…"*

◈

---

I could see, so we borrowed it. With a lace from one of Dad's shoes (to tie the bag shut), we were ready to pick cherries.

Bill and I walked 2 miles to the hollow that led to the Renalds' backyard. And there was the cherry tree. What a beautiful sight! It was loaded with cherries the size of walnuts.

There was just one problem. Farmer Renald was sitting on the back porch in his rocking chair, puffing his pipe and staring right at the tree. Bill and I withdrew to the hollow to discuss the situation.

We hadn't seen a gun on the porch, and the farmer looked pretty old, so we figured we could outrun him. We'd just keep

our eyes on him. If he stopped rocking, we'd head for the hollow. I approached the tree first. As soon as I reached the trunk, I checked the farmer. Still rocking. Bill came next, and up the tree we went. The farmer kept right on rocking.

There I was, a skinny little boy sitting in the top of a cherry tree, eating juicy, delicious cherries under a beautiful summer sky. It was as close as a barefoot boy would ever get to Heaven. Bill and I filled the bag, and the farmer kept rocking.

### Never Left His Rocker

We laughed all the way home about stealing the farmer's cherries while he just sat on his porch. "I'll bet he's still rocking," Bill chortled.

When I got home, I set the bag on the kitchen table in front of Minnie. She let out a squeal. "If that's the pillow slip off my bed, I'll skin you alive!" she said. She calmed down when she opened the bag and saw all those luscious cherries.

Minnie told me to go do my paper route, and she'd have the pies cooling when I got back. A cherry pie all my own! I didn't even plan to eat it—at least not right away. I was just going to *look* at it, and then eat it only when my willpower weakened.

When I returned, I ran into the kitchen. Minnie was sitting at the table. "Where are the cherry pies?" I shouted.

"No pies," Minnie said.

I grabbed my chest. I actually felt faint. "What do you mean, no pies?" I demanded.

"That's what I said—no pies," Minnie said. "Every one of those cherries had a big fat worm in it."

No wonder that farmer didn't try to stop us. Now I know why George Washington chopped down his dad's cherry tree. ▨

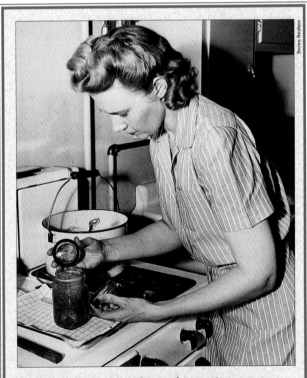

**SURVIVAL IN A JAR.** When refrigeration was not an option for most folks, the ability to can food for use later in the year was a crucial skill.

# CHAPTER EIGHT

# All the Okies Weren't from Muskogee

*CALIFORNIA AND/OR BUST.* When farms (and opportunities) dried up, families like this one packed up and headed west in a desperate search for work. (Photo: American Stock Photos)

# From the desk of Clancy Strock

Dear Katie,

Bad as the Depression was, it was only a piece of the misery suffered by North Americans during the '30s.

The country also suffered the cruelest stretch of rotten weather anyone could remember. The summers were the hottest and driest in history, and the winters were the coldest and snowiest. Many of those records still stand today.

It didn't rain for so long that many people thought the middle of the U.S. had become a desert. The worst-hit areas—especially Oklahoma and Kansas—were soon known as the "Dust Bowl". Wells dried up. Crops couldn't grow. Windstorms simply picked up the top layers of soil and blew them away.

To top things off, the farming areas also were ravaged by huge swarms of grasshoppers and other ravenous bugs.

Eventually the people who had settled those areas had to get out, leaving behind the farms they had worked so hard to establish. But it was either find a better place to live, or stay there and starve to death.

California sounded like the new Promised Land. So the desperate families loaded their few belongings onto a rattletrap old car or farm truck and headed west. Or they jumped a freight train, as you read in Chapter 3.

Since so many of the hardest hit came from Oklahoma, these migrant families soon were called "Okies". There was only one major highway leading to California, and the Okies became a river of misery. They had no food, little clothing and rarely any money. They were eager to work, but there was no work to be found.

The towns on their route hardly rolled out the welcome mat. They already had more than they could handle just trying to feed and clothe their own people. These ragged nomads from the Midwest were a new and unwelcome burden.

Katie, I must confess that despite all I've read through the years about the plight of the Okies, these next stories told by people who actually made the migration west stunned me. They are remarkable stories of bravery and suffering that will stay with you for a long, long time.

*Your Grandpa Clancy*

# Battered Trophy Symbolizes Oklahoma Family's Struggles

*By Walter Combs, Tahlequah, Oklahoma*

TWO-TIME OKIES. Walter Combs and his family (Walter's the "towhead" in the middle of his brothers at left) made the Oklahoma-to-California trip twice. And that deer head at left spent plenty of time on Route 66, too.

MY PARENTS were farmers in Cherokee County, Oklahoma. Although we weren't in the so-called Dust Bowl, times were very hard with eight children (seven boys and one girl) to feed.

When Dad sold the farm in 1929, we joined the other travelers on their way to California and settled in Tulare County. In 1931, my grandfather died in Oklahoma, so we returned. On the way home, while we were camped under a Joshua tree, a stray dog came to our camp. After we fed him, "Old Polo" became part of the family.

Things were rough after our return. Our horses died, apparently from eating poison ivy. At one point Dad was working for $1 a day, cleaning Bermuda grass out of a yard to make a garden. He was thankful for that wage—but imagine trying to feed eight children on it.

### Back West Once Again

June 1935 found us headed back to California, crammed into a 1929 Chevy sedan that towed a trailer full of household and canned goods. Old Polo and I rode on the running board all the way.

"Old Billy" was part of the family, too, so he went with us. Billy was a five-point buck my grandfather had bagged in Montana in 1924. After having the head mounted, Grandpa had given it to us.

Somewhere along the road, the trailer tongue broke and Old Billy went scooting down Route 66 on his chin!

Back in California, I joined the CCC, served 5 years in the Army and married an "Okie" gal. Years later, when we retired and returned to Oklahoma, it took a moving van, a pickup, a car, a dune buggy, a motor home and the help of our three sons to move all our stuff...including, of course, Old Billy. ▨

---

## Riverbank Squatters Sold Footstools Door-to-Door

NO MATTER WHERE they came from, people who migrated to California during the Depression were called "Okies". A lot of Oklahomans did make their way west, but many came from other states as well. Some stayed in Oklahoma until they earned enough money to move on.

At Watonga, Oklahoma, where I was raised, many travelers camped along the North Canadian River. There was a stand of willows along the bank, and some travelers used tree branches and ingenuity to create items to sell.

They built footstools from wooden apple boxes salvaged from a merchant's trash pile, with willow branches for legs. The fabric tops were stuffed with "lost cotton" that had fallen from the cotton wagons. Families walked the dirt and gravel roads in search of this cotton, then took it back to camp and cleaned it as best they could.

When a family had several stools, they brought them to town and sold them door-to-door. The asking price was 50¢, but they'd sell them for less if a buyer didn't have the money. Some were traded for food.

Those were lean years, and a lot of people did things they didn't like in order to survive. Hunger made thousands swallow their pride and ask for help.
—*William Woolman, Shell Knob, Missouri*

Brown Brothers

**WHERE TO NEXT?** Dust Bowl refugees were photographed in Bakersfield, California. These desperate people had nowhere to go for shelter. It was a time when destitute families wandered the land.

# Trip West on 'Bloody 66' Was Filled with Hazards

*By Lois Curnutt, Odessa, Texas*

IN THE MID-'30s, hard times forced my family to move from Pittsburg, Kansas to a farm outside town. Payments would be made to the bank after harvest.

We skinned by the first year. The second year was so dry we didn't even harvest enough to pay our seed bill, and the hard times got a lot harder. We decided to move to Bakersfield, California, where Daddy would look for work in the oil fields.

To my sister and me—and Daddy's 16-year-old brother, who would go with us—it was big adventure. We had no idea how worried our parents were.

It must have been especially frightening to Mama, 7 months pregnant at the time. But they seemed hopeful and excited about joining the thousands who'd already migrated to the "land of milk and honey".

Daddy built a sturdy stock rack for our old pickup and covered that with a tarpaulin. We hung tubs, pans, canvas chairs, cooking utensils and spare tires from the stock rack, piled our possessions on the truck bed and laid two mattresses on top. My sister and I traveled atop the mattresses, waving at those behind us.

Everyone seemed bound for California—most in dilapidated vehicles, many on foot—and Route 66 was the only way to get there. That narrow two-lane road was teeming with multitudes who'd lost everything.

At midday, we'd pull onto the shoulder to cook a meal on the camp stove, walk a bit and let the truck cool down. When we pulled over for the night, we were joined by other travelers in little camps. The women shared stories and chores while the men discussed jobs, cars and road conditions.

## Hymns Were Comforting

Some carried instruments and played for impromptu church meetings, which were a comfort. Owls coasted overhead and coyotes yipped in the distance as hymns like *Rock of Ages* and *Amazing Grace* drifted through the night air.

At that time, about 800 miles of Route 66 were paved. The remaining 1,648 miles were graded dirt or gravel, asphalt-covered bricks or wooden planks. The unexpected dips, curves and hills caused so many violent collisions that the road was nicknamed "Bloody 66".

Just outside Groom, Texas, the load shifted on our truck and a rear tire nearly caught fire. Daddy fixed it, drove into Groom and asked the storekeeper if we could auction some home-canned food to lighten our load.

The next morning, we found local folks were lined up waiting to buy our dewberries and our kidney beans.

The mountains were a stunning sight, but crossing them was perilous. The road through Oatman, Arizona was terrifying. There were horrible gooseneck curves, and the road fell away at the edge of the highway to endless ravines.

Some drivers froze in fear and tried to back their cars to safety. Charred remains of loaded pickups were visible in the brush.

It was here that our truck lost its low gear and then the foot brakes. We feared we'd plummet to our deaths, but somehow Daddy managed to stop safely.

## It Was an Uphill Climb

The truck often overheated on the upgrades, forcing us to stop for an hour or so. Many times, we simply made that our stop for the night. If we didn't pamper the truck, we weren't going to get to California.

Next we had to cross enormous spans of blistering desert. Water became scarce and expensive—up to 15¢ a gallon. Gas cost more, too, and drivers had no choice but to fill up before attempting to cross the open desert.

We arrived in Bakersfield at last, out of money and food. Mama and Daddy began searching for jobs. Daddy found temporary work in the oil fields, and Mama was hired as a hospital aide. We rented a tiny one-room cabin with a single bed. My sister, uncle and I slept on pallets.

Eventually, Daddy saved enough to buy a 24-foot plywood trailer, and he got a good job in the building trades. After 2 years, we'd saved enough to pay off the mortgage on the farm and return to Kansas.

Going west in search of a new life was extremely risky. But the folks who made this journey were hardy. They'd learned long ago to live on very little, and they were determined to survive. ⊠

**HAD TO HIT THE ROAD. Lois Curnutt's family posed outside a Kansas farmhouse in better times. That's Lois kneeling in front, second from the right. She and her relatives somehow survived the obstacle course that was Route 66 in those days.**

# Veteran's Bonus Provided Hope for New Life in Oregon

*By Norma Hucka, Eugene, Oregon*

DROUGHT and low crop prices forced my parents to give up their South Dakota farm early in the Depression. We moved to a small town and Dad took whatever jobs he could find, often riding the rails to get to work.

Our situation improved when he was hired by a lumber mill, although we had to buy all our groceries at the company store. The mill closed in 1936, leaving us with little hope or money.

Then the "bonus army" demonstrators marched on Washington, demanding payments for World War I veterans. Dad received a bonus for his service in France. It was small, but it offered a way out.

My folks and their friends talked often about the great opportunities out west. Oregon was the "land of milk and honey"—if only one could get there. With Dad's bonus and careful planning, now we could. We had no other options, and moving offered a ray of hope.

### Slept Beneath Stars

We bought a used car and two-wheeled trailer, and the six of us set out in July of 1936. We slept outdoors most nights, and Mom cooked over open fires. I thought it was fun, though I recall problems, too—flat tires…poor campsites…a broken trailer hitch.

When we reached the Oregon border, we were so happy we had a little cele-bration. We had no idea what lay ahead! Finding work proved difficult, and the bonus money was running low. I can still see the disappointment on Dad's face as he returned to the car after being turned down for yet another job.

Mom and Dad took whatever work they could find, and we children picked beans and other crops. We lived in a former chicken coop once, and we often stayed in run-down rental houses that came with short-term jobs.

In 1940, Dad found a job as a night watchman. Then came a job in a plywood plant, and we moved to better housing in town. With World War II looming, the economy picked up.

It took courage for my parents to move us from the hopelessness of South Dakota to a better life in Oregon. Thanks to them, we never really suffered or went hungry. Maybe our experiences made us stronger and built character; they certainly didn't hurt us.

The "hard times" are among my best childhood memories. ⊠

**MOM AND DAD TOOK THE LEAP.** Norma Hucka's parents are shown at upper left in about 1920, some 16 years before the local mill closed and the family left South Dakota and set out for the "land of milk and honey". Unlike the "Okies" who rode in this wagon, they traveled in a car and trailer.

## Cramped Trip West Left Her With Fear of Tight Spaces

WHEN I WAS 3, my parents, grandmother and I left the Dust Bowl of Tulsa, Oklahoma behind and set out for California. Dad, Mom and Grandma were scrunched in the front seat of our two-door car. I was placed in the cramped backseat, on top of all our belongings.

When we crossed the mountains, I became frightened. As the trip progressed, I cried quite a bit. After telling me a number of times to quit crying, Dad lost his patience, stopped the car and gave me my first spanking. To this day, I have a phobia about mountains and enclosed places and try never to sit in the backseat of a two-door car.

**BACKSEAT BAWLER.** As a child, Charlene Rodriguez (with her family above) found riding on top of a bunch of luggage didn't suit her at all.

In later years, I was told something about the trip that I didn't remember. My great-grandfather rode all the way on the running board, leaning back into the space that held the spare tire. We must have been quite a sight.

—*Charlene Rodriguez, Palm Desert, California*

**THE "FLUFF TWINS".** Working in the California hops fields was a necessity for Clay Matthews' family. That's Clay and his sister in front.

## At Harvesttime, These Youngsters Hopped to It

IN 1933, our family lived in San Francisco. I don't know what the rent was, but our upstairs flat was home to nine people—my mom, stepdad, younger sister, grandpa, two aunts and their husbands and me.

One day we all packed up the family car, a 1931 Chrysler sedan, and drove to Watsonville to pick fruit. We shared two one-room cabins and worked throughout the season.

What I remember most is working the hops fields. After a half day of school, my sister and I had to fill two baskets with hops before we could play with the other kids. I was 8 at the time and she was 6.

One extra-hot day, I talked my sister into "fluffing up" the hops, which are very light, instead of pushing them down into the basket as we were supposed to do. When we called our mom over to show her we'd finished, she just said, "You were awful fast today." Then she sent us off to play.

Months later, she told us, "I know what you did—don't think you got away with anything!" —*Clay Matthews, Rio Linda, California*

## Tough Times Led Texas Family to Colorado

IT WAS getting hard to make ends meet in Guymon, Oklahoma in 1932. Dad put a tarp on the back of our old Model T truck and moved our family of seven to Brownsville, Texas. We arrived on my ninth birthday.

None of us kids went to school that fall. We spent the winter camped on the outskirts of town. Daddy worked for some of the farmers in the area, and people who ran a packing shed nearby gave us culled cabbages and other produce.

In spring of 1933, we returned to Texas to live with my grandfather. But the dirt was rolling, so we didn't tarry long. It was time to move on again.

We were fishing between Gunnison and Montrose, Colorado when some fellow travelers told Daddy the peach harvest was about to start near Palisade. Daddy got a job in an orchard there, and Mom canned 50 gallons of peaches over an open fire. They sure made good eating that winter.

Our family remained in that area until the war began. All five children were in the service during World War II. —*Arlene Standafer, Bronston, Kentucky*

**FOLLOWED DAD AS HE LOOKED FOR WORK.** Arlene Standafer (in the inset photo and above, playing in a stream with her brother) traveled with her family from Oklahoma to Texas to Colorado. Wherever they stayed, Arlene's mother (above right) was the "camp cook".

## Gold Mine Became Their Campground

I WAS ABOUT 7 when my dad lost a good job at Lockheed in southern California. We "downsized" from a lovely home first to a small apartment—and then to tents.

My grandfather owned an unproductive gold mine in the Trinity Mountains, and government regulations demanded annual assessment work there. So we loaded up a jalopy and headed for Trinity. The dirt road out of Weaverville was almost impassable—we had to move huge rocks out of the road just to get through.

We left that road to follow a rutted wagon trail 1 mile to Union Creek, where we camped. Our campsite turned out to be a watering hole. We saw deer as well as an occasional bear, and we had to watch out for rattlesnakes.

One night my sister and I heard something poking around our tent flap. When she turned on our flashlight, the golden eyes of a mountain lion were

staring at us! We were scared stiff, but the lion just turned and walked to the creek for a drink.

Our diet consisted mostly of red beans. Mother started a pot every morning on a man-made tin stove, then left for the mine with Father and Grandfather. Sis and I were to keep the fire going, but sometimes we forgot. On those days, we had "bony" beans for dinner.

Bread was bannock, made with self-rising flour, salt and water, then fried on top of the stove. Our dessert was a few raisins and peanuts Mother kept in a mason jar. We also found wild hazelnuts and chokecherries, which were delicious.

Other families camped in the area, too, and none of us ever found enough gold to live on. But poor as we all were, we learned more about caring, sharing and being good neighbors than we've experienced since.

—*Marjorie Thompson West Sacramento, California*

# Family Left Dust Bowl Behind in Search of A Better Life

*By Ruth Sparks, Bellevue, Washington*

MY PARENTS homesteaded a dryland farm in Baca County, Colorado, near the Kansas border in the 1920s. By the early '30s, times grew hard. The drought and the Depression went hand in hand.

We'd wake to a nice sunny day, only to have the dust blot out the sun by afternoon. We had to stay inside to be able to breathe. The farmers hadn't had a crop in years and were forced to dispose of their livestock because there was nothing to feed them.

In spring of 1934, when I was 15, Dad told us that if we lost our crops again, we'd have to move. There was no way to make a living for a family of seven.

He replanted twice that year. Finally we got a little rain, and Dad planted a third time. This crop grew to 6 feet…and then a hailstorm beat it to the ground. In July, we had no choice but to leave and find work. The land would be returned to the government to pay back taxes.

### Make Room for Soap!

My brother, whose wife was expecting a baby, would drive our 1929 International truck, which Dad rigged with a canopy for sleeping quarters. Dad and Mother, who was expecting her sixth child, would take our 1930 Chrysler car.

As we packed the truck, Mother insisted we make room for a small wooden barrel of homemade soap. "There may not be money to buy soap," she said, "but we must be clean."

The saddest moment came when Dad took his team and wagon to his parents' house a mile away. My brothers, sisters and I rode in the wagon, with the neighbor kids and our old dog walking

**WELL-SCRUBBED GROUP.** Ruth Sparks' mother, with Ruth at left, insisted on cleanliness. Below is the farmhouse the family found and "cleaned up" so they could live in it.

**STEINBECK HAD IT RIGHT.** John Steinbeck's *Grapes of Wrath* chronicled the lives of farmers fleeing the Dust Bowl. This scene is from the movie made about it.

alongside. We were all in tears.

We left early the next morning. I can still see my grandmother standing in the yard, waving good-bye and wiping tears from her eyes.

Our destination was a community in Idaho that had sent literature to many Dust Bowl farmers. As we traveled, we worked in fruit orchards, camped along the road and cooked over fires. We met other families doing the same thing. It was like a scene from *The Grapes of Wrath*.

When we reached our destination, we were disappointed —it wasn't a suitable place to settle. We set out for Sacramento, California, where my mother's sister lived.

But while picking apples in Washington, we found a deserted farmhouse on 80 rocky acres in the Kittitas Valley. We could live there with an option to buy.

### A Home at Last

On October 3, we set up camp in the yard and began cleaning the house to make it livable.

The house had no windows, and cattle had been running through it, so we made good use of Mother's lye soap. We papered the walls with newspaper, and Dad bought a second-hand cookstove and wood heater on credit. After lots of work, we moved in.

Dad traded the Chrysler for two cows, which supplied us with milk and butter. We built a herd through the local dairymen's association, using half of each milk check to make the payments. Then Dad found a job with the WPA, and my siblings and I started school.

When my brother and nephew were born that winter, there was no money for a hospital, so both were delivered at home. I remember the nurse saying, "These people may not have money, but they sure are clean!"

I look back now and marvel at the fact that Mother and Dad never complained about their life. Through all the hard times, they always assured us that with a strong faith in God, the love of our family and all of us working together, everything would turn out fine.

And they were right—the Good Lord blessed us. All six of us children have done well, and my parents grew prosperous and lived the rest of their lives in the Kittitas Valley.

# Widowed Mom and 11 Children Worked The Fields to Survive

*By Jean Taylor, Corvallis, Oregon*

MY FAMILY made a good living on our southeast-Colorado farm until the drought struck. Then everything changed completely. In 1930, when I was 7, my widowed mother moved her 11 children to northern New Mexico and homesteaded a square mile of land.

We planted potatoes and pinto beans, but it was so dry we only got a few back, and the potatoes were no bigger than marbles.

Finally we had no choice but to join the migration west. We left with a small trailer packed with one bed, a few clothes and very little else.

We found work picking cotton near Phoenix, Arizona, and all 12 of us lived for several days on a loaf of store-bought bread. We were that close to starving. When we received government-issued graham flour, rice and beans, we were so grateful.

A day's work in the cotton fields paid no more than a dollar, and often less. We had to walk two blocks to fill a bucket with cold water, and there were only two outdoor privies for more than 100 workers. But we slept in tents, which seemed like Heaven to me.

When the cotton ran out, we moved to California's Salton Sea Valley to pick peas. We slept on the ground for several days, until the government provided 9-by 12-foot tents. We were very glad to get one.

Our next stop was Brentwood, where we picked more peas. Then we moved on to Lodi to pick cherries. That was the first fruit we'd eaten in years.

From California, we traveled about 600 miles north to The Dalles, Oregon, where the cherry trees grew on steep hillsides. We had to climb 40-foot ladders to work, and gale-force winds almost knocked us down.

## Bean and Potato Diet

Winter was coming, so we rented a tiny cold-water shack with one and a half rooms, a small stove and an outdoor privy. My brother was the only one who could find work—cleaning a chicken house twice a week, for $2 a day. But he could keep any eggs he found in the litter, and we loved those. Otherwise our diet was mostly beans and potatoes.

That fall, I started high school. Only one other person in my family had gotten that far.

Traveling in search of work became a way of life. We worked the crops in summer and rented a tiny cabin every winter.

After the war began, my brother found work running a bulldozer. He was drafted soon afterward, and we lived on the $40 a month the Army sent to Mama.

Our mother died in April 1943, but somehow we managed to keep body and soul together. I finished high school, received a scholarship to college and became a teacher. I was the first in my family to get a college education. ⊠

**CHERRY HARVEST SAVED THEM. If it weren't for the opportunity to pick crops like peas and cherries, Jean Taylor and her family might have starved.**

*H. Armstrong Roberts*

---

## Dad Turned Truck into "RV" for Journey West

WHEN TIMES GOT BAD at my father's Iowa pharmacy, he started driving a truck in Missouri. By 1929, my mother was tired of living in poverty and told Dad she was taking us four children to San Francisco, where our three oldest siblings had already moved. Fortunately, Dad said he'd go, too.

Dad sold the pharmacy and built a house on the truck bed for our trip. Our makeshift "recreational vehicle" had white shingle siding, a pitched roof and a stove. We kids, in our bib overalls and cardboard-lined shoes, were crammed inside like sardines.

We must have been quite a sight in that beat-up truck loaded down with water bags, tubs and mattresses, but that wasn't unusual. We saw many others heading west, driving—and living in—whatever kind of vehicle they could find. Some even drove makeshift covered wagons drawn by horses.

*Brown Brothers*

**HOME ON WHEELS. Trucks like this were turned into year-round campers by men like L.N. Buckmaster's father.**

When we arrived in San Francisco in the fall of 1929, we were amazed by all the sights on Market Street—the tall buildings...the four lanes of streetcar tracks...the 12-foot-high clocks. I'm very thankful my mother put her foot down and insisted that we move.

—*L.N. Buckmaster, Woodland, California*

# CHAPTER NINE

# Now *That* Was Entertainment

**BIG THRILLS IN THE BIG TOP.** The circus was a low-cost form of entertainment enjoyed by many during the Depression. Saturday matinees and radio programs also remain memorable. (Photo: SuperStock)

# From the desk of Clancy Strock

Dear Katie,

This chapter is going to test your imagination quite a bit, because it's about a world you've never experienced. It's about a time when there was no television--which many of your friends often watch 5 or 6 hours a day.

It's about a world with no computer games of the sort your brother finds so endlessly enchanting. And there was no Internet to prowl either.

In fact, it was a world in which very few people even had tele- phones!

That's what the Depression years were like, Katie. I expect it sounds awfully dull, but we really did have a lot of good times.

To begin with, movies were only 10¢--or sometimes just a nickel. And if it was Saturday, kids really got a lot for their money. There was always an animated cartoon...usually a cowboy movie...and also a scary movie of some sort that ended with the hero or heroine in horrible danger, which meant you had to go back the next week and see how they escaped.

So you got at least 4 hours of entertainment in a theater packed with kids. For several months, our local movie house had a super- deluxe red bicycle on the stage, softly lit by a little spotlight.

The bicycle was to be awarded to some lucky kid in a drawing, but they never said exactly when the drawing would be held. You had to go every Saturday so you didn't risk missing out when the big day finally arrived.

As far as toys go, if you had three or four, you were really lucky. But no matter, you got good at inventing and making your own.

My sister and I were lucky, because we grew up on a farm where there were endless places to play hide-and-seek and all sorts of scraps of lumber and old junk we could turn into toys. We got to exercise our imagination every day.

As you'll read on these next pages, both kids and grown-ups, poor as they were, have good memories of the fun they had together in those days.

*Your Grandpa Clancy*

# Ladies Card Party Trumped Her Distaste for Pinochle

*By Ruth Polchek, King of Prussia, Pennsylvania*

THERE weren't many diversions on summer afternoons in the 1930s. Few people could afford cars, and there was no such thing as a paid vacation.

But people found ways to enjoy themselves. For lots of the older women in our predominantly German neighborhood in Philadelphia, playing pinochle was a good way to spend a warm afternoon.

Mother was usually too busy to join a game. So every few weeks, our nice neighbor Mrs. Kraus would ask Mother to send me over to make a fourth at a game with her friends.

I never wanted to go. I was only 12 or 13, and the other players were in their 50s and 60s. But my kindhearted mother would coax me into it, saying, "It won't hurt you to help them out."

After lunch, I'd put on a clean sundress and reluctantly walk up the hot street to Mrs. Kraus' dim house. She and her friends would be seated in the cool breakfast room, at a round oak table with curved legs and carved feet.

## Uniform of the Day

All three would be wearing dark print "afternoon" dresses with crochet-edged white collars and good white summer oxfords. Two of the ladies had permanently waved white hair covered with hair nets. The more fashionable one wore her hair in a stylish marcel.

Each place at the table had a glass of grape juice or ginger ale. The ladies had large water glasses, but a small juice glass was considered sufficient for me. There was also a pink glass bowl of thin pretzels for us to share.

But these were lean years, and the treats were just that. I had strict instructions never to ask for a second drink and to limit myself to two or three pretzels, since "Mrs. Kraus has to make them last all afternoon".

The ladies were all smiling when I arrived, their eyes friendly behind thick, steel-rimmed glasses. They asked politely about my mother and grandmother.

But they were sharp card players who took their game seriously. I wasn't. None of them really wanted me for a partner, so they "drew", and the loser was forced to play with me.

For the first hour, things weren't too bad, and the ladies laughed and talked in English. But after that I grew tired of playing, forgetting to count tricks or the number of trumps played, and we'd begin to lose.

Then my partner would stop laughing and start muttering in German—although the gist of her remarks was understandable in any language.

At the end of the afternoon, I'd go home, telling Mother and myself nothing could make me go back. But we both knew in a few weeks, the whole scene would be repeated.

After I left, the ladies would relax, eat a late-afternoon snack of assorted wursts, pumpernickel and Mrs. Kraus' delicious German potato salad. And my partner would start smiling again. ☒

RELUCTANT PARTNER. Ruth Polchek (right) played cards in her mother's place (her mom is on the left below). Ruth's grandma (on left below right) and a friend are wearing typical dresses of the day.

**DOUGH TO GO.** Unlike the folks in the story below, these men standing in a New York City breadline didn't get to see a movie with their bread.

Brown Brothers

# 'Bread-Wrapper Movies' Got Money Flowing...for a Night

*By Robert Cloyd, Lafayette, Indiana*

PEOPLE DIDN'T LOSE their sense of humor during the Depression's early years, though it was sorely tested. One old story involved two housewives discussing hard times. "Well, it's this Depression," one said. "It came at such a bad time, when everyone was out of work."

A man discussing his unprecedented streak of bad luck was nearly elevated to hero status when he quipped, "If it was raining soup, I'd be standing with a fork in my hand."

When the last of some 25 to 30 deep-shaft coal mines closed near our town, the place became a virtual "temple of doom". The big mines had employed thousands and generated most of the area's income.

The next 2 years deteriorated into a nightmare. Simple survival was a continuing challenge. There was no work, no poor relief (the township itself was broke) and no such thing as food stamps.

Banks closed, businesses failed and haircuts dropped to 15¢ with no takers. Clothiers advertised going-out-of-business sales but couldn't sell enough merchandise at any price to close up, so they remained open.

Where the money disappeared to was a complete mystery. Anyone who had a dollar in his pocket in 1932 or '33 was wealthy. Some weeks went by when families, including

ours, never had a cent in the house. The fact that bacon was 10¢ a pound, potatoes 15¢ a peck and sugar a quarter for 6 pounds didn't mean a thing.

One enterprising gentleman came up with what he thought was a surefire idea to generate some business—reopening the ornate Capitol Theater. His plan involved a bakery.

On selected days, theater admission would be free with a used wrapper from a designated brand of bakery bread, and the two businesses would split the proceeds. It wouldn't be much, but it was better than the nothing they had coming in at the moment.

The first of the bread-wrapper movies was a huge success. The theater was packed, and the movie manager and baker congratulated each other for making a few dollars.

The second time around was a disaster. Nobody had any money for another 10¢ loaf of bread. Kids besieged the bakery in droves, pleading for wrappers. The bakery workers didn't have the heart to refuse those ragged, entertainment-hungry kids, but they admonished everyone to "wrinkle 'em up real good so they'll look used".

The second bread-wrapper night didn't even bring in enough to pay the theater's light bill. After that, the Capitol Theater closed forever. 🔲

# Giveaways Added Excitement To Small-Town Theater

*By Joseph Galinis, North Royalton, Ohio*

THE MAIN SOURCE of entertainment in our small coal-mining town of Hastings, Pennsylvania was the grand Hollywood Theater. Movies played every night of the week.

Wednesday night was "Bank Night", with a double feature. After the first movie, the houselights came up and the manager chose a child from the audience to come onstage and draw a ticket from a wire cage. The person holding the matching ticket number won a sum of money.

On two occasions, I was the little boy chosen to draw the winning ticket. Both times, the winner gave me a 50¢ piece. To me, that was a lot of money!

Another night was designated "Dish Night", with a set of dishes going to the holder of the winning ticket. But I didn't care about any old dishes.

Friday was "Western Night", featuring cowboy stars like Hoot Gibson, Ken Maynard, Buck Jones, Tom Mix, William "Hopalong Cassidy" Boyd, Gary Cooper and John Wayne. There was always a long line of people waiting to buy a ticket on Friday night.

## Cowboys to Classics

My favorites were John Wayne and Gary Cooper. They had a rugged screen presence the other cowboys lacked. For other movies, I liked Clark Gable, Spencer Tracy and Wallace Beery. I also enjoyed seeing Charlton Heston and Victor Mature in the Biblical classics produced by Cecil B. DeMille.

Although Hollywood had many great actresses, my favorite was Bette Davis. None of those pretty girls could play tough roles the way she did.

I also liked Maureen O'Hara, Jean Arthur, Jennifer Jones, Claudette Colbert, Lana Turner, Marjorie Main and Thelma Ritter. And everyone loved Shirley Temple. Her movies filled our theater to capacity.

Tickets for kids 12 and under were 10¢ each, but the Sunday matinee was only a nickel. At those matinees, the manager and his assistants gave a candy bar and comic book to each child. We sure enjoyed those treats.

We kids spent an awful lot of dimes and nickels at the Hollywood, and it brought much joy into our lives. Sadly, television spelled its demise. I'm glad I was able to enjoy it in its glory days. ▨

**TO THE RESCUE. Tom Mix** was one of the biggest cowboy heroes of the day. A former Texas Ranger and rodeo cowboy, Mix did all his own stunts. Some say he "invented" the action Western.

## A "30-Bottle Day" Would Pay His Way

EVERY Saturday morning, I cruised the alleys of Columbus, Ohio, searching for trash cans that featured milk bottles. These could be refunded for half a cent per bottle. If I could find 20, I could go to the movies.

The bottles were dirty, and no store would take them unwashed, so I'd fill a galvanized tub on the back porch, twist a rag around a stick for a bottle brush and scrub away.

On a really good day, I might scare up 30 bottles. The extra nickel bought a *huge* bag of popcorn. I was in heaven on a 30-bottle day.

Of course, I could've asked my parents for 15¢, and on rare occasions I might have even gotten it. But it was more fun to go it on my own and say "I've got the money" when I asked for permission to go to the show.

Luckily I didn't know I was poor. Otherwise I wouldn't have enjoyed it half as much.
—*Glenn Williams*
*Colorado Springs, Colorado*

### Rare Outing to Movies Delighted Sisters

WE NEVER HAD extra money during the Depression. Whatever we had was set aside to buy food. One time the relief office gave us food, blankets and jackets, and my sister and I refused to wear the jackets. We thought everyone would where they came from.

We were too young to realize everyone was in the same boat.

I don't know where Dad found the money, but one day he took us to the Shirley Temple movie *Bright Eyes*, which features the song *On the Good Ship Lollipop*. I've never forgotten what a joy it was to be able to see a movie during those troubled times.
—*Ruth Hunter, Brisbane, California*

### Theater's Promotion Spelled Success

THE SMALL THEATER in my hometown changed movies three times a week. The manager offered free tickets to any students who scored 100% in spelling for 6 weeks.

Of course, we became pretty good spellers. I didn't have to pay to go to a movie for most of my grade-school years.

Later, when I worked as a secretary for an attorney, he said he never had to worry about my spelling or even check it. —*Dlores DeWitt Colorado Springs, Colorado*

**GOAT POWER.** Doris Tietz (getting a ride with her brother) tells below how her grandma almost got an unexpected ride.

### After Movie, Grandma Was Ready to Ride

FEW PEOPLE had cash in the 1930s, so goods and services were often traded. In exchange for renting a truck from my father's shop once a month, a movie theater in Oakland, California let our family go to the movies for free.

Grandma loved movies, so she saw every one that was shown. Dad would drop her off at the theater, then pick her up at a designated location when the movie was over.

One time Dad got caught on the phone and was late leaving to pick up Grandma. In the meantime, Grandma found an empty car in the agreed-upon spot and climbed in the backseat to wait.

A few minutes later, two young men approached their car and saw an unfamiliar old lady sitting in back. When they looked at Grandma, she just smiled and gave a friendly wave. They were so confused that they walked behind the car to check the license plate! Luckily, Dad drove up and resolved the problem. —*Doris Tietz, Redding, California*

### Young Moviegoers Saw Many "Instant Replays"

MY CHILDHOOD TRIPS to the movies were few and far between. About the only theaters I could afford to visit were the two in our neighborhood on the east end of Youngstown, Ohio.

We got the chance to visit a top-of-the-line movie house once a year, when The Palace admitted children free if they donated a can of food for the needy. The Palace had wonder-

ful stage shows, and the lines extended for blocks as people waited to see Horace Heidt and his Musical Knights, Cab Calloway or the Andrews Sisters.

We loved the serials about Rin-Tin-Tin and cowboy films featuring Tom Mix, Buck Jones and Ken Maynard. Many times we got our dime's worth by sitting through the same movie two or even three times. One of my all-time favorites was James Cagney in *G-Men*.

As the Depression wound down, we could even afford after-movie treats like sundaes, milk shakes and floats at downtown teenage hangouts. Then we could drop a coin in a jukebox selector at our table to hear Glenn Miller's *Moonlight Cocktail* or *Sunrise Serenade*.

It was a much simpler life then, and we enjoyed the simple pleasures. —*Michael Lacivita, Youngstown, Ohio*

### Money for Movie Tickets Was in the Bag

IN THE LATE 1930s, we lived on 5 acres just outside the Chicago city limits (that's me in the photo). We had food, but no money. In those days, if you thought you had a quarter in the house, you didn't stop looking until you found it or were dead sure it wasn't there.

Going to the movies was a treat, and I had two small children who wanted to go. We didn't have any money, but we had plenty of chickens. With the help of my son, we caught three.

I placed the chickens in a shopping bag and went to catch the bus. My plan was to take the birds to a poultry house and sell them.

When I got off the bus downtown, it was raining and the bag got torn up. A complete stranger offered to hold my chickens while I went around the corner to the Piggly Wiggly and bought a paper grocery bag for a nickel.

I stuffed the chickens in the new bag, carried them to the poultry house and sold them. I don't remember how much I received for the chickens, but it was enough to take my children to the movies.

—*Dorthia Turnbo*
*San Diego, California*

# Movie Adventure Was Ours for Mere Pennies

*By Leonard Peterson, Holiday, Florida*

IN THE 1930s, a few pennies clutched in a grubby hand were enough to open wide the gate to romance and adventure.

For one modest nickel, the Buckingham Theater on Chicago's Clark Street treated us to the irresistible combination of two feature films, a cartoon, one episode of a 12-part serial and a tiny but adequate Baby Ruth or Butterfinger.

One film would be a Western with Tom Mix, Bob Steele, Ken Maynard or Hoot Gibson riding a spangled horse and sporting pearl-handled six-guns. The girl was always pretty and, much to our relief, usually allergic to kissing. The other film was often a detective story.

The serial was our bread and butter, the magnet that drew us back week after week. Our favorites were *The Phantom Empire* with Gene Autry and *Flash Gordon* with Buster Crabbe. Both kept us on the edge of our seats.

On the rare occasions when I went to an evening movie with an older sibling, it was *Dracula*, *Frankenstein* or *Werewolf of London*. I'd usually be under the seat, trembling and asking whether the spooky part was over and it was safe to come up.

I loved the Vic on Sheffield Avenue, where every night was Bank Night and some lucky ticket holder went home about $80 richer.

My older brother won once and came home with a wallet stuffed with greenbacks. He stacked them one by one on the kitchen table while we younger ones watched in envy. We ate a little better than usual that week.

The Vic was the movie palace most vulnerable to sneaking in. When the first show ended, I'd wait near one of the side doors. As the adults came pouring out, I'd work myself against the outward tide and gradually move up the stairs to the balcony. I'd grab a seat in a dark corner, my heart pounding as I waited for the long arm of the law to grab me. Amazingly, it never did.

In that balcony, I lived and breathed marvelous adventures—*Things to Come*, *San Francisco*, *Captain Blood*, *Les Miserables*, *It Happened One Night*, *The Good Earth*, *Lost Horizon*, *The Prisoner of Zenda*. These epics made a real impact on a boy's imagination.

The Julian on Belmont Avenue was a favorite haunt for us kids, because if you didn't have a nickel, two pennies would suffice. And you always got your money's worth.

## Western Had Him Hooked

One afternoon I got hooked on a Western with an odd twist at the end. I simply had to see the ending again—and again and again.

Late that evening, during the last show of the night, my older brother came storming down the aisle with the usher, who speared me with an accusing beam from his flashlight. My brother inquired solicitously about my sanity, then marched me home to face the court-martial.

During one Sunday matinee around Easter, the Julian was giving away bunnies. Lo and behold, my sister Ruth's ticket number was called. Squealing with delight, she ran up to the stage to claim her prize. From the back row, I grumbled that she had all the luck…then I stood up in shock when they called my number next.

We kept the rabbits in a makeshift hutch for 2 weeks. But the price of rabbit food became prohibitive. One evening there they were, pretty as you please, served with hot gravy on the dinner table. The rest of the family was pleased, but Ruth and I ate nothing that evening—or the next. ⊠

## For Family Outing, Every Penny Counted

WHEN I WAS about 10, my entertainment was taking the bus to downtown Winston-Salem, North Carolina with my parents to go to the movies.

One day Mother and I planned to meet Daddy downtown but couldn't find enough money for bus fare, which was 7¢ per person. We searched all through the house and finally came up with 13¢. We needed one penny more.

Mother looked down the hot-air register and saw a penny sitting on a tiny ledge. She stuck a piece of chewing gum on the end of a thin cane, reached down into the register and retrieved the penny.

Whenever I see a penny on the street, I always pick it up and say, "Thank you. This is bus fare."

—*Carolyn McDonald, Alexandria, Virginia*

## They Pooled Pennies to Keep Multicolored Vehicle on the Move

MY HUSBAND and his friends had great fun in 1936 with a disreputable excuse for a car, a battered 1927 Chevrolet. John doesn't remember who owned it, but everyone pitched in to keep it running.

There was no money for a decent paint job, so the boys brought a multitude of colors from home and created a one-of-a-kind vehicle. They cut lawns, bagged groceries and shoveled driveways to keep the car gassed up.

These teens were students at the Baltimore Polytechnic Institute for Boys, so they named their treasure the "Poly-lop". Only one boy had a driver's license, so he was always assured a seat. The rest had to draw lots, as the car only held three in front and three in back.

This may sound like tame entertainment today, when many teenagers have their own wheels, but during the dismal years of the Depression, ingenuity took the place of money. You can just imagine the fun to be had mixing the exuberance of youth with one crazy-looking automobile.

—Ina Valentine, Massapequa, New York

**NOT YOUR BASIC CHEVY.** Those are definitely not the original factory colors on this beat-up old 1927 car. The vehicle did attract attention, though.

## "Low-Tech" Toys and Games Kept Them Busy

OUR FAVORITE swimming hole was on the site of a former coal mine. The water was always a beautiful green. Although the banks were steep and the water deepened quickly, this was where I dog-paddled and learned to swim. A few experts would dive off the higher cliffs.

We played basketball, softball, football, ice hockey and games like green light-red light, kick-the-can and run sheep run.

We made our own kites, slid down steep hills on cardboard boxes and crafted homemade toboggans out of sheets of metal.

At the creek, we made our own boats and played hide-and-seek among the bridge girders. Roller skates got a good workout on the town sidewalks and later were used to make orange-crate scooters.

I often wonder if today's youngsters would be content with what we had. I think about how lucky they are, with all the high-tech, battery-operated toys available. Or are they?

I wouldn't trade the great memories of those Depression days for anything.

—Paul Schmidt
Mt. Bethel, Pennsylvania

**GIRL NEXT DOOR.** Paul Schmidt posed in 1932 with a Bridgeville, Pennsylvania neighbor.

## Boredom Was Simply Not an Option

AS CHILDREN, we never ran out of things to do. We made dolls out of socks or scraps of worn-out clothing. We packed a lunch and hiked for miles. We cut paper dolls from newspapers and colored them with crayons.

We played dominoes, checkers, cards and jacks. We jumped rope, had races and invented tag games. Almost everyone had a tire swing. There were neighborhood picnics. We set old bedsprings on crates and used them for trampolines. We roller-skated in summer and flooded garden plots for ice-skating in winter.

People didn't complain much back then. There were too many in the same boat, and no one expected the government to pick up the slack. —Hazel Kemp, Forestville, California

## Depression "Flowered" With a Lump of Coal

I WONDER how many readers remember making those pretty "Depression flowers". Just mix a lump or two of coal, 2 tablespoons of laundry bluing, 2 tablespoons of salt, mercurochrome and food coloring if you like.

The mixture becomes very colorful, spreads out and takes many forms. It's fun to watch its progress, and if the "flowers" dry out, all you have to do is add a little water.

—Ruth Hartman, Cincinnati, Ohio

### Fiddling Grandfather Created Center for Village Social Life

MY GRANDFATHER, E.R. Calkins, owned a woodworking and basket-making shop that was the center of social activity for the village of Steiner, Michigan in the 1930s.

At first, Grandfather's 11 children and their families gathered at the shop every Saturday night. Grandpa, an accomplished fiddler, provided the entertainment. One of my earliest memories is of dancing with my cousins as he played tunes like *Turkey in the Straw*.

Soon these gatherings grew to include the entire village. Every weekend, the shop was filled with farm families eager for music and dancing. The Depression had made their lives hard, and this small diversion quickly became the highlight of their week.

In its heyday, the shop hosted square dances, wedding receptions and political rallies. One of the most memorable visitors was Henry Ford, who stopped by during a trip to nearby Monroe, where he was buying a gristmill for his museum. He spent the whole afternoon chatting and even took a turn on my Grandpa's fiddle.

Today, Steiner is all but gone. The only remaining business is the old sawmill and basket factory. Two of my uncles own and operate it now, although it's more of a hobby than a business.

Whenever I drive by the old shop, it never seems like it's been 60 years since my last dance. It seems more like yesterday, and I walk away whistling *Turkey in the Straw*.

—*Clyde Mainzinger, Southgate, Michigan*

**SATURDAY NIGHTS WERE SPECIAL.** The building shown above (photographed most recently in 1979) once rang with music and laughter, courtesy of E.R. Calkins (below right and with his wife below). Photo at left shows the Calkins family long before the couple's 11 children grew up and attended dances at the shop.

# Radio Gadgets Fell Far Short Of Their Billing

*By Edward Braun, Danville, Indiana*

WHEN DAD BOUGHT our first radio in 1932, I couldn't wait to get home from school and tune in Chandu the Magician. It takes a special kind of fan to believe in tricks performed over a radio, and I was a faithful believer.

One day Chandu offered a magic disappearing black ball in a secret container for only two box tops and 25¢. I just had to have one.

I saved my pennies and Wheaties box tops, and Mom mailed them off to Chandu. I watched the mailbox like a barn owl waiting for a mouse. Finally it arrived. The minute I tore open the package, I realized I'd been swindled.

Inside the package was a cheap plastic "urn" with a liftable top. Lift the top and it exposed what looked like half a ball. Replace the top, then lift it again (this time reaching a bit farther down the urn and picking up the false bottom of the lid). No "ball" was there to be seen!

Chandu lost a loyal listener that day.

### Mars Preferable to Earth

I turned my radio devotion to Flash Gordon and his ongoing fight with Ming, emperor of the evil empire on Mars. Flash Gordon never had a more faithful listener. I fought by his side every afternoon. Together we foiled every plot the evil Ming could conjure. Then Flash offered a genuine simulated disintegrating ray gun. It cost only 25¢ and two box tops.

I squirreled away every penny I could. I had to have a genuine simulated disintegrating ray gun. At long last, I could mail my order. I hounded the mailman, and after 3 weeks,

**FLASH IN THE PAN?** One of Flash Gordon's most loyal listeners, Edward Braun was disappointed by the "disintegrating" ray gun he sent for.

my ray gun arrived. It was a piece of colored cardboard with a picture of a ray gun on it. The gun folded to conceal a flap of paper, which snapped when you waved the gun. But the big rocks I aimed at were still there. Flash lost a loyal listener, too.

My next hero was Og, Son of Fire. Every afternoon I'd hurry home to plop down on the floor in front of the radio and tune it to Cincinnati's WLW, waiting anxiously for Og to wake in his cave and begin looking for burning embers from forest fires.

### The Wizardry of Og

Thanks to radio's sound-effects men, you didn't just listen to a story like Og's, you lived it. I walked with him every day in a desperate quest through dense primeval forests. We heard terrible growls from grizzly bears and saber-toothed tigers.

Eventually Og discovered how to start a fire by rubbing two sticks together. After that, he could build a fire with a piece of flint, which he carried in a pouch around his neck. When he got hungry, Og would kill a small animal with a spear, start a fire with the flint and cook supper.

I was also hooked on *The Pirates*, which aired right after Og. I thought I'd learned my lesson with the box tops-and-quarter scams, but Captain Jack had a secret cryptographic decoder that I really needed to decipher the secret messages at the end of every program. I decided to try again.

This time I wasn't disappointed. The decoder was a pretty card with the alphabet in a circular pattern and a circle of numbers that rotated inside the alphabet. It was probably worth about a nickel.

The decoder worked just fine until a contest came up to unscramble a super-secret message. One clue was given every Friday afternoon for 9 weeks, and the winner would get a new bicycle. Naturally, my decoder wouldn't do the job. But I could buy one that would…for two box tops and 25¢.

The show's sponsor probably received 20,000 quarters from kids trying to win a $20 bike…and one of those quarters, of course, was mine. ⊠

---

## Radio Entertained Farm Clan—But Only on Weekends

ENTERTAINMENT on our farm came from a radio powered with A and B batteries—while they lasted. During the week, the radio was turned on only for weather reports. On Saturday nights, we listened to *Barn Dance* on Chicago's WLS and also the *Grand Ole Opry*.

We played Chinese checkers and rummy. We also read a lot of books (and did our homework) by the light of kerosene lamps.

In winter, we took turns with the neighbors hosting card parties. Our parents played until the wee hours while we kids played games like Monopoly.

—*John Zimmerman, Nampa, Idaho*

# They Were the 'Dance 'Til You Drop' Entertainment

*By Wally Aldrich, Grove City, Florida*

IN SPRING of 1934, my friend Joey Adams and I were just out of high school and "in between jobs". We hitchhiked from Waukegan, Illinois to Bloomington. We were hoping to participate in a walkathon being held at the Coliseum.

Joey and I were outside in the lobby when I spotted a girl standing about 10 feet away. Not having a partner yet, I walked over, introduced myself and asked if she'd enter with me.

Her name was Ann Williams, she lived in Bloomington and was looking for a partner, too. She called home to let her parents know what she was doing.

As it turned out, she was with me almost 'til the end of the contest (Joey never did find a partner and left for home the next day).

In the beginning, we were allowed 2 hours of sleep every 24 hours. But as the weeks went by, nap times were reduced. In the last week, sleep was only allowed on your partner's shoulder.

## No Resting in Rest Room

Bathroom breaks were allowed on request and by permission of the judges, but the times were closely monitored. We had shower breaks every day, along with four meal breaks (which also got shorter every week).

Most participants entertained the audience by singing or performing skits. One song that I remember singing was *Little Dutch Boy and Girl*. At night, a five-piece dance band played while the couples danced and walked. During the day, recorded music played hits from the era.

During the middle of the walkathon, Red Skelton showed up to be master of ceremonies for about a week. He really livened things up.

We also had fun when local merchants performed a comedy routine as a spoof on the walkathon (see the large photo below). And two dancers were even married during the contest (small photo).

## They Lasted 600 Hours

The entire walkathon ended after 700-plus hours. Each day was progressively harder as the rules grew more strict and times for eating, showering and bathroom breaks became shorter.

After 600-plus hours (about 25 days), Ann and I were too exhausted to continue (the contest would go on for another 4 days). But even after all those hundreds of hours, it was a hard decision to quit.

After agreeing we couldn't go any further, we still waited a day before actually telling the judges we'd be unable to continue. Both of us left the dance floor in tears that day and, although we never saw each other again, we didn't go unrewarded for our efforts.

The first prize of $500 was out of reach, but because we managed to finish fifth out of 33 couples, we were each awarded $100—a considerable sum of money in those days. ⌧

**GAVE 'EM THE BUSINESS.** Local merchants spoofed the walkathon participants (above), including Wally Aldrich, at far right next to the boy in the striped shirt. In wedding photo, he's second from right.

# Circus Suffered Hard Times, Too

*By Dorothy Lambert, Barboursville, West Virginia*

MOST of us can remember the first time we went to the circus, but I can remember when the circus came to *me*. It was during the Depression, when we were living on the outskirts of West Hamlin, a small town on the banks of the Guyandotte River in West Virginia.

There was a gravel road near our home with a high bank nearby. That's where my brother and I spent most of our time, playing and watching the few cars that did go by.

One morning as I looked up the road, I saw a large gray shape moving slowly toward me. Although I'd never seen an elephant in person, I was an avid reader and had seen pictures of them in books.

I got so excited that I ran home as fast as I could and shouted, "There's an elephant coming down the road!"

Well, of course, my busy mother and older sisters didn't believe me. "You're making that up—you read too many books," they said.

### Beast Was Moving Closer

So back I ran to my post. By this time, the great, slow-moving beast was much closer. Now I could see it wasn't alone. There were men walking on either side of it.

Then came a camel, a giraffe and beautiful show horses pulling the wheeled cages of lions, tigers and monkeys. There were also people walking, carrying bundles and children.

When they saw these two big-eyed kids watching them, they'd smile and wave—some of the clowns even did a few capers right there in the gravel road. What a sight for two country kids!

We learned later that the circus (a small one) had fallen on hard times while performing in Logan, about 60

**HORSE-DRAWN WAGONS**, like this famous bell wagon, couldn't carry a circus far without the aid of a train.

miles upriver. There was no money for the train and no gas for their trucks.

So they *walked* all the way to West Hamlin down that gravel road, uphill and downhill, sleeping out at night. They marched right on past us to the bridge over the Guyandotte River about a quarter mile away.

They set up their big top on a vacant lot. I think they stayed a week and, of course, we had to attend a time or two—I might have died if I hadn't gotten to go after all that excitement!

Thinking back, I believe that even then, as a small child, I realized circus folks had a spirit that could not be crushed. And you can be sure I never forgot "my elephant". ⊠

**BIG TOP TRAVAILS.** As you'll learn from Dorothy Lambert's story at left, even circus performers struggled to survive hard times.

## Thrilling Sight of Circus Train Didn't Cost a Cent

THE CIRCUS was coming to our Nebraska town, and big posters went up everywhere. How my brother and I longed to go! Though the admission price was small, it was still more than our parents could afford. My mother came up with a wonderful solution.

The circus train was to arrive about 3 a.m. and stop on a railroad spur a few blocks from our house. Mother woke us at 2:30, and we walked over to see the train pull in.

From our perch on a warehouse loading dock, we could see the brightly painted wagons and the animals inside. The roars of the lions as they were jostled in their cages sent shivers down our spine.

The elephants were unloaded first and used to move the wagons off the flatcars. It was wonderful to see these huge animals obeying their trainers' commands. Beautiful horses were hitched to the wagons to move them to the field where the circus would take place.

We didn't see clowns or trapeze artists, but we experienced a side of the circus many never get to see. When the calliope went down the street the next day, we felt we'd already seen a good part of the circus—and it hadn't cost us a cent.

—*Marjorie Lori, Anchorage, Alaska*

## With All That Excitement, Who Needed Tickets?

WE COULDN'T afford tickets when the circus came to town, but we still considered ourselves lucky. The circus train parked practically in our yard, and the grounds were only two blocks away!

We reveled in the anticipation of the colorful train's arrival. Everyone from blocks around got up in the wee hours to welcome it. We walked up and down the tracks, trying to catch a glimpse of the tigers, elephants and other beasts.

When it was time for the train to unload, boys of all ages went to the grounds in hopes of being hired to help erect the tents. Whatever they earned would be enough to buy a ticket to the big performance.

Though we couldn't afford tickets, I didn't really mind. I was satisfied just to see the parade with all its colorful wagons, the elephants draped with glittering blankets and the clowns that made us giggle.

At night, we'd sit on our porch, listening to the cacophony of sounds from the circus grounds—music, hawkers, laughter. The air felt electric with excitement.

Our friends owned a small gas station and lunch counter on the edge of the grounds, and they grilled hamburgers and hot dogs outside during the circus and carnivals. Sometimes we were able to buy one of these treats and appreciate being so close to all the merriment.

Those memories will stay with me forever.

—*Dolores Eggener, Marinette, Wisconsin*

## Big Top Setup Was Best Show of All

MY FATHER never forgot the thrill he'd received as a boy when the circus came to town, and he wanted my sister and me to experience it, too.

That's why, one morning in the summer of 1936 in South Bend, Indiana, he got us about 4 a.m. to watch the circus arrive and set up the big top.

Sleepy as we were, we gladly jumped into our clothes and followed Dad down to the railroad tracks south of town. We were soon rewarded by hearing the station whistle herald the coming of the long circus train.

As the wide freight doors slid open and people inside started pulling out tons of equipment, we were amazed at how fast they worked. Even the star performers helped get the wagons rolling toward the vast open field where their temporary new home was being set up.

Our eyes opened wide as we saw cages of snarling lions and tigers added to the long procession. Then came the real stars of the show—the great elephants!

They were put to work promptly, hauling the huge canvas tents into place, lifting giant poles with their curling trunks and hoisting endless yards of heavy canvas skyward.

Meanwhile, the roustabouts worked feverishly. A few local boys were hired on the spot to fetch and carry equipment—tasks they did gladly, knowing they'd be rewarded with free tickets to the big show.

We watched all this activity from the fringes and it was awesome! Before the sun had even fully risen, all was in place and those hardworking men were headed for the food wagons for a well-earned rest and breakfast.

Downtown that afternoon, performers and animals attired in glittering finery marched down Main Street in a long parade designed to entice people to come see "The Greatest Show on Earth".

As far as we were concerned, we'd already seen it!

—*Margaret Markham, Lynnfield, Massachusetts*

# Friendly Gypsies Left Vivid Memories

*By Raymond Good, Tucson, Arizona*

IN THE 1930s, my mother and I lived with her grandparents near Newman, Illinois. Whenever summer neared, I eagerly awaited the return of the Gypsies.

They always camped at the creek near our house. Just watching them troop down the street with their heavily laden wagons made me jump with joy.

"Mom! Here come the Gypsies!" I'd shout, then I'd run out the door to wave and follow along with the caravan. I was supposed to wait until they set up camp, but that seemed like eternity to a 7-year-old boy.

I had such fun playing with the boys and girls in camp. Mom would let me stay there until dusk. Then she would come after me, and sometimes we'd both eat supper with the Gypsies.

I don't remember what the food was like, but I vividly recall the beautiful music that filled the camp after supper. Those who did not play musical instruments danced around the fire. Mom and I always joined in—she had as much fun as I did.

### Had Nothing to Fear

Most people in our town were afraid of the Gypsies, believing they'd steal anything they could get their hands on. We never had one thing stolen…maybe because we didn't have anything!

Once the Gypsies traded us a horse for some milk and eggs. I was so proud of "Old John"—he was my very own. I thought I took good care of John, but he died soon after. I felt sad then, but looking back now, I realize that old horse had to be on his last legs for the Gypsies to trade him for milk and a few eggs.

These days, whenever I return to Illinois, I make a brief trip to go see the spot where the Gypsies once camped. As I stand and ponder, I can still hear their beautiful music coming through the cottonwood trees.

I can still see the dancers, joyfully turning around and around the campfire. My mother is there, too, tapping her foot to the lively music.

As I stand there remembering, I can't help but wonder, where are my friends, the Gypsies, now? ☒

**GYPSIES AT HEART. Raymond Good and his mother (with Sis in the middle) looked forward to the arrival of the Gypsies' caravan each summer.**

# Dad's Rail Pass Took Boys on Trip of a Lifetime

*By Edward Braun, Danville, Indiana*

MY FATHER HAD a railroad job in Cincinnati, and every year he applied for a free pass that let us ride wherever we wanted. Dad couldn't afford "real" vacations, but those trips on steam locomotives were the most thrilling and memorable events of our young lives.

One summer day in the mid-'30s, Dad asked my brother Bill to fetch an envelope from his jacket pocket. When Dad opened it, we recognized it immediately as a railroad pass.

"How would you boys like to take a trip to New York City?" Dad asked. "Maybe we can stay in a hotel 1 night, but we'll have to scrimp on what I have."

I was about 11 then, Bill was around 14 and Bob was 9. Dad figured Bob was big enough now to stand a long trip, so with a B&O timetable and a geography book, we started planning.

We'd leave Cincinnati at night, travel 2 days and 2 nights, spend a day in New York and catch a train home the next night.

### Learned Geography Firsthand

We pulled out of Union Terminal the evening of August 16. The next morning, at a stop in Parkersburg, West Virginia, Dad pointed out the Blue Ridge Mountains, draped in a beautiful blue haze. We learned more about geography on our trips with Dad than we did in the classroom.

The train pulled into Washington, D.C. about sundown. Suitcases in hand, we took a bus to the Capitol and walked past the White House.

We returned to the terminal about 9:30 p.m. and climbed aboard the milk train, which left at midnight. (The joke was that these trains stopped to pick up milk every time the engineer saw a cow.)

We chugged into New York's Grand Central Station about 7 a.m. August 18. There seemed to be a zillion people on the enormous concourse. "You boys hold hands and stay close," Dad said. We didn't intend to let him out of our sight.

**THREE FOR THE ROAD.** Edward Braun (on the left), his little brother, Bob, and older brother, Bill, were delighted when their father offered to take them on a trip to New York City.

For breakfast, Dad took us to the Automat, a huge diner that had vending machines spread across an entire wall of one long room and a steam table along the opposite wall. We thought it was incredible.

We registered at the Penn Post Hotel, which charged $5 a night for the four of us, then set out for New York Harbor. The Statue of Liberty was a hundred times bigger than it looked in our history book. We took the elevator up 13 stories to the shoulders, then climbed a circular stairway to the statue's head.

In the afternoon, we visited a museum, an aquarium and Wall Street. I was disappointed when I saw the spot where the stock market had crashed. It was just a narrow dirty street lined with tall buildings.

The next stop was St. Patrick's Cathedral. I'd never seen anything that could compare with its breathtaking beauty.

The next morning, we were up at dawn to check out of the hotel and see Coney Island. We didn't have swimsuits, so we just jumped into the Atlantic in our clothes. Getting knocked over by the waves was thrilling.

### Top of the Town

When our clothes dried, we took the subway to the Empire State Building. Dad told us each of the 48 states had donated a block of marble or granite for its construction. It took two elevators to get to the top, where an observation deck surrounded a restaurant 102 stories above the street. The people below looked like ants.

After a bite at the Automat, we returned to Grand Central Station and caught the train. Around 5 a.m., we pulled into Baltimore for a 4-hour layover. We walked to a grocery and bought a quart of milk and four bananas.

We had about $2 left of the $20 we'd started with. Dad was worried sick about spending all our money.

When we pulled into Washington, D.C. about 10 a.m., we had just enough

for bus fare to the Capitol and carfare when we got back home. We were hungry for some real food—we'd had only two good meals the entire trip—but there was no money to spare. We'd just have to tough it out.

God must have heard our prayers, because when our bus turned onto Pennsylvania Avenue, we saw the American Legion was having a convention in Lafayette Park.

The entire park was covered with box lunches stacked high at the base of every tree. The Legionnaires invited us to join them. The lunches were free, and we could take as many as we wanted. Each box had two sandwiches and fruit.

### Had Lunch on the Legion

After eating our fill, we tucked a couple extra boxes under our arms and went off to see the Capitol, the Lincoln Memorial, the Washington Monument and the Smithsonian Institution.

When we walked past Lafayette Park to catch a bus to the depot, there were still boxes all over the place, so we picked up as many as we could carry. Dad was relieved and started smiling again.

"This trip was pretty hard on you guys," he said, "but I'm sure you'll remember it for a long time." He was right. Sixty-odd years is a long time.

We got a little tired of those sandwiches on the trip home, but we didn't complain. We just thanked the Good Lord we had that much. ⊠

# Teen Bicycled 3,200 Miles in 28 Days

*By Lee Van Allen, Penfield, New York*

WHEN I GRADUATED from high school in 1937, I dreamed of working in the then-new field of radiology. But there was no money for college. My father had died when I was 12, leaving my mother with nine children to raise.

When my aunt in California told me that college was free there, I got an idea.

I was 19 years old and didn't drive, but I was an accomplished bicyclist and even had my own small delivery service. I could easily ride 30 miles at a stretch, and I was sure I could ride from our home in Rochester, New York to California in a month.

And I did. I rode 3,200 miles in 28 days. I started out with two friends, but they dropped out at Cleveland, Ohio, and I made the rest of the trip alone.

I took $30 I'd saved, budgeting to spend $1 a day on the road. I packed a raincoat, a warm sweater, a change of clothes and an imitation-leather tarp. I wore shoes with 2-inch heels to help keep my feet on the pedals.

### Kindness Across the Country

The trip was the adventure of a lifetime and enabled me to see the country in a unique way. I was warmed by the kindness of people who were generous with me even though they had little to share. People let me sleep on their porches and barns in inclement weather or offered me a meal in exchange for stories of the road.

Sometimes I traveled with "Okies". One family let me sleep in the backseat of their car while they dozed in a nearby tent.

Occasionally I'd arrive in a town and discover I was a celebrity, since people had learned about my trip from newspapers in nearby towns. I met mayors and governors, and in one "Wild West" town, the authorities invited me to spend the night in a jail cell to ensure my safety.

The scenery was spectacular and the weather dramatic, but most of the miles were hard, lonely work. The only negative experience I had was having my pocket picked in Denver.

In Reno, Nevada, worried about stories I'd heard about the steep Sierra Nevada, I decided to take a stage to Sacramento. It was the only time I rode anything but my bike, and the ride cost $5.

After visiting my aunt in Stockton, California, I rode on to San Francisco. The Golden Gate Bridge was under construction, and the foreman let me walk my bike across it.

As it turned out, I didn't go to college in California. I returned to Rochester by bus. My destiny was back East. But I received a different kind of education on the road.

I learned there are many wonderful people living on the backroads of this land, and that the spirit to survive hardships can sometimes inspire you to do more than you ever thought possible. ⊠

**PEDAL PUSHER.** When two of Lee Van Allen's friends decided to turn back on their cross-country trip, Lee rode on to California all by herself.

## Shoe Game Kept Family Harmony on Solid Footing

OUR FAVORITE GAME had no name, and there were no stated rules. Mom, my brother, Rex, and I played it at noon-time and suppertime. It could be slow or fast, depending on Mom's eagle eye and sharp ears. The game involved Mom's shoes, and it continued for as long as she owned them.

During the Depression, clothing was mended patch upon patch, and shoes were resoled and reheeled countless times. Only when shoes were completely worn out did we get new ones.

Mom's shoes had reached the point of no return, so she went to Elstrom's clothing and shoe store to buy a new pair. Mr. Elstrom didn't have a large selection, but Mom finally settled on a pair of black leather shoes with medium heels.

After a few days, Mom began to complain about how uncomfortable the shoes were. She finally took them to Mr. Elstrom, but he wouldn't take them back. He assured her they'd be fine after she'd worn them for a while.

After another week, Mom began wearing the shoes for a couple of hours, then taking them off and leaving them wherever she happened to be. Dad kept asking her why she didn't wear shoes, and he got quite insistent about it.

That's when Mom invented the game. Actually, it was more like a race, with the promise of double-dip ice cream cones on Sunday.

Whenever we saw Dad coming up the road from work, Rex and I would start looking for the shoes. We had a big two-story house on a very large lot, and there was no telling where Mom might have left them.

"Hurry up! Hurry up!" Mom would say. "Can't you find them?" One of us generally did, and we'd race to the kitchen just in time for Mom to slip them on before Dad walked in the door. I'm sure Dad felt he'd won his point, because Mom was always wearing shoes (at least when he was home).

We never told him about the game. I don't think he would've seen the humor in it.

Mom finally gave the shoes to Aunt Zelma, who gave them to my grandmother. By then they were broken in, and Grandma never complained about the fit.
—*Donna Smith*
*Springfield, Oregon*

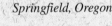

**SEARCH UNIT.** Donna Smith and her brother, Rex (left), raced around the house looking for their mom's ill-fitting shoes every time Dad (at far left with Mom) came home from work.

*ONE OF THE GUYS.* Singer Gene Autry loved baseball so much that he couldn't resist joining a kids' pickup game—even if it meant getting dirty.

## Dive for Ball Was No Big Deal

WHEN THE KIDS in my Illinois neighborhood put together a softball team, the only place we had to play was a high open area. First base looked down over a brick sidewalk and a steep grassy area that sloped to the street.

We were playing about 3 o'clock one afternoon when a car stopped. Out stepped a fellow in complete Western gear, including boots and a 10-gallon hat. He watched us play for a while, then asked if he could join us. We put him on first base.

Everything went well until the third baseman made a wild throw to first. The stranger grabbed for the ball but missed it and tumbled down the slope. He landed in the street with a hole ripped in the knee of his pants, but he just walked back up the hill as if this was an everyday affair.

We were still playing when another car pulled up and a fellow jumped out, mad as a wet hen. He approached the "Western dude" and said, "Gene, you know your program goes on the air at 4, and it's now 3:50!"

Our first baseman replied, "Well, I guess I'd better get going." He thanked us for letting him play, then left.

We later learned "Gene" was none other than singer Gene Autry, who would go on to become a movie star! His radio program was broadcast from WMRO in Aurora.
—*James Tate, Apache Junction, Arizona*

## Children Spent Summer "Reading the Walls"

WHEN I WAS 8 years old, our family moved into a modest frame house where all the interior walls were papered with pages from magazines.

Someone had removed the staples from the broad pages of *The Saturday Evening Post*, *Collier's* and *Ladies' Home Journal*, then neatly pasted them side by side, so every word was visible. For a family of compulsive readers, this proved to be great fun.

My three older siblings and I spent that summer "reading the walls". One of us might find the start of a good story above the kitchen table. Days later, someone would spot the rest of the story near the ceiling in the living room. It was like a fascinating mystery!

We never knew what we'd find to read behind a bed or in a corner behind a door. Of course, we couldn't see what was on the backs of the pages, so we had to use our imaginations to fill in the blanks. It was frustrating, yet fun.

I don't recall that we ever tired of this game. We improved at finding things as the summer wore on, and all of us became better readers. More than 50 years later, I'm still grateful for the skills I learned from that "wallpaper".
—*Jnita Wright, Miami, Florida*

## Insurance Man Colored Her World with Kindness

GROWING UP on a farm in the little town of Flatwoods, Pennsylvania wasn't easy in 1938. Dad was working for the WPA but wasn't making enough to meet the mortgage payments.

We children didn't ask for, or expect, little things to entertain us.

My favorite pastime was coloring, but there was no money for coloring books or new crayons. Mom would hold a picture up to the window and trace it on another sheet of paper so I'd have something to color, but those pictures got repetitious after a while. That was where our insurance man came in.

When I heard his old car chugging down the hill, I'd run to meet him as he pulled into our dirt driveway. He visited our house monthly to collect our 39¢ premium and always gave me three different coloring books advertising his company. Each book had about eight pages. Once he even brought me a box of six crayons, which I wore down to stubs.

One day when I ran to meet the insurance man, he was all smiles. He had a surprise for me in his satchel—a book of cutout dolls. What a happy day! I'd wanted some ever since I'd seen a book of Dionne quintuplet cutout dolls 4 years earlier.

This book didn't advertise the insurance company, so I'm sure the insurance man paid for it out of his own commission. His generosity kept a little girl happy for weeks. —*Betty Cunningham*
*Parma, Ohio*

## Operetta's Fantasy World Launched Writing Career

THE GLORIOUS operettas of the 1930s filled my preteen years with melody and magic at the Broadway Theater in Burlingame, California.

With one dime for the show and another for two Hershey bars, I was in a fantasy world with the Casquette girls of New Orleans in *Naughty Marietta*. I'd glide home, thinking of Jeanette MacDonald singing *The Italian Street Song* to a handsome Nelson Eddy.

Then came the rough-and-ready Mounties and the booming drum of *Indian Love Call*. On the way home, I'd climb to the top of hill, all alone in my fantasy world, and sing my heart out to the blond hero.

Then I'd walk down the hill and spend hours writing my own operetta, where I lived in the same town as the *Girl of the Golden West* and ran my own thousand-acre ranch with a blond baritone ranch hand.

Those days kept me writing through a lifetime of legends, fantasies and musical plays as a free-lance writer. —*Alice Kennedy*
*Keaau, Hawaii*

# Granddad and His Bear Made an Entertaining Pair

*By Mike Clavette, Franklin, Wisconsin*
*(as told to Trudi Bellin)*

MY GREAT-GRANDFATHER, John Akey, was a logger, woodsman and lumber camp cook in Merrill, Wisconsin. But back in the days when vaudeville was big, he traveled North America with a performing bear—"Queenie, The Bear that Made Merrill Famous".

Maybe you recall seeing Queenie and John perform during the early Depression years. Great-Granddad and his bear toured as entertainers from 1915 through 1933. John was 55 the year he met Queenie. When he brought that little bear home, the local newspaper reported, "She caused no little commotion on the streetcar. Several women screamed and a near panic ensued, until they found the bear was chained."

John trained Queenie, and she was performing tricks within 3 months. Soon, the duo took their show on the vaudeville circuit. That left Great-Grandmother Cora with all the family responsibilities while her gregarious, fun-loving husband entertained the nation.

Queenie knew a marvelous array of tricks. She could waltz, ice-skate and climb a ladder. She could swing, skip rope, push a baby carriage, swim, drink from a bottle and perform on a trapeze. Her real claims to fame, however, were roller-skating and driving!

### Didn't Need a Learner's Permit

Postcards were printed of Queenie on roller skates. But the highlight of every show, fair or vaudeville stop was when John let her drive a Ford. Local dealerships welcomed the publicity.

One newspaper reported, "Queenie sits in the front seat and places her paws on the steering wheel. She does this alone with nobody sitting in the front seat and takes the corners by the best of driving. She obeys traffic laws by keeping on her own side of the street."

John periodically sent word home during his travels to every state in the Union. He was optimistic that he and Queenie would eventually travel to South America and Europe. They entertained in Canada and Mexico but never crossed the ocean before their adventure ended.

Years later, my family uncovered an interesting newspaper clipping that reported the duo's Depression-era income at $225 a week! Maybe that explains why Cora never complained about John's travels but always welcomed him home!

Shortly after John and Cora's 50th wedding anniversary, John came down with pneumonia and died. Cora sold Queenie to a Chicago amusement park owner and animal trainer who planned to have her perform for the Chicago Century of Progress Exposition.

That was the last we ever heard about Queenie, but we hope she entertained plenty of people at that 1933 World's Fair. My fun-loving great-granddad would have wanted it that way. ◻

**BEAR IN A CHAIR.** Like this bruin, Queenie was multitalented.

# Message in a Bottle Added Extra Thrill to Boat Trip

*By Genevieve Bertram, Payson, Arizona*

OUR LIFESTYLE during the Depression was sparse, but I was content—largely because of my mother. She had a magical way of making the simplest things seem like treats beyond compare.

One example was the once-a-year summer trip we'd take across Lake Michigan. This $1, all-day excursion took us from the Chicago River to Milwaukee, Wisconsin or Benton Harbor or Grand Haven, Michigan.

But to my mother, this was no simple trip. She spelled anticipation with a capital "A".

Weeks before, we'd begin discussing which of those three cities to visit. Mother researched places to see in each one, and many dinners were spent planning our precious layover time.

### Imagination Ran Wild

There was so much to plan. What would we put in our picnic basket? Would we have enough saved to eat in the dining room? What books should we take for the luxury of reading on a reclining deck chair? Lists were made, crossed out and written again, while my excitement and anticipation grew.

The trip in July 1932, when I was 13, stands out in my memory because of Mother. She suggested I write a note, attach my photograph and seal it in a bottle. My father would calculate when we were halfway to Grand Haven, and I'd throw the bottle into Lake Michigan.

Would the currents carry it? Who would find it? Would that person write to me? Mother's enthusiasm was contagious, and my playmates listened to her plan in awe and admiration.

The day of the trip arrived at last. As I walked up the swaying gangplank, I clutched the bottle deep in my pocket. My father settled us in chairs at the front of the ship, and soon we felt the powerful engines vibrating under our feet. Our journey had begun.

It was torture waiting for the time to pass. Finally my father looked at his watch and nodded. I followed him down a narrow hatchway to the hold of the ship, where bare-chested stevedores were stacking cargo.

We stopped at a low, wide-open doorway near the level of the water. Only a few chains separated us from the churning, foamy water, and a cold spray stung my face.

When I reached into my pocket for the bottle, I felt the exhilaration of an adventurer daring the unknown. I flung the bottle into the lake and breathlessly watched it sink out of sight. Then it rose to the surface and jauntily bobbed away over the waves.

### Mother Never Doubted

Two weeks passed, then 3. Even my best friends began to doubt I'd hear from someone who'd find my bottle. But not Mother. With love and wisdom, she faithfully assured me that months could pass. And they did.

One cold November day, the mailman delivered a letter to me in unfamiliar handwriting. Someone had found my bottle! A 17-year-old boy who lived in Spring Lake, Michigan had found it while hunting ducks near Muskegon.

We enjoyed corresponding, and the following summer, he accepted Mother's invitation to visit us and see the 1933 Chicago World's Fair.

The image of opening our door to that tall brown-haired boy still lingers brightly in my memory. He and I continued to write for several years.

Wherever you are, Harry Edwards, have you told your grandchildren the story of finding a bottle in Lake Michigan during the Depression? ⊠

**ENTHUSIASM WAS CONTAGIOUS.** Genevieve Bertram (riding pony below) got caught up in her mother's exciting plans.

# CHAPTER TEN

# City Life Was a Challenge

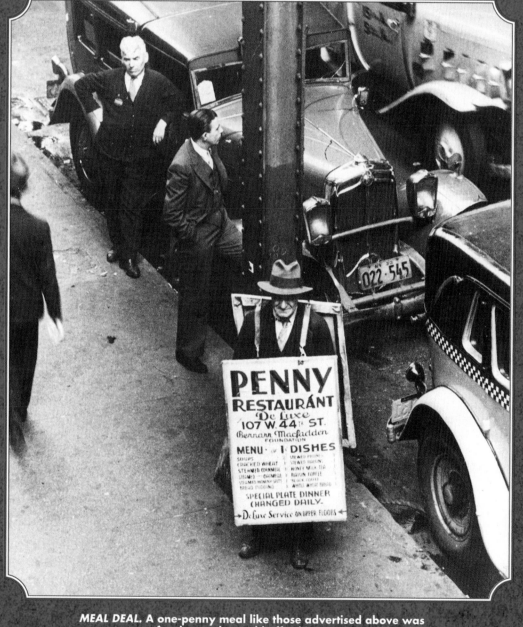

***MEAL DEAL.*** A one-penny meal like those advertised above was a great way—for those who could afford it—to stave off hunger. Unlike farmers, city folks couldn't grow most of their own food. (Photo: H. Armstrong Roberts/American Stock Photography)

# From the desk of Clancy Strock

Dear Katie,

I realize that your Social Studies treat the Depression and World War II as separate events. You know...like the Revolutionary and Civil Wars.

Actually, they weren't separated by much more than a heartbeat. And to those of us who went into the military, the Depression was very fresh in our minds. So fresh, in fact, that having new clothes, medical care and three good meals a day was a real treat for most of us.

In our spare time, we compared notes about who'd had it toughest during the Depression. I was thoroughly astonished to have the city guys tell me how lucky I'd been to have lived on the farm.

How could they say that?

"Hey, at least you always had food on the table because you grew your own. Lots of nights we went to bed hungry."

"Wait a minute! We sure didn't grow our sugar and cornflakes and bath soap. We bought stuff the way you did."

"Well, I suppose so. But your dad wasn't out of work for nearly 3 years the way mine was."

"Ha, what a deal! Dad worked from dark to dark 7 days a week all year long and what did he get for it? In both 1934 and 1936, he actually lost money."

"My brother and I weren't even teenagers when we had to get after-school jobs. And every Saturday night, we turned our pay over to our mother to help cover the rent and buy groceries."

"Yeah, like I didn't have chores to do and help Dad with the crops in the summer. And I didn't get paid a cent."

It was an argument no one ever won. But it was quite an education for both sides. Those who were raised in the big cities could not begin to imagine what farm or small-town life was like.

On the other hand, I had no idea what it was like to live in an apartment house or tenement building, where the sidewalk was your front porch and kids played baseball in the street.

What I did come to understand was that there was a whole different level of desperation and suffering for people in places like Chicago and Philadelphia and Pittsburgh. There was a terrible aloneness to it, probably because big-city life tends to be so impersonal.

Quite a lot of the memories in other chapters of this book describe troubles faced by folks on the farm. And that's as it should be, because years ago, a bigger percentage of the population lived out in the country. This chapter was included to provide city folks' unique perspective. Katie, things were tough all over!

*Your Grandpa Clancy*

# Purloined Meals Took Bite Out of Food-Service Jobs

*By Robert Talbot, Houston, Texas*

I LEFT COLLEGE in 1933 with 3 years of engineering training, but there were no jobs. I walked the streets of New York with a few dollars in my pocket, looking for any work. I rented a room at the YMCA for a dollar a night and lived on egg sandwiches and milk.

When I finally heard about a job at Bickford's cafeteria in Brooklyn, I leaped at it. I was down to my last 60¢.

My first task was stacking dishes for the dishwasher in sweltering heat. I worked 9 hours a day, 6 days a week, with a half hour off for lunch. The pay was $11 a week, with one free meal a day. After a few weeks, I was promoted to counter man, with a $2 raise.

When my shift ended at 4:30 p.m., I'd hit the streets around Times Square to look for an evening job.

One night I saw a "Help Wanted" sign at the Brass Rail restaurant. It was a meat-carving job, and I applied. Asked where I'd carved, I named a hotel and a couple of restaurants, taking pains to think of good ones. I got the job and was outfitted with a starched white uniform and chef's hat.

The carving and sandwich-making counter was right in the window at the

> *"That knife was huge—I'd never held one like it..."*

end of the long mahogany bar, so passersby could watch. Experienced carvers put on a good show, then slid the sandwiches down the bar with a flourish.

I took my place behind the counter, and the other carver handed me a carving knife and fork. That knife was absolutely huge. I'd never held one like it.

My first order was a ham on rye. I hacked away at the ham, trying to remember how Dad did it at home. Somehow I got the meat onto the bread, chopped the sandwich in half and slid it down the bar without incident. Now all I had to do was bluff my way through while I learned how to carve.

I struggled through the next two sandwiches, trying not to cut off a finger. I was sweating almost as much as when I'd been a dishwasher.

One of the bosses called me over and asked where I'd carved. "I've never carved in my life," I confessed, "but I need the job." I was ordered to leave and never set foot in the place again.

I'd turned in my uniform and was trotting for the door when the other carver motioned me over. He slipped me two of the biggest corned beef sandwiches I'd ever seen, wrapped in newspaper with two huge dill pickles.

I took a 3-hour evening job at the Metropole, a corner lunch counter that sold nothing but soup and crackers. Employees weren't allowed to eat unless they worked a 9-hour shift, but I got darn good at bending down behind the counter and slurping split pea soup right out of the pot.

My part-time night job at Horn & Hardart Automat was hilarious. I got that one by mentioning my "experience" as a carver at the Brass Rail. The manager never asked why I'd left.

## Up to the Mayonnaise Room

A woman named Flossie took me up to the fourth floor in a rickety wooden freight elevator that ran on a rope pulley. We went to a spotless room with three large mixing machines, each holding 20 gallons of mayonnaise. Alongside sat an old-fashioned Victorian bathtub mounted on a wheeled platform.

Flossie handed me a half-gallon ladle and showed me how to dredge the mayonnaise into the old claw-footed tub. I started ladling, wondering which one of us was more nuts—Flossie or me.

When the bathtub was full of mayonnaise, we rolled it back to the elevator and worked our way down, stopping at each floor to fill an astonishing number of mayonnaise jars. *We used every drop.*

Taking that tub back upstairs wasn't easy—it didn't roll well when empty, and it was hard to steer. Back on the fourth floor, the tub was scrubbed, disinfected and rolled into a special closet, ready for the next evening.

The mayonnaise detail was my entire job, and the first day I did it on my own, it took 5-1/2 hours. It was supposed to be done in 4, so that's all I got paid for. The fastest I ever managed was 4 hours and 15 minutes.

There was only one drawback to working at the Automat—there were so many people around that I couldn't snitch anything to eat. I sure couldn't make a meal out of mayonnaise. ⊠

**BICKFORD BOYS. Robert Talbot (far right below)** was one of the lucky men who had a job at Bickford's Luncheonette in Brooklyn. He worked there during the day, then hit the streets looking for an evening job.

## He Pedaled Windy-City Wares

AFTER MY MOTHER died of pneumonia in 1932 and Dad lost his job, I started delivering Chinese food for a restaurant on Western Avenue in Chicago. I'd inherited an old 28-inch Ranger bicycle from my grandfather, and Dad made an insulated wooden box to mount on the handlebars.

On this trusty steed I made deliveries for 2 years in the best post office tradition—through heat, rain, snow, sleet and dark of night.

I worked every day after school, from 4 to 7:30 p.m., and from 1 to 7:30 p.m. Saturdays and Sundays. I was paid the amazing sum of $1.25 a week. After a year, my pay was raised to $1.50.

I received some small tips—and a few complaints when the food wasn't as hot as expected. In winter, the snow, ice and near-zero temperatures slowed me down a bit. But generally the customers were gracious and understanding.

My pay always went into the family pot, but I usually was given some change for goodies. Because I worked through the dinner hour, I ate for free in the restaurant's kitchen—consuming about 700 consecutive Chinese dinners. I enjoyed those meals, and they relieved my family of some of the burden of feeding a growing boy.

I also found a way to earn a few pennies when unex-

**HAPPIER TIMES.** Robert Nelson posed with his parents and sister Laverne in spring of 1931, before his mother died, his dad lost his job and he began working as a restaurant delivery boy.

pected rainstorms hit in spring and summer. I'd don a heavy rubber raincoat, head over to the streetcar island on Western Avenue with one or two large black umbrellas and offer unprepared passengers some protection as they walked to their destination.

Sometimes I got a small gratuity, a cup of cocoa or a soft drink for my efforts, and sometimes I just received a pat on the head and a "thank you". I took my chances.
—*Robert Nelson, Nampa, Idaho*

**SOLE SURVIVOR.** Charlotte Costello (at left with her sisters) found herself in debt to a shoe repairman.

## Holey Shoes Had Her Scrounging for Cobbler's Fee

IN 1931, I took my shabby oxfords to the shoe repair shop down the alley from our home on Chicago's south side. Both soles had holes the size of quarters, and school was starting in a week.

When I returned and told Dad the half soles would cost $1.50, he nearly had a fit. "Go back and get the shoes!" he yelled. "I'll fix them myself."

I ran down the alley as fast as I could, but the cobbler was already working on them. I couldn't ask him to give them

back now. I'd have to earn that money myself.

On the walk home, I spotted a milk bottle someone had discarded and got an idea. I persuaded my brother to help me look for more bottles to turn in at the store. We found 40¢ worth, and I earned a quarter baby-sitting that night, but it wasn't enough. It was time to confess.

I gave Dad the 65¢ and told him the cobbler still had my shoes. He smiled and said, "I know. I met Joe coming home from work yesterday, and we had a talk. He has a family to support, too. I'm proud of you for trying to help out."
—*Charlotte Costello
Winamac, Indiana*

## Just Being Near the World's Fair Was Entertainment

I GREW UP in Chicago, and a big attraction in 1933 was the World's Fair on the lakefront. A trip to the fair was simple—we boarded the bus outside our apartment and got off outside the gates.

If we were entertaining visitors from out of town, we'd pay the admission and spend the day seeing the wonders. But since this was the Depression, there were plenty of times we took the bus to

the lakefront, saved the admission and enjoyed the activities *outside* the gate.

Sometimes, on hot summer evenings, a ride on top of a double-decker bus provided pleasant relief from the heat. The round-trip to the Loop and back was enjoyable, provided you paid attention when the driver warned about standing up as the bus passed under the elevated tracks! —*Mary White Reiter
Villa Park, Illinois*

**WAY OUT WEST?** This photo was actually taken at Chicago's Century of Progress Exposition in 1933. Mary Reiter (shading her eyes) went with sister Ann (left) and cousin Marian.

# Trusty Wagon Got Them Through Grammar School

*By Robert Miller, Philadelphia, Pennsylvania*

**WAGON MASTERS.** Robert Miller (left) and his brother, Tom, went on many "scavenging" missions on Philadephia streets with their little coaster wagon.

I BEGAN TO understand what the Great Depression was about in 1933. I was 8 and my brother, Tom, was 7 when I overheard Dad and Mom discuss how hard it was to make ends meet. Christmas was coming, so I told Tom we probably wouldn't get any presents.

On Christmas morning, Tom and I shuffled downstairs, sure that Santa Claus had skipped us. We peered into the parlor and saw Dad and Mom standing in front of our scrawny tree. They smiled and wished us a Merry Christmas, then moved aside. Tom and I were struck speechless. Under the tree was a present—a new coaster wagon!

Tom and I were stunned. Wouldn't the kids on the block be envious! We could hardly wait to take it outside.

Our introduction to reality began the next day. After breakfast, Dad told us to put on hats and coats and follow him. He dragged the wagon into the yard and tossed in a shovel and three gunnysacks. "We need coal," he said. "Come along."

## They Dug Coal in Philly

Our neighborhood was in a Philadelphia river ward, amid factories and railroad spurs. I trudged behind Dad, pulling the wagon with Tom in it. After about an hour, we reached an electric generating plant and walked through the gate to its huge ash pile.

Dad began digging and told Tom and me to pick up pieces of unburned coal and put them in the sacks. We had to work quickly, because a dozen other people were doing the same thing.

As we walked home, I asked Dad why he didn't just buy a hundred pounds at the local coal yard. "We can't afford it," he replied. "The mill is on slack time and I don't know when I'll be called back to work."

Then I realized our Christmas present was meant to be a work tool, not a plaything. Every Saturday morning that winter, we dragged it to the ash pile to scrounge coal. Soon, Tom and I went alone while Dad searched for work. Scavenging became a way of life.

On trash day, Tom and I rose at dawn and pulled our little wagon through the neighborhood, looking for newspapers, rags or bits of metal we could sell at the junkyard. Then we'd take it home, get some breakfast and hurry to school. After classes, we'd take our haul to the junk dealer and turn over the profit to our parents.

As we gained experience, Tom and I ventured into more affluent neighborhoods, where people discarded things we considered treasures. Some were sold to secondhand stores; others we kept to furnish our home.

We scoured industrial trash piles for firewood to burn when our coal ran out, and we looked for cardboard boxes to sell to the wastepaper man. Factory floor sweepings sometimes yielded nails, screws and other hardware we could use.

## Enjoyed a Sweet Reward

One favorite trash pile was at a candy factory, where we found packages of damaged candy. The wrappers might be torn and the contents smashed, but sweets were too good to pass up. We rarely got candy at home. Tom and I grabbed all we could and stored them in the basement.

In 1934, a cut-rate supermarket opened about 2 miles away, and the wagon was pressed into service for shopping trips. Tom and I were proud we could help.

Despite our efforts, things grew worse. We gained a baby sister, and Dad lost his job. I was sent to live with Grandma on a small farm in northwestern Pennsylvania.

Meanwhile, Dad secured an apprenticeship with an elderly paperhanger. He learned the craft, and when the old craftsman passed away, Dad went into business for himself. As business picked up—with some jobs far from home—Tom used the wagon to deliver tools and materials to the job sites.

When I returned home to begin fifth grade, I became Dad's second unpaid helper. At 10, I learned how to trim, measure, match, cut and paste wallpaper. As I became more skillful, Dad conceded my presence was a big help.

Dad couldn't afford to turn down any jobs, so we worked constantly. Quitting time was whenever Dad said it was, so my homework often had to wait until the next morning before school. My career as a paperhanger continued until eighth grade, when Dad found a job at a paper mill.

Tom and I continued scavenging and found occasional work as errand boys, storekeepers' helpers and soft-pretzel vendors. We picked up the pretzels early in the morning and sold them on the street from baskets. I usually bought 200 for $1 and cleared another dollar if I sold them all.

Today, Tom and I are proud we never accepted charity even during the worst of those hard times. With our trusty wagon, we worked our way through grammar school! ⊠

## "Call Waiting Service" Was a Money Maker

WHEN I was growing up in Philadelphia in the '30s, there weren't many opportunities for a boy of 12 to pick up some spending money. But my friends and I found a way.

There was a drugstore or a candy store on nearly every downtown street corner. All those stores had one or two telephone booths inside. The phones received a lot of use because so many people couldn't afford a phone.

Hanging around downtown, my buddies and I saw a business opportunity. We'd stand in a store, waiting for the phone to ring. The first guy to answer the phone was the lucky one.

He would take the name and address of the person being called, then run to that house or apartment and inform the party a call was awaiting them.

The guys left in the store would protect the incoming line to prevent it from being used and thereby disconnecting the incoming call. It was an honor system among friends.

The standard fee for our service was a nickel. On a good day, a kid might make as much as 25¢.

—*Joseph Miller*
*Pembroke Pines, Florida*

## Big Money Wasn't Needed For Big-Apple Fun

MY WIFE and I were married in 1934 and found the Depression did have its advantages. Although it was a time when most jobs only paid $12 to $20 per week, we could "do the town" on a Saturday afternoon in New York City for "four bits".

The trolley was 5¢, a cottage cheese and nut sandwich with orange juice was 15¢—and for 25¢, you could spend the entire afternoon at the movies.

That included an organ number, a vaudeville act, a serial and comedy, plus the main feature and a newsreel. It all added up to 4 hours of cheap, but welcome, entertainment.

—*William Stitt, Clewiston, Florida*

**ANOTHER WORLD. Movie-goers during the '30s were glad to escape—if only for an afternoon—to a place where people didn't worry about their next meal.**

**THE SUN STILL SHONE. Like these happy kids, Patricia West enjoyed the simple pleasure of ice cream in summer.**

## Lean Years Were Full of Fun for Boston Family

THE DEPRESSION years are often described as hard times, but all I remember are good times and lots of family fun.

In Boston, Massachusetts, spring meant May processions and band competitions at Boston College's Alumni Field. Marching with the band in the Charlestown parade on June 17 was always fun. Our heavy twill uniforms were hot, but the free ice cream at the end of the procession made it all worthwhile.

Growing up during the Depression taught us frugality. The car was sold, the telephone was taken out and we all learned the discipline of "FHB" (family hold back) when we had company for dinner.

My father was a captain with the Boston Fire Department. One day he responded to a fire in a bakery. Rather than see all the pies go up in flames, he put one inside his coat and went back to work.

After leaving the scene, he opened his coat to remove the pie and found it crushed all over his shirt. It was blueberry. He never tried to "save" a pie again.

—*Patricia West*
*Weymouth, Massachusetts*

# Family's Holidays Were Joyous Despite Hardscrabble City Life

*By Coleen Roche, Woodhaven, New York*

MY GRANDFATHER grew up in a large family in Brooklyn, New York. Money and food were scarce, but the family received "home relief", which was a state distribution of food and money.

Grandfather once told me that he patiently stood in line for hours waiting for a single can of "Not to Be Sold".

When I asked what that was, he explained it was can of Spam, specially labeled.

He had fond memories of Thanksgiving and Christmas, when he'd pull a sled or wagon to the police station to pick up a long-awaited turkey dinner.

On Christmas Eve, his father would wait in the cold until the tree lot closed, then bring home a discarded evergreen that couldn't be sold.

He'd proudly pull the bare tree through the streets and up three flights of stairs, where eight smiling children were waiting eagerly to decorate it. Although there was little or no money for toys, Christmas was still a joyous time because the family was together.

## Two Shoes, Two Bits

My grandfather once bought a pair of unclaimed shoes from the shoemaker for a quarter. Although they were girls' shoes, he wore them until the soles wore down. Then his mother lovingly lined them with cardboard or newspaper so that his feet wouldn't touch the pavement.

Jobs were scarce, and many people worked only 1 or 2 days a week. His father participated in a program where the boss picked a limited number of workers each day. Since he never knew when he'd be chosen to work, he left the house early every morning and didn't return until late at night.

As the oldest son, my grandfather felt he should do something to help, but there wasn't much a 10-year-old could do. So he and a friend built a shoe-shine box. Every day after school, they sneaked onto the subway and hopped from one car to the next, shining shoes for a nickel.

He was so proud to help out. But when his father discovered what he was doing, he made him stop. My grandfather was too young to understand, but as he got older, he understood he'd hurt his father's pride.

Although I always enjoyed listening to my grandfather's stories, I often took them for granted. Now that he's gone, I'd give anything to hear them again. He was proud to tell me these stories, and I'm proud to repeat them. ▨

**SIDEWALK ENTREPRENEURS.** Like these young businessmen, Coleen Roche's grandfather and a friend built a shoe-shine box and used it to make a little extra money. But they shined shoes on the subway.

J.C. Allen and Son

# Poor Boy Made Rich Memories In Detroit

*By Harold Ceaser*
*Port Richey, Florida*

MY FATHER was an Italian immigrant who worked as a barber in Detroit. For our family, money was always scarce. I remember him leaving a dollar bill on his dresser so my mother could buy food for our family of seven.

Mother sometimes made a pan of scalloped potatoes and called it "surprise steak". When we asked where the steak was, she'd tell us to keep eating. At the bottom, we'd sometimes find small flat "hamburgers" made with lots of bread crumbs.

After school, we made sandwiches with bread and salad dressing or uncolored oleo sprinkled with sugar.

When Mother could afford it, she'd buy a chunk of bologna and grind it with pickles, onions and salad dressing for sandwich spread.

### Address Changed Often

Whenever we couldn't pay the rent, we'd move. I think we lived on every street in Detroit. Sometimes we'd come home from school to an empty house. When that happened, we knew what to do. We'd sit on the porch and wait, and soon our parents would arrive to take us to our new apartment.

Shoes were a never-ending problem. Dad cut out cardboard liners to cover the holes in our shoes. Once he made liners from sheet metal. When we ran down the sidewalk at night, we could see sparks. I made rubber bands out of an old inner tube and wrapped them around my shoes so the soles wouldn't flap.

Clothes were in short supply, too. At my eighth-grade graduation, only one boy had a suit coat. As he left the stage with his diploma, he handed his coat to another boy.

The second boy ran behind the curtain, put on the coat, got *his* diploma, then passed the coat to the next boy. All 26 boys in our class wore the same coat that night.

For fuel, we walked down miles of alleys, sifting ash piles for usable bits of coal. Sometimes we walked to the railroad tracks and put metal slugs on the rails to bump the cars and shake off pieces of coal.

When we could afford to buy coal, we ordered half a ton. It cost 25¢ extra to have the deliveryman wheel it into the coal bin, so my brother and I hauled it to the bin in bushel baskets. We had to wrap the basket handles with rags so our hands didn't get cut.

In 1936, my little sister had scarlet fever and the whole family was quarantined for 3 months. We made a complete Monopoly set from memory, did lots of crafts and made model airplanes with a paste made of flour and water.

My brother and I passed the time by playing catch on the second-story back porch. When the ball fell into the backyard, none of the neighbor kids would throw it back. They teased us about being quarantined.

So I'd sneak out the back door and get the ball, then run at the kids and scatter them like a flock of crows.

Everyone made kites, but we didn't have money for string. One day I went into a store and grabbed the string that hung from a spool on the ceiling, then ran like all get-out. I got a good block away before the string was cut. I was top dog at our kite-flying field that day.

One Christmas was especially memorable. We kids went to bed Christmas Eve with no sign of a tree or presents. The next morning, we had a beautiful tree and a few gifts.

My father had gone out after midnight, found a tree at an abandoned lot over a mile away and dragged it home through heavy snow. He and Mother stayed up late to decorate it. We had a great Christmas after all.

Though we didn't have much money, we did have lots of love, and all of us grew up to lead successful lives. As poor as we were, we had a very rich childhood. ⊠

**TOTAL SURPRISE.** Harold Ceaser (inset) was no less delighted than these youngsters when he discovered a tree on Christmas morning.

# New Yorkers Rode Out Storm with Move Upstate

*By Martha Snyder*
*Media, Pennsylvania*

Ewing Galloway

**BIG-CITY BLUES.** The situation in New York City during the early '30s was not very healthy for the Snyder family. So they picked up stakes and moved to the country.

WHEN THE DEPRESSION reduced our family to poverty, my father decided the best way to ride out the storm was by moving from Staten Island to a smaller town in western New York.

We arrived in East Aurora in the winter of 1932. We found a market for Papa's building skills and a nice house to rent for $25 a month. It was still a struggle, but everyone else was in the same boat, just trying to make ends meet.

Life in upstate New York was like living in the country, and we all liked that. There was a lot of snow when we arrived, and we learned to toboggan, ski and ice-skate. I also remember a wonderful sleigh-ride party with a group from our church.

No one got allowances in those days. If help was needed around the house, children just did their jobs. Everyone in the family cooperated to make things work.

For spending money, I did baby-sitting, worked at a store (I was paid $1 for an 8-hour shift) and picked strawberries, earning a nickel for every 2 quarts. In high school, I played the organ at church for $1 per Sunday. It was a real workout pumping those foot pedals.

The Depression restricted our spending, and we had to make do with what we had. But we got through it. When a family cooperates and the parents set an example, that makes all the difference. The kids in our family came out winners, and we always thanked God for the parents we had. ⊠

# 'Good Life' in Los Angeles Didn't Pan Out

*By M.E. Fitzpatrick, Salem, Oregon*

IN 1930, Uncle Kent urged our family to move from small-town Oregon to Los Angeles, California, where the opportunities were better. Dad could work at Uncle Kent's washing machine store, and my sister Marge and I could find work.

Seventeen and fresh of out high school, I went to California full of hopes and dreams. Dad began working for Uncle Kent, Marge got an office job, and I found work at a radio store. We were slow to realize what the Depression meant, until Uncle Kent had to close his store. Dad returned to Oregon, where we still had our homestead.

My two younger sisters began carrying their shoes when they walked to school to save wear and tear on the soles.

When the store where I worked closed, looking for a job became a daily struggle. I'd get up at daybreak and go downtown, walking from one shop to the next, sometimes finding an hour or two of work. Minimum wage was $16 a week, but for part-time work, I gladly took anything offered.

### Sister Supported Them

Marge met a young fellow who ran a service station and wanted to get married. Since she was our family's sole financial support, she'd continue giving us her salary, and the newlyweds would live on the groom's meager income. I felt guilty I couldn't do my share.

When I heard I could get work at a cannery in Oregon, Mother scraped together $9 for bus fare and I went back home. I worked there until the canneries closed for winter.

The Depression wasn't over, but things seemed more hopeful back in the country. The Depression there seemed to lack much of the futility of Depression in the city.

A neighboring farmer piled squash in his yard with a sign reading, "Help Yourself". Another laughed when I offered to pay for the blackberries I'd picked from his hedgerow. I scrounged fruit jars and canned 400 quarts, determined I'd have at least one thing to eat every day for the next year.

Back in California, Marge made a wedding dress with material from a used-clothing store. Mother fashioned her veil from a lace curtain. A cousin loaned his car for a honeymoon trip to the Grand Canyon. I sent my wedding present, $2, to buy gas. Of course, I missed the wedding.

For me, the Depression ended in January 1934, when I got a wonderful job in a bank. I remained there for many years. But even now, 60 years later, the mental scars of the Depression remain. Sometimes I still wake in a cold sweat, thinking I'm late for work and someone else will be hired for my job. ⊠

**HOMEGROWN GOWN.** M.E. Fitzpatrick's sister (with new husband) made her own wedding dress.

## Iceman's Visit Thrilled South Philadelphia Lass

**THE ICEMAN IN PHILLY.** For Lori Moore, the man who refreshed their icebox was a welcome sight.

MY MOM was known as "the queen of clean" in our neighborhood in South Philadelphia, Pennsylvania—and that meant a painstaking cleaning of our wooden icebox before the iceman's delivery.

All the food was stacked on a table and covered with newspapers so it wouldn't melt. I scrubbed the metal shelves with creosote and scalding water, cleaned the drain tube with a coat hanger and bottle brush, then scoured the drip pan with Brillo pads and Old Dutch cleanser until it sparkled. When the box passed Mom's inspection, we were ready for the iceman.

The horse-drawn ice wagon was driven by 19-year-old Jim, as handsome an Irishman as a girl of 13 could hope to see. He'd yell up the stairs so we'd open the door for him, and he worked quickly to keep drips to a minimum.

Jim would place the ice just so in the chamber, then sniff. Mom was always pleased when he told her how clean our box was—nothing like the lady's in Apartment 1.

Then came my reward. Jim would chip off a piece of ice that shimmered like a diamond and hand it to me. Then he'd run down the stairs with his ice tongs clinking, and my heart would slow to a normal beat.

Do I miss those days? Sure do. —*Lori Moore*
*Santa Rosa, California*

## Family Swept Away by Dreams of Cash-Paying Job

MY FATHER was a printer and lost his job when our local newspaper in eastern Washington went out of business. He occasionally worked for a farmer, bringing home a sack of potatoes, carrots or onions at the end of his day. He was never paid in cash, and we had no money to spend.

Then Dad was hired for a special week-long printing job in a city 20 miles away. He took a folding cot with him and slept at the print shop, because we couldn't afford the gasoline for him to drive back and forth every day.

My mother, brothers and I spent that week thumbing through the Sears, Roebuck catalog, dreaming about what we'd buy when Dad brought home his pay. We chose items, changed our minds, and made new selections over and over.

At last, the long week ended and Dad pulled into the driveway. When he climbed out of the car, he handed our mother an electric vacuum sweeper. We just stood and stared at it. That was his pay for a week's work—and we didn't have electricity!

Six years later, the Grand Coulee Dam was built and electricity came to our valley. But for years, that vacuum sweeper sat in our front closet, a symbol of dashed dreams.
—*Maxine Strane*
*Rancho Cucamonga, California*

## Friendly Bronx Neighborhood Had Small-Town Atmosphere

CLASON POINT, a remote area of the Bronx, was a wonderful place to grow up in the 1930s. Though close enough to the city for the men to commute by trolley or subway, our community had a neighborly, small-town feel. There was open space for kids to play, and the adults helped us build our own ball field.

We had a volunteer fire department, and when the alarm sounded, everybody pitched in. The men fought the fire, the women helped the affected family and the older kids ran messages to the church if a priest was needed.

When jobs got scarce, grocers gave credit to their customers. The women cooked a lot of casseroles and soup, and if a man lost his job, the neighbors made sure the family was fed.

On Sunday afternoons, the neighboring families would take the ferry across Long Island Sound to College Point. The fare was a nickel. My mom made lemonade to take along. Often someone played the guitar or accordion, and the ride turned into a party.

Times were hard in those days, but I don't remember enjoying life as much since. —*Al Wilson*
*San Diego, California*

**FANCY OUTFIT.** Everyone wore their best clothes for this photograph of Al Wilson's family (plus assorted aunts, uncles and cousins). That's Al seated on the right. His parents are the couple standing at right.

# Summer Move to Farm Offered Break From Big-City Woes

*By Margaret Chaiet, West Hills, California*

IN 1930, my father's dress-manufacturing business in New York City failed. Then our house in Brooklyn was in foreclosure and we had to move to an apartment. Papa began selling dresses on commission, but we still couldn't pay the rent.

A farm in the Catskill Mountains was looking for families to rent rooms, so we rented a small apartment for the summer for $60. Mama would stay there with us four children while our father remained in the city and decided what to do next.

We put our furniture in storage and loaded our suitcases and bedding into the old Maxwell sedan. We no longer had a home, and none of us kids wanted to go to the farm. I was 15 years old and miserable.

"Papa, what am I going to do on a farm?" I sobbed. "We'll be miles from the movies or my friends."

"Don't worry," he said. "I'll come up every weekend and bring you whatever you need. The farmer has fresh food, cows, chickens—plenty to eat."

We arrived at dusk, and the farmer and his wife were on the porch waiting for us. Their children, Pauline and Max, helped us carry in our things.

### Apartment Was Small But Clean

Our apartment had three bedrooms, with two small iron beds and a dresser in each. Everything was shining clean. Our dining table was covered with a red-and-white checked oilcloth, and there was a jar bursting with colorful wildflowers on top.

The next morning, we explored the rest of the rooming house. I followed Mama as she was shown the big communal kitchen, its walls lined with iceboxes. Some of the other women were cooking breakfast on little two-burner stoves. Everyone seemed happy, calling to each other and shooing the children out to the porch. The aroma was heavenly.

Later, I followed Pauline while she gathered eggs in the noisy henhouse. Then Max, who was about 17, came along. "A group of us kids are walking down the road to a hotel for a dance tonight," he told me. "Wanna come?" Did I ever!

I'd been teasing Max about being a hayseed, but he didn't look like one when we left for the dance that night. He was dressed just like everyone else, except that he'd slicked back his blond hair with pomade.

Nine of us went to the dance, and I had a wonderful time. Maybe summer on the farm wouldn't be so bad.

### Had Fun After All

Our stay was more enjoyable than I'd expected. On some nights, Max hung a sheet on the dining room wall and showed old movies. On rainy days, we sat on the front porch and played cards, using Necco wafers for money.

Before we knew it, 2 months had passed and we were saying tearful good-byes. Papa had found an apartment in the East Bronx for $33 a month, and we were going back to the city.

When we walked into our tenement apartment, I said, "Mom, we're back in the Depression." She just gazed around and said, "When we hang up our curtains and arrange the furniture, it will look very nice."

That night at dinner, I thought about what was happening back on the farm—Pauline candling eggs...Max helping with evening milking. Staying on the farm had briefly freed us from the worries of the Depression, and it had been fun after all.

**EGG-CITING WORLD.** Like this girl, teenager Margaret Chaiet came to enjoy life on the farm.

H. Armstrong Roberts

# 'Taking in' a Broadway Show Had a Whole New Meaning

*By Bill Einhorn, Fairfield, Connecticut*

WHAT DID New York teenagers do for fun during the '30s? Well, I was part of a group of seven that had plenty of fun.

Without much money, we needed ingenuity and imagination to take advantage of the many amenities the big city offered. Broadway and the New York stage was an intriguing challenge. But we were equal to it. We saw many Broadway shows for the cost of a nickel subway ride from 181st to 42nd Street.

Once we'd figured it out, it was really very simple. Most stage plays were written in three acts. The first act, usually the shortest, was followed by a 10-minute intermission.

During that intermission, many ticket holders gathered in the lobby to smoke and discuss the show. All we had to do was mingle in with them until the blinking light signaled the next act. Then we'd walk in and find some empty seats.

### A Few Hurdles to Cross

But there were some hurdles.

First, all the people in the warmed outer lobby were coatless. Solution: We left our coats at a nearby fraternity suite at the Hotel Lincoln.

Second, how do you recognize empty seats? We noted that when theatergoers leave at intermission, they do so without raising their seats after them.

All we had to do was look for a group of non-turned-down chairs. As we spotted them, we'd turn into the row and unobtrusively slide into them.

But most important of all, we found, was attitude. You had to act nonchalant and worldly, betraying neither hesitation nor indecision. Then you'd sit quietly until the lights dimmed and the curtain went up. If no one tapped you on the shoulder, you were home free. I don't recall ever being challenged.

We were very discriminating playgoers. We only went to see the biggest stars and the best plays. We saw greats like Paul Muni in *Counsellor-at-Law*, and Noel Coward and the Lunts in *Private Lives*.

When Fred Astaire danced with his sister, Adele, in *The Gay Divorce*, we were there. Other names I recall from that era are Phil Baker, Victor Moore, Ethel Merman and Jimmy Durante. How exciting it was!

Once, we even managed an opening night! It was the fabulous Beatrice Lillie in *Walk a Little Faster*. At this play we had to stand in the rear of the theater with the paying standees, a concession we normally wouldn't have considered.

Of course, on the downside, we only saw two out of three acts of each play (and only one act of the musicals). But we couldn't complain—not at those prices! ☒

Brown Brothers

Ewing Galloway

***NO BUSINESS LIKE "SNOW" BUSINESS.*** **Bill Einhorn and his friends found an ingenious way to sample exciting New York nightlife like that shown above. And, the incredible thing was they were able to do it without paying for the ticket! All it took was a little planning—and a lot of attitude.**

# CHAPTER ELEVEN

# It Was My Lucky Break

***DOWN AND OUT...THEN UP.*** This man won some money in a radio contest, quite a lucky break when times were tough. He decided to share his lucky break with those less fortunate. Folks who caught such a break during the Depression never forgot it, as the stories in this chapter attest. (Photo: American Stock Photography)

# From the desk of Clancy Strock

Dear Katie,

It seems the only luck most people had during the Depression was bad luck. Just when you thought things couldn't get any worse, they did.

What we call "welfare" today was almost unknown in the 1930s. But it didn't matter a lot, because even starving people were ashamed to accept handouts or relief. There they were with no jobs but too proud to accept charity and too law-abiding to steal.

That's why the rare piece of good fortune was never forgotten. These days when you see someone picking up a penny in the parking lot, it's almost certain to be an older person. They still recall when finding a penny was an important piece of luck. And many, like me, harbor a deep-seated superstition that failing to pick it up would bring down an immediate spell of bad luck.

The biggest single piece of good luck I can recall during the Depression years was the day Dad spotted a wolf prowling one of our farm pastures, probably hoping to find a tender young calf.

We couldn't imagine where it had come from, because wolves hadn't been seen for years in Illinois.

Well, your great-grandfather loaded his rifle and stalked the wolf until he got a clear shot. Then he took the carcass to the courthouse, where he learned that there not only was a county wolf bounty, but also one from the state.

The two rewards came to $20 or so--more money than we'd seen in weeks. We were rich!

The wolf bounty was our one memorable piece of Depression luck. Good luck for us--bad luck for the wolf! Dad even got his picture in the newspaper, standing beside the critter. I, the son of the Great Wolf Hunter, was famous at school for a whole day.

Times have changed, of course. The days of bounties offered on wild predators that kill farm stock are pretty much gone, because most of those predators themselves are long gone.

State and federal governments have come full circle in their thinking and now reintroduce some of the same animals to woods and fields because they're so rare. It was lucky for us the bounties were in place during the tough years of the Depression and that the critter happened by.

Sometimes luck came in the form of an accident like that. Other times it was the result of a chance meeting with someone more fortunate than you, who generously shared what they had. As the following stories make clear, these folks never forgot the day they caught a lucky break.

*Your Grandpa Clancy*

THE DEPRESSION YEARS were, believe it or not, the happiest of my life. Dad was the caretaker at the old Lancaster fairgrounds. He didn't get paid after the Depression hit, but we lived there rent-free. It was just the first of many lucky breaks that helped us through those years.

My mother was a saint, and she made great meals out of anything she could lay her hands on. There were lots of elderberry bushes around for dumplings, pies and jelly.

She also made delicious meals from edible weeds—seasoned lamb's-quarters, dandelion greens with a hot bacon-and-egg dressing, and purslane with a sweet-and-sour dressing.

### Kindness Disguised

One day a Mennonite grocer who knew about our situation told Dad to come to his store. Mr. Moseman claimed he had a couple items that "weren't moving" and sent us home with huge bags of flour, cornmeal, navy beans and oatmeal. Mr. Moseman had told Dad a white lie, of course, but that was his way of helping a friend in need. Dad was too proud to accept alms.

Later, Dad got a weekend job at a meat store that was a godsend. When the store closed late Saturday night, Dad was given anything that wouldn't keep in the walk-in icebox, especially pork loins and sausages.

We all pitched in to help Mother can the meat in half-gallon jars, working well into the wee hours of Sunday morning.

# Series of Lucky Breaks Kept Family Warm And Well-Fed

*By Albert Lohr, Lancaster, Pennsylvania*

**SOMEONE WAS WATCHING OVER THEM.** Albert Lohr's family (he's standing on the right) didn't make much money, but the satisfaction of getting by without it was great.

But we always made it to church. "The Lord sent us this meat," Mother would say. "We must now go and thank Him."

Once a farmer invited our family to glean potatoes after the picking machine went through his fields. We collected enough to last a year.

We often gathered coal along the railroad tracks. The firemen caught on and started tossing off the larger lumps so they didn't have to hammer them into smaller pieces to burn.

### Free for the Taking

The biggest coal bonanza came with a call from the railroad yard master. "Fred," he told my father, "I'm not supposed to tell you this, but a coal car gate broke as we were shifting on the siding next to you. There are 30 to 40 tons of hard coal spread down the track. Whatever you collect, we won't have to clean up tomorrow."

Dad got two large wooden barrels from a friend at the Coca-Cola plant, sawed them in half and strapped them to the bumpers of our car. We cut a hole in our fence to get the car as close as possible to the siding.

The whole family collected coal far into the moonlit night. Each time the barrels were filled, Dad drove back to the house, dumped them under our black walnut tree and returned for another load.

When we finished, I was dead-tired but exhilarated. What a joy seeing that big pile of coal under our tree...and knowing it might be enough to last us 2 years! ▨

**WARMTH IN A SACK.** These people are receiving their coal rations at a relief station in New York City. The photo was taken in the '20s, but by the time Albert Lohr's family faced the Depression dilemma of keeping warm without money (see story above), they, like so many others, were scavenging coal from the railroad tracks.

American Stock Photos

# 'Angel' Helped Destitute Student Stay the Course

*By Hazel Donaldson, Carmel, California*

I WAS a high school sophomore in 1933, the worst year of the Great Depression for our family. One day during morning classes, I found runs in my last pair of stockings. I would have to quit school. We didn't have enough money even for necessities.

My heart was heavy. I knew that without an education, I could spend the rest of my life in poverty. But in those days, most people were too proud to ask for charity. They'd almost rather starve than go on relief.

I spent the entire morning shivering with nerves and indecision. By the time the noon bell rang, I'd made up my mind. I'd rather suffer the humiliation of asking for help than drop out of school.

Miss Keiser ran the relief office in our small town of Meridian, Idaho. I left school and began walking the five blocks to her house. With snow falling softly around me, I felt like the only person in the world.

### Would She Be Able to Help?

For several seconds, I stood on Miss Keiser's doorstep, trying to muster the courage to knock. When I did, I half hoped she wouldn't hear me, but she did. I've often wondered what she thought when she saw me standing there, shivering and covered with snow.

Miss Keiser wasted no time with questions. She practically lifted me into the warmth of her cozy house, which was filled with wonderful aromas drifting from the kitchen.

For a moment, I felt as if my guardian angel had dropped me into Heaven. Angels aren't always dressed in white, with beautiful faces and golden hair. I learned they can be quite ordinary, plump and smelling of good things to eat.

Miss Keiser went to the cupboard, took out an extra soup bowl and set a place for me across the tiny table. She glided around the kitchen, making comforting sounds to herself as she dished up a stew so delicious that just thinking of it still makes my mouth water.

Only after I'd thawed out a little did she ask why I'd turned up on her doorstep on such a day. Warmed by the stew and so much unexpected kindness, I told her I could no longer attend school without books and clothing.

She sat silent for a moment, just looking at me. Finally she said, "Go back to school and check in with the principal. She will help you. It was so nice having company for lunch."

I thanked her and returned to school. But it was Friday, and the principal had taken the afternoon off.

When I returned to school Monday, I was asked to report to the principal's office. The gift of books and clothing I received that day made it possible for me to continue my education. Two years later, I became the first person in my family to graduate from high school.

God bless those wonderful women who answered my prayer for help. Without their compassion, I would have been a dropout—without the skills to make a decent living when my husband died later, leaving me with two young children to support.

As I reflect on my life today, I realize that much of what I'm thankful for dates back to that memorable day in 1933. ⊠

## Surprise Awaited Sisters At End of Mysterious Line

IN 1933, my sister and I noticed a long line leading into the church next door to our home in Portland, Maine. Out of curiosity, we got in line. I was 9 and my sister was 11.

As we entered the church, we were handed tin plates. We continued moving with the long line, and eventually our plates were filled with hot baked beans and a slab of brown bread.

We cleaned our plates, and as we left the church, we each were handed two pink marshmallows. "What fun!" we thought, and ran home to tell our parents.

Of course, we were soundly reprimanded for depriving some homeless, destitute person of a hot meal.

I supposed it was lucky to run into free food during the Depression, but the real break my sister and I received was some needed education. How naive we were!

—*Ann Mountford, Fairfield, Connecticut*

**WARM MEAL WAS A LUXURY.** The men in this photo are dining at a shelter in November of 1933. For the homeless and unemployed, church and shelter meals were godsends.

**BRIGHT BUT POOR. This young girl was fortunate to encounter Sara Riola's schoolteacher aunt (see story below). Sara's aunt saw potential that deserved to be fulfilled.**

## Teacher's Intervention Took Mountain Girl to New Heights

MY AUNT was a schoolteacher in Harrisonburg, Virginia in the early '30s when she heard about Hallie, a bright young mountain girl of 13 whose family couldn't afford to continue her education past grade school. They'd been hard-pressed to allow her to go that far.

Aunt Sallie knew the girl would probably end up taking a low-skilled job or marrying early in order to survive. So she decided to intervene.

During Hallie's high school years, she lived with my aunt, helping with household chores in exchange for room and board. Hallie's main responsibility was cleaning up after dinner.

When Hallie graduated from high school, she earned a scholarship to Georgetown University, where she met and fell in love with a fine young man the State Department was grooming for an overseas appointment.

The couple decided to marry rather than be separated, and the young man soon left for the Middle East with the girl from the Blue Ridge Mountains at his side. I guess you can call this a Depression-era success story—or maybe a lucky break for a young girl from the mountains. —*Sara Riola Lakewood, New Jersey*

## "Write Stuff" Brought Welcome $5 Windfall

THE DAY of Franklin D. Roosevelt's inauguration in March 1933 remains vivid in my memory. On that eventful day a registered letter arrived for me.

I'd won a handwriting contest sponsored by Chicago radio station WGN, and the envelope contained my prize—a crisp new $5 bill. Can you imagine? In the deep Depression days, this money felt like it was hundreds of dollars.

Mother marched me to the shoe store and bought me a new pair of tennis shoes and school shoes for a total of $2.35. The store owner couldn't make change for a $5 bill because all the banks were closed. He gathered his family together and eventually came up with our $2.65—all in coins.

For dinner that evening, Mom fixed a big pot roast. We hadn't seen a meal like that in Lord knows how long. It was quite a lucky day! —*Cliff Erickson Leslie, Michigan*

### "Can-Do" Attitude Fed Two Families

IN 1932, my family lived as tenants on a farm in Cameron County, Texas. Everyone was struggling to keep their heads above water when we hit it lucky.

The Home Demonstration Office launched a search for the largest family in the county. My 29-year-old mother had seven children, so she filled out the form and sent it in.

The county presented her with a large pressure cooker and a can sealer-opener, which cut cans below the rolled edge so they could be used again.

Mrs. Teal, a friend of Mother's, had a little money, so she bought tin cans and Mother furnished the vegetables. Working together, they canned vegetables, chicken, veal and pork for both families to share. They could put up about 100 cans a day.

I especially remember canning tomatoes and corn. The children took the skins off the scalded tomatoes and placed them in the cans, which went into a big black pot in the yard. I felt very useful, because it was my job to keep the fire going under the pot.

At corn-canning time, children shucked and de-silked the ears. Ladies cut off the kernels and packed them in cans prepared with special linings. Then the cans were processed in the pressure cooker.

When World War II started, the government stopped allowing private individuals to buy cans, because tin was essential to the war effort. Mother and Mrs. Teal were the only people I ever knew who did home canning in tin cans. —*Stella Morris, Port Lavaca, Texas*

## Honesty Was Rewarded With Answered Prayer

**MONEY MATTERS.** Claire Stickel (shown at right above with her mother and siblings) was praised for returning cash that didn't belong to her.

DURING THE HEART of the Depression in 1932, I found a $5 bill and a $10 bill rolled together in an aisle at a public market. I took the money to the office upstairs to turn it in to the lost-and-found department.

The manager was sitting with his feet up on his desk. When I handed him the money, he said he'd just lost that exact amount and gave me a 10¢ reward for finding it.

Of course, I knew he was lying. No one who'd just lost that much money would be sitting around. He'd be frantically searching for it.

When I got home and told Mama, she said she was proud that I'd done the honest thing, as I'd been taught. What I didn't know was that she had been praying for $15 to pay a doctor's bill.

The next afternoon, the mailman brought a letter from a local attorney who knew Mama had witnessed a bad accident on our street corner. He wanted her to testify at the trial…and would pay her $15 plus carfare.

—*Claire Stickel, Gresham, Oregon*

## Starving Family's Decision to Share Had Happy Ending

IN THE EARLY 1930s, our family had no food and no work.

One afternoon, an elderly black man came across the fields from the railroad tracks to our house, one of the few in town. The man asked Dad for something to eat, and Mother gave him homemade bread with jelly and a glass of water. We had nothing else. Dad hadn't worked for a long time.

The visitor dropped to his knees and thanked God for my parents. He said he was walking from South Jersey to Sussex, where he'd been promised a job, and other people along the way had sent their dogs after him.

Two or 3 days later, my dad got a job. The Lord does work in mysterious ways.

—*Harry Henning Pompton Plains, New Jersey*

## "Christmas Angel" Answered Child's Plea

DADDY SUPPORTED our family of seven by working as a mechanic in the small town of Wilmington, Ohio. Mother took in washing and ironing to help, but pennies were few and far between.

The Christmas when I was 8 years old, Daddy didn't have any business and we couldn't afford a tree. For days, I begged Daddy to get one. Finally he said, "If I have a customer, we can have a tree."

Christmas Eve came, and still he had no customers. A winter storm covered the ground with heavy snow and ice.

It was getting dark when a car suddenly pulled into Daddy's garage. I ran out to Daddy and blurted, "Now we can have a tree!"

Standing beside the car was a lady with beautiful white hair like an angel. "My dear, don't you have a tree?" she asked kindly. "This storm just blew over my blue spruce tree. As soon as I get my car repaired, we'll cut the top off for your tree."

How excited I was! When Daddy finished with her car, we went with her

**TOUGH SLEDDING.** Even a Christmas tree was beyond reach for some poor families like Dorothy Lauman's (she's on the left with her brothers).

to cut the tree, and she returned to help us trim it.

On Christmas morning, we were surprised by a knock at the door. There stood the lady with the beautiful white hair, carrying a basket of fruit and candy. I've always remembered her as my Christmas angel.

—*Dorothy Lauman Davie, Florida*

# Pancake Breakfasts Just What the Doctor Ordered

*By William Allan, Pittsburgh, Pennsylvania*

I DIDN'T REALLY UNDERSTAND my father until years after his death. At a banquet, an older man at my table mentioned he was from Turtle Creek.

"I was born and raised in Turtle Creek," I told him. "My dad was Doc Allan."

"Doc Allan!" he fairly exploded. "My goodness, when I think of the people in Turtle Creek who owed Doc Allan money…"

Somehow it all started to come together.

My father, Alex Allan, was a dentist in a small factory town east of Pittsburgh during the Great Depression. He was a little man who wore special shoes to make himself look 5-foot-7 (he was actually 5-foot-5).

Doc Allan also put up a gruff exterior to mask the fact that he was soft inside. He was a sucker for people in pain.

It's difficult to imagine today how prevalent hunger was during the 1930s. With no welfare, Medicare, food stamps or food banks, families were struggling. Most were too proud to accept help, but people found ways to provide it anyway.

Dad always did. In addition to his private practice, Dad was the school dentist. He painted the walls of his school office with Mother Goose characters to ease the children's fears.

There was a nurse's office, too, but she sent quite a few children who "didn't feel good" to see Doc Allan. After a quick check, the conversation would go something like this:

"What did you have for breakfast?"

"Nuthin'."

"And you're hungry?"

"Yeah."

So the child would get 35¢ and be sent across the street to Shorty's diner, where Dad had a standing arrangement to provide an all-you-can-eat pancake breakfast.

Years later, when I was in high school, those breakfasts provided a side benefit for me. I had gotten in way over my head in a fistfight. Suddenly an immense football player grabbed my opponent, almost pulling him off his feet.

"That's Doc Allan's kid," the athlete growled. "Leave 'im alone." The big guy told me later that he'd filled up on Doc Allan pancakes more than once.

I'm not suggesting things were better in those days, but maybe people were. Looking back, I don't recall Dad ever indicating he was doing anything special.

I think if someone had asked, he would've just passed it off with a shrug of his shoulders and said, "What in the world would you expect me to do?" ⊠

**DR. SOFT TOUCH.** Alex Allan's stern exterior masked a kind heart that provided pancakes for countless hungry schoolkids. He posed with son William (above left) just before William left for Europe and World War II.

# Ice Cream Fan Handed His Dream Job

*By Frank Kastner, Clearwater, Florida*

BEFORE the Depression, ice cream cones were only available in pharmacies and confectioneries—and flavors were limited, too. But with the advent of bad times, dairy prices plunged.

The stage was set for the eye-catching, mouth-watering, gigantic double-dip cones. And that's when a new chain called Brown and Simpkins opened in our Detroit, Michigan neighborhood.

The store featured over 45 different flavors, including Rainbow, Banana Nut, Butterscotch, Hawaiian Pineapple …even Chop Suey!

No wonder visions of giant scoops of ice cream constantly danced in my head. But first I needed money. I started scavenging alleys for empty bottles I could turn in for pennies and nickels. Then I went door-to-door searching for grass cutting jobs.

With my new hoard, I dashed down to Brown and Simpkins. My goal was to sample all 45 flavors and, being at the growing stage in which a boy's appetite is boundless, I was at that place morning, noon and night.

Soon I was recognized by the clerks as one of their best customers. One morning after polishing off two dips of French Chocolate Delight, I was leaning against the far wall of the store when I noticed the boss of the crew (a college student) staring at me intently.

Suddenly, he yelled over to me, "Hey kid, how would you like a job?"

## Too Good to Be True?

My response was, "Boy! You mean I could work for Brown and Simpkins?"

"You sure can," he said. "Follow me and I'll show you what I have in mind."

He took me into a back room and there sat 10 or 12 empty 10-gallon ice cream cans. I looked in one and saw the residue of ice cream clinging to its bottom and sides. Nearby was a sink, some boxes of soap and a pile of towels.

"Your job," I was told, "is to scrub these cans, then dry and polish them to a mirror finish. You can report in three or four times a day and I'll have empty cans waiting for you."

I must still have looked eager as he searched my face for a response, because he continued with his pitch.

"Now as to your pay," he said, "we don't pay in money…we do something better. You get yourself a nice big spoon and I'll see to it that an extra layer of ice cream is left on the bottom of every can, plus you get any left clinging to the sides. What do you think of that?"

My answer? "Wow! When can I start?" What a lucky break!

My strict German father had taught me: When you take a job, do it thoroughly. This, in addition to my enthusiasm, meant those cans were cleaned to a flashy shine. And the ice cream? Boy, I got my fill!

Even the Chop Suey tasted swell!

**AN IRRESISTIBLE OFFER.** The devotion Frank Kastner (left) had to his favorite dessert eventually caught the eye of a smart young businessman. The two worked out a deal that let Frank indulge his love while also providing a valuable service.